BRANSON

The Official Travel and Souvenir Guide to America's Music Show Capital

BY JORDAN SIMON

Fodor's Travel Publications, Inc.
New York • Toronto • London • Sydney • Auckland

First Edition

ISBN 0–679–02817–X

Fodor's Branson: The Official Travel and Souvenir Guide to America's Music Show Capital

Editor: Alison B. Stern

Editorial Contributors: Steven K. Amsterdam, Susan Bain, Robert Blake, Hannah Borgeson, Lara Edelbaum, Laura Kidder, Elizabeth Kuka, Stacey Kulig, Rebecca Miller, Linda K. Schmidt

Creative Director: Fabrizio La Rocca

Design: Alida Beck

Desktop Production: Tigist Getachew, Carol Nelson

Cartographer: David Lindroth

Cover Photograph: Paul D'Innocenzo

Acknowledgements

The following people and organizations provided invaluable assistance along the way: American Airlines, American Eagle, and the indefatigable Susan Young at USAir; all of my friends at the Springfield and Eureka Springs chambers of commerce; John Bowers, Dawn Erickson, and Terry Winters of the Branson/Lakes Area Chamber of Commerce, who were unstinting with their time even when they had none to give; the stars and their managers, all of whom were unfailingly accessible and cooperative; the good people at Silver Dollar City, Mutton Hollow, and Shepherd of the Hills, who made sure I could relax and enjoy the Ozarks while I was there; family and friends, who accepted deadline craziness without batting an eye; and of course my editor, Alison Stern, who puts up with the writer's usual occupational hazards.

ABOUT THE AUTHOR

Whenever New York noise, traffic, grime, and crime overwhelm him Mr. Simon escapes to the countryside. He loves Branson and the Ozarks because there he can have the best of both worlds: the beauty, peace, and warmth of small-town life and the excitement, entertainment—and traffic—of a large city. Mr. Simon has worked in nearly every aspect of the entertainment industry, as a child actor in commercials, an off-Broadway director, a story editor, and, currently, producer of the International Ski Film & Video Festival, held annually in Colorado. He defected to the world of journalism in 1987. The former contributing editor of *Taxi* has written on various topics for *Elle, Modern Bride, Travel & Leisure, Ski, Physicians Travel & Meeting Guide, Wine Country International, Ski Impact, Food Arts, California, Snow Country, Travelage, International Entertaining, Travel Agent,* and *Fodor's Caribbean* and *Virgin Islands,* among others. He is also the author of *Fodor's Colorado* and the *USA Today Ski Atlas.*

CONTENTS

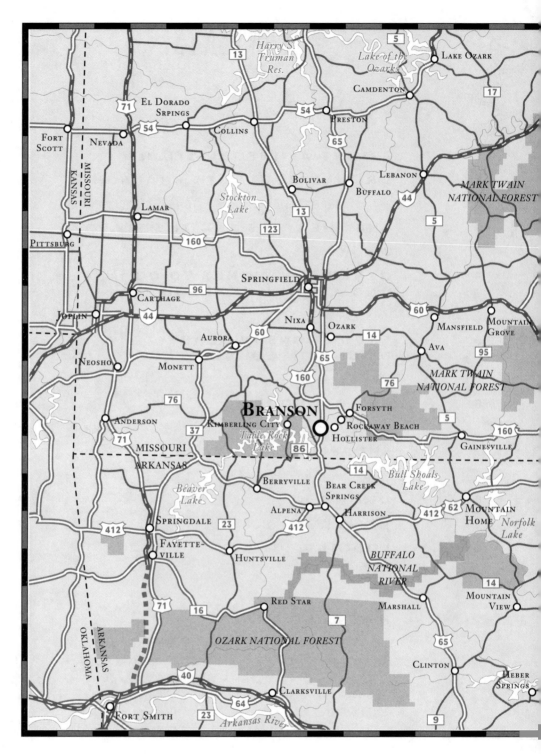

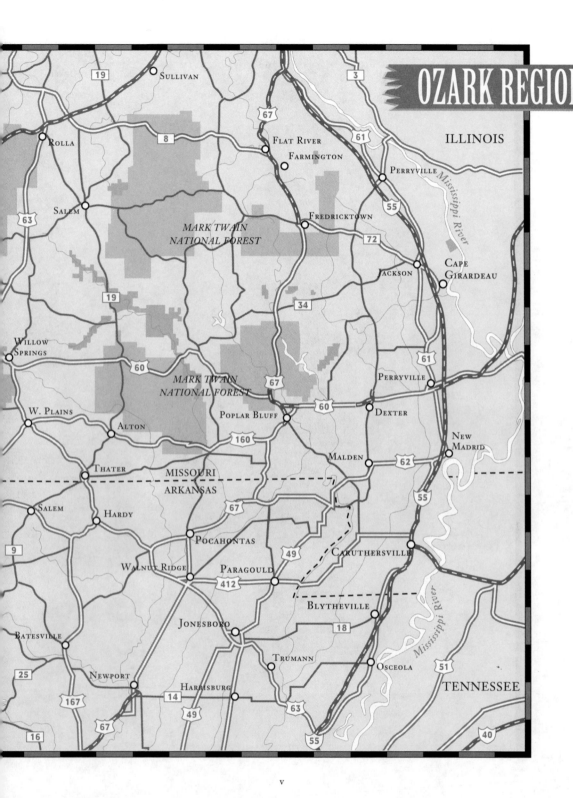

OZARK REGION

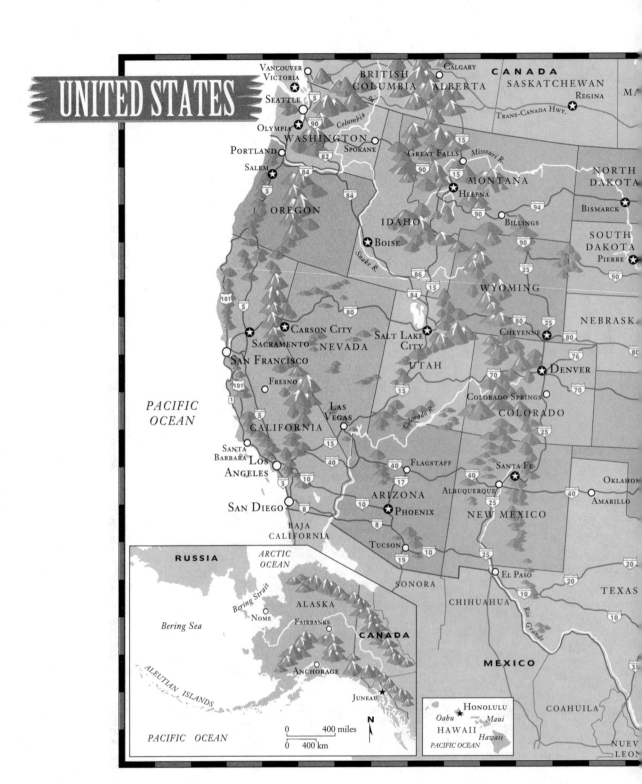

UNITED STATES

Vancouver
Victoria
Seattle
Olympia
WASHINGTON
Spokane
Portland
Salem
OREGON
5
84
84
82
5
101
5
NEVADA
Carson City
Sacramento
San Francisco
Fresno
101
1
80
CALIFORNIA
Santa Barbara
Los Angeles
5
10
San Diego
8
5
40
15
LAS VEGAS
BAJA CALIFORNIA

BRITISH COLUMBIA
ALBERTA
Columbia R.
Snake R.
IDAHO
Boise
86
84
GREAT FALLS
15
90
MONTANA
Helena
90
Missouri R.
Billings
90
WYOMING
84
15
UTAH
SALT LAKE CITY
70
15
Colorado R.
40
17
Flagstaff
ARIZONA
Phoenix
8
Tucson
19
10
40
Santa Fe
Albuquerque
25
NEW MEXICO
El Paso
25

CALGARY
CANADA
SASKATCHEWAN
Regina
Trans-Canada Hwy.
NORTH DAKOTA
Bismarck
94
SOUTH DAKOTA
Pierre
90
25
NEBRASKA
80
25
Cheyenne
80
76
80
Denver
70
70
COLORADO SPRINGS
COLORADO
25
Oklahoma
40
Amarillo
20
TEXAS
10
10
MEXICO
CHIHUAHUA
SONORA
Rio Grande
COAHUILA
NUEVO LEON
35

PACIFIC OCEAN

RUSSIA
ARCTIC OCEAN
Bering Strait
ALASKA
Nome
Bering Sea
Fairbanks
CANADA
ALEUTIAN ISLANDS
Anchorage
Juneau
N
PACIFIC OCEAN
0   400 miles
0   400 km

Honolulu
Oahu   Maui
HAWAII
Hawaii
PACIFIC OCEAN

ONTARIO

QUÉBEC

NEW
BRUNSWICK

ITOBA

CANADA

FREDERICTON ⭐

⭐ Winnipeg

95

29

QUÉBEC ⭐

MONTRÉAL ⭐

MAINE

Lake Superior

MINNESOTA

⭐ AUGUSTA

95

Fargo ○

DULUTH ○

MONTPELIER
VT

CONCORD ⭐

35

MICHIGAN

OTTAWA

Lake
Huron

N.H.

BOSTON ⭐

29

94

WISCONSIN

Hudson R.

ST. PAUL

GREEN
BAY

Lake
Ontario

90

TORONTO ⭐

ALBANY ⭐
HARTFORD

MASS.

R.I.

⭐ PROVIDENCE

MINNEAPOLIS ⭐

90

MILWAUKEE

LANSING

Lake
Michigan

Buffalo
Lake
Erie

NEW
YORK

87

CONN.

Missouri R.

MADISON ⭐

DETROIT ⭐

CLEVELAND ⭐

PENNSYLVANIA

N.J.

⭐ NEW YORK

80

IOWA

90

CHICAGO ⭐

90 80

PITTSBURGH ⭐

Harrisburg ⭐

76

TRENTON

80

DES
MOINES ⭐

55

65

OHIO

70

⭐ PHILADELPHIA

Lincoln ○

INDIANA

COLUMBUS ⭐

Baltimore ⭐

Dover

80

ILLINOIS

Omaha ⭐

75

MD.

DEL.

SPRINGFIELD ○

INDIANAPOLIS ⭐

WEST
VIRGINIA

Annapolis ⭐

KANSAS
CITY

Topeka ⭐

MISSOURI

55

CINCINNATI ⭐

CHARLESTON ⭐

95

WASHINGTON, D.C.

70

70

LOUISVILLE ⭐

Frankfort ⭐

RICHMOND ○

35

JEFFERSON
CITY

St.Louis ⭐

Ohio R.

NORFOLK ○

KANSAS

Mississippi R.

KENTUCKY

VIRGINIA

65

75

SPRINGFIELD ○

85

RALEIGH ○

35

BRANSON ⭐

NASHVILLE ⭐

95

HARRISON ○

40

NORTH
CAROLINA

CITY ○

TULSA ○

ARKANSAS

40

TENNESSEE

40

65

55

MEMPHIS ⭐

COLUMBIA ○

OKLAHOMA

40

LITTLE
ROCK ⭐

Tennessee R.

85

SOUTH
CAROLINA

75

20

35

30

BIRMINGHAM ○

ATLANTA ⭐

20

Savannah R.

Dallas ○

MISSISSIPPI

20

GEORGIA

85

16

45

Mississippi R.

55

ALABAMA

Montgomery ⭐

Savannah ○

20

JACKSON ⭐

65

95

75

Austin ⭐

BATON ROUGE ⭐

12

10

JACKSONVILLE ○

10

10

MOBILE ○

TALLAHASSEE ⭐

San Antonio ○

HOUSTON ○ LOUISIANA

New Orleans ○

FLORIDA

ATLANTIC
OCEAN

Gulf of Mexico

ORLANDO ○

4

Bahama
Islands

75

95

41

MIAMI ⭐

NASSAU ⭐

N

0   200 miles

0   300 km

Introduction

When I travel, I hope to be surprised, edified, to have my expectations confounded. And the more I heard about Branson, the more intrigued I became.

The statistics were staggering. Nearly 40 theaters boasting a seating capacity of over 50,000—more than all the Broadway theaters combined. From virtually out of nowhere, Branson had become the second-most-popular drive-vacation destination after Orlando/Walt Disney World, with more than 5 million visitors annually. The number keeps growing. Branson is a certified boom town. Construction proceeds at an astounding rate: a new hotel, theater, restaurant, or shopping mall seems to sprout every day. No surprise, Branson is legendary for its traffic along the two-lane highway known as 76 Country Boulevard, or the Strip. "The longest parking lot in America" (as locals joke) is part of the Branson aura; it allows people to look around to their hearts' content, absorb it all. The city actually keeps traffic counts (there's a meter on the strip). On an average day during the first half of 1994, some 300,000 vehicles inched by. Branson had construction, traffic, and theaters: three things that ought to make a New Yorker feel at home.

My first glimpse of Branson was in winter. It was a perfect time to take stock and meet the locals without the craziness of high season.

I went into the delightful Dick's Five and Dime, which seems frozen in the 1920s. One of the cashiers struck up a conversation. Within a few minutes I had heard all about the town, her family (going back a couple of generations), how excited locals were that people were now coming in winter. She concluded, "You stop on back and tell me how you're enjoying yourself." My second night I attended a show at the tiny 76 Music Hall. The usher had run out of programs and suggested I ask the box office. I offered to bring a stack back, and the cashier smiled brightly, "Why bless your sweet heart, darlin'": I was entranced, reminded of Ellie Mae's closing line in the *Beverly Hillbillies*, "Y'all come back now, ya hear?" (I later learned that scenes of the Clampetts' hometown were filmed right here in the theme park, Silver Dollar City.) No wonder the region once marketed itself as the "Land of a Million Smiles." With more than 5 million visitors annually, that's not enough to go around, but they keep trying.

So far the warmth seems genuine, unforced. When one theater runs out of popcorn, it's not uncommon for a concessionaire to duck into the theater next door. It's the good-neighbor policy of borrowing a cup of sugar, writ on a grander scale. That spirit of sharing and generosity extends to the top of the totem pole. The stars promote each other's shows. By and large the boosterism is astonishing. "You be sure to go stop by my friend Mel's . . . or Jim's . . . or Glen's theater," runs the constant refrain. They're no fools: what's good for one is good for all. But they mean it. Most of them have been working together for years, doing grueling road tours or two-a-night Vegas acts. They support each other's charitable efforts. There's a real sense of community in Branson. Jimmy Osmond (the mogul of the family) says, "We're tight-knit. We meet once a month as theater owners and entertainers. We talk about ways to herd cattle versus fighting over a piece of meat."

Of course, the stars are businesspeople, too, and Branson is big business. No less a corporate titan than Lee Iacocca has invested (he's associated with Glen Campbell and Will Rogers theaters). The Disney people have been snooping around, studying the feasibility of an exchange of acts (they've since adopted a wait-and-see attitude). Although most stars wax even more rhapsodic than the brochures put out by the chamber of commerce, some, like Bobby Vinton, take a more pragmatic view, speaking of the inevitable competition for audiences, even creating the impression that for them Branson's primary attraction is commercial.

But in many cases, stars talk frankly of their debt to Branson and its audiences, which have revived or extended their careers. They're appropriately humble. As a result, Branson is one of the entertainment world's great values. Some people might snipe (you get a lot of it in Nashville and Vegas) that the performers are on the downside of their careers, but you wouldn't know it from the energy and enthusiasm on stage. That's 20 to 40 years of honing their craft up there. Nowhere else will you get shows of this caliber (at twice the length of a typical Vegas or Atlantic City show, mind you) for under 20 bucks a pop (and mom and grandma . . .).

And the stars are remarkably accessible and approachable. I'm interviewing Yakov Smirnoff in a restaurant near the Osmonds Theater (where he was performing at the time of the interview) when the waitress comes over and says, "That man there doesn't believe you're really Yakov." Yakov points to the enormous billboard of himself across the street. "But that's a good-looking guy," the man teases. "If you were half as good-looking as that picture, I'd believe you." Some celebrities would consider it an intrusion on their privacy. Yakov shrugs. "He'll have something to tell all his friends back home, that he ribbed Yakov Smirnoff. I *like* the contact you get here. New York and L.A., you're barricaded inside. That's the magic of Branson." Celebrities go out into the audience during the performance, talk to their fans, pose for pictures, spend an hour in the lobby or on tour buses after the show signing autographs. Tellingly, stars who feel the need to isolate themselves don't fare as well. As Mel Tillis comments, "Wayne Newton's bodyguards looked awfully out of place."

Perhaps inevitably, Branson has attracted more than its share of negative press. It has its problems, to be sure, most of them stemming from the lack of infrastructure to support its explosive growth. There are fears of inadequate drainage (the sewage-treatment plant, built for 4,000 people, is flush with the waste of nearly 10 times that number during high season). There's even the specter of homelessness, as the town tries to cope with the influx of would-be performers and service-industry workers. Most of them live in mobile homes on the fringes of town or travel 40 miles to find affordable lodging. Then there was the hoopla over buildings completed without such details as permits, inspections, or compliance with fire laws. Most locals scoff. As Tony Orlando says, "You think I'd let my daughter in this theater if it was unsafe?" He points out that the negative publicity has had a beneficial effect. "So many fire marshals descended on this town it's probably the safest in America."

Far more disturbing are those who paint Branson as a neo-Nazi stronghold: homogeneous and exclusionary. Don't bother coming if you're black, Jewish, gay, or liberal, they claim.

Some feel Branson is being unfairly singled out. Others are philosophic, recognizing it goes with the territory. Jimmy Osmond laughs. "My mother used to have a saying, 'Birds always pick at the best fruit.'" And residents wonder, What's wrong with wholesome? Despite increasing comparisons to Vegas and the undeniable economic potential of legalized gambling, citizens are dead set against it.

Branson sits snugly in the buckle of the Bible Belt, and most folks talk seriously of

Christian lifestyles and family values. Yet because of the tremendous influx, not only of audiences but of performers, designers, and technicians, Branson is a lot worldlier than most towns its size. Suddenly the belt is loosened a notch. For example, most Bransonites shudder the first ADOPT-A-HIGHWAY sign you see when you cross into Arkansas on I-65: this stretch of road has been adopted by the Knights of the Ku Klux Klan. Bransonites welcomed Charley Pride with open arms. Tony Orlando (Greek–Puerto Rican New Yorker), Shoji Tabuchi (Japanese) and Yakov Smirnoff (Russian Jew) all rave about the friendliness and openness of the locals. For them, Branson truly represents the American Dream, where the poor boy or immigrant makes good. All of them feel at home. We hope that you will, too.

With this book in hand, you should become quickly familiar with all that Branson has to offer. We've planned it to help you not only zero in on the shows that you'll find most entertaining but also to direct you to the most comfortable places to stay, the most distinctive places to dine. The bits of Ozarks wisdom, the archival material, the interviews with the stars, and their photographs should make the book a wonderful souvenir of your visit as well as an excellent guide.

To ensure the accuracy of the information provided here, we have taken enormous pains, checking our facts, then checking them again. Still, although all prices and opening times were current at press time, it's a good idea to call ahead: Especially in fast-changing Branson, the passage of time always brings changes. Finally, please let us hear from you about your trip to Branson and the Ozarks, whether you found that the establishments you visited surpassed their descriptions or the other way around. Send your letters to the editors of Fodor's Travel Publications, 201 East 50th Street, New York, New York 10022. And have a wonderful trip!

Branson, Through the Years

Branson today may appear a ready-made phenomenon with a sort of "Build it and they will come" inevitability. Indeed, gazing down the neon landscape of the Strip, it's difficult to think of Branson as a place with a past, only a continually expanding future. Yet there was a Branson even before the watershed 1991 *60 Minutes* segment arguably put it on the national map. The largely positive, slightly incredulous report focused on a booming theater town that seemingly sprang up overnight, anointing Branson the "Country Music Show Capital of the Universe." The nickname stuck—somewhat to the chagrin of locals who wanted to stress the region's variety of attractions.

Pribble family; photo courtesy Virginia Belfiore

The tale begins, as these stories usually do, with life-giving water: The roaring White and James rivers created opportunities for fishing, drinking, and transport, and so enticed a number of peoples to settle the region. The region's first inhabitants, the Osage tribe (whose roots can be traced back over five centuries), took full advantage of the splendid setting. Alas, little remains of their once-thriving culture. A few trappers and explorers ventured into the wilderness in the late 18th and early 19th centuries, emerging with tales of the startling clarity and purity of the water. Gradually, as land grants opened up in the middle of the 19th century, the Ozarks were homesteaded, mainly by English, Scots, and Irish families that branched out from Tennessee and Kentucky in search of a better life. Whether they found it is debatable, for the limestone soil is porous and poor, with a low crop yield. Yet they persevered, and even today local families such as the Olivers and Moores trace their lineage to those early hardscrabble days.

During the mid-1800s there was no Branson, just a patchwork quilt of farms interrupted by the occasional gristmill or cotton gin. The only town here at the outset of the Civil War was Forsyth, a megalopolis of 88 souls at its peak, among whom were six merchants, two doctors, a druggist, a blacksmith, and a carpenter. But the War between the States ended growth and progress in the region. As a border state with only a cursory allegiance to the Union, Missouri was subject to the ravages of both sides. The Ozarks were particularly hard hit: the area's bountiful forests provided ideal cover and its hills perfect lookout points for guerrilla warfare. Blue and Gray troops lived off the land, seizing livestock, grain, and crops from families that could ill afford the loss. The end of the war brought no relief, as bands of outlaws roamed the hills under the guise of Reconstruction. Veterans returned to confiscate land under the new bounty rights. Sympathizers on both sides continued their petty feuds. What little civil government existed was riddled with graft. Murderers were set free by corrupt courts. Anarchy prevailed.

A scene from "Shepherd of the Hills"; photo courtesy Shepherd of the Hills Homestead.

The breakdown of law and order led to the formation of a vigilante group in 1883 under the leadership of a charismatic veteran named Nathaniel Kinney. Dedicated to redressing grievances and imposing a semblance of control over the rampant murder and mayhem, they met on treeless mountaintops called "bald knobs." A grateful populace dubbed them the Taney County Baldknobbers, and the name stuck. But as often happens when groups take the law into their own hands, the Baldknobbers began to think of themselves as judge and jury. Anyone who disagreed with their views was subject to their justice: swift vengeance. The locals soon came to fear their trademark calling card, a bunch of switches on an intended victim's bed, as much as the rapacity of the lawless. Splinter groups attracted an unsavory lot who marauded under the pretext of keeping the community safe.

When the Baldknobbers voted on April 15, 1885, to lynch notorious criminals Frank and Jubal Taylor without due process, a cadre of outraged citizens formed the "anti-Baldknobbers." This ushered in a three-year reign of terror as the two groups vied for control of the county. The original Taney County Baldknobbers finally agreed to disband at the governor's request, but not before Kinney was brutally shot by one Billy Miles (who earned the "right" by losing a poker match among several anti-Baldknobbers) on August 20, 1888. Ironically, the Baldknobbers saw themselves as a beacon of civilization and, indeed, many historians credit such vigilante groups with making the frontier safe.

In 1882, in the midst of the anarchy, Reuben S. Branson, an enterprising schoolteacher, moved his family to the mouth of the Roark Creek and opened a general store. Locals had discovered a profitable trade in timber, and thick stands of oak, cedar, hickory, and walnut were gradually denuded. Logging camps sprang up and Reuben prospered. In 1886, he applied for and won the position of first postmaster, a political appointment in those days, which carried with it the right to name the town: Branson sounded good. But Reuben's luck soon changed. His land was flooded by the White River, and he had to move to higher ground; his brother, Galba, was appointed sheriff and was promptly shot dead by the Miles brothers, whom he had intended to arrest for Kinney's killing. Reuben was eventually elected county clerk and headed for the county seat of Forsyth, leaving the town that still bears his name.

That town was little more than a collection of homes and a few mercantile establishments in 1903, when it was transformed forever by the Iron Horse. There's no doubt that the railroad was the single greatest contributor to the opening of the frontier. It also provided an opportunity to exploit America's natural resources and encouraged unscrupulous business practices among some. A man named B.B. Price formed the Branson Town Company to buy land from homesteaders. In a typical transaction Price purchased a plot for $1,500, then sold it to the Branson Town Company for $25,000. A fierce competition between developers ensued. A new municipal plan was drawn up; the town even briefly changed its name to Lucia, named for one of the developer's daughters.

Branson grew dramatically in the three years before the completion of the railroad line in 1906. The Branson Hotel (still standing and today functioning as a B&B) was constructed in 1904, followed by the Bank of Branson in 1905, when the local newspaper, the *Branson Echo*, touchingly reported, "We've become quite a little city; we have three mercantile stores and a bank being built." Even destructive fires in 1912 and '13 didn't dampen the locals' enthusiasm; they simply rebuilt the structures in concrete.

The new Branson was designed to be a railroad town: The Missouri Pacific Company encouraged locals to grow so-called cash crops—cotton, tobacco, tomatoes—then use the railroad to move the freight. But the Iron Horse primarily made Branson and the White River accessible to vacationers, who had always known about the area's superb fishing but had to travel for days by wagon or

3

Vacationers at Ozark Beach, 1918. Photo courtesy Ionamae Rebenstorf and the Branson Tri-Lakes Daily News

oxcart for their holiday. The first major realtor, the Colony Farm Homes Association, issued pamphlets as early as 1908 extolling the wonders of the region, its clean air and clean lifestyle. This became the enduring base for tourism in the area.

Also around the turn of the century, the first Branson phenomenon occurred. It started in 1896 when a minister and landscape painter named Harold Bell Wright rode into town. His father and brother had fallen gravely ill during a trapping expedition, and Wright planned to cross the White River to come to their aid. But a swift current and abnormally high watermark convinced the operator of the Compton Ferry service to cease operation for the day, so Wright rode up the hillside and found shelter for the night in the cabin of John and Anna Ross. He awoke to a scene of unparalleled splendor—a panorama of mountains, rivers, and valleys extending for more than 40 miles. Entranced, he returned several times over the next few years, always staying with the Rosses and their young son Charles.

In 1904 Wright was diagnosed with tuberculosis and decided that a healthy dose of fresh mountain air was just what the doctor ordered. He set up camp on a knoll in the Rosses' cornfield and over the next two years labored on a manuscript he called *The Shepherd of the Hills*, whose characters were thinly disguised portraits of his friends. The themes it sounded still resonate today: the wholesomeness and integrity of the people, the bewitching beauty of the countryside. Published in 1907, it became a runaway bestseller and eventually spawned four movie versions; at one point it was the best-selling novel of all time (first eclipsed by *Gone with the Wind*, then others). Today its imprint can be found in the names of many attractions and locales; it even created an official geographic subregion, "Shepherd of the Hills Country."

Taking advantage of the White River Railroad, tourists descended in ever-increasing hordes, seeking the people and places of their beloved book. They became such a nuisance that they drove the Rosses (Old Matt, Young Matt, and Aunt Mollie in the novel) to abandon their original dwelling. Sadly, the Rosses never forgave their friend for what they regarded as selling them out.

It was about this time that an event with far-reaching implications for tourism occurred. The Powersite Dam was completed in 1913 as a way to harness the White River for electrical power. It was reputedly the largest power dam in the country at that time. The impoundment of the river formed Lake Taneycomo (after Taney County, Missouri), around which resort communities like Rockaway Beach sprang up almost immediately. Even more tourists came to take a pleasure cruise on the riverboat *Sammy Lane* or marvel at the dam itself, and the calm waters of the lake provided a more efficient means of transportation for the locals. The Ozarks Playgrounds Association was formed in 1919 to promote "the true Ozarkian spirit of hospitality and fair dealing" and coined a catchy slogan, "the Land of a Million Smiles." The population swelled.

That's how things stood for a decade, until Jim Owen moved his family from the middle of the state to Branson to open a drugstore. His son, also named Jim, would become a major player in the commercial development of the town. A sharp operator and opportunist, Jim Jr. saw the perfect way to bolster Branson's tourism. Realizing that most city slickers envisioned the locals as hillbillies, he decided to capitalize on the image. By

Watermelons transported by johnboat to the shore of Lake Taneycomo, 1920s. Photo by Carl Mayhew and courtesy of Ionamae Rebenstorf and the Branson Tri-Lakes Daily News

Top: Jim Owen, Frog Millhouse, and Steve Miller (left to right) in front of the Owen Theater, 1930; photo courtesy Jim Gibbs and the Branson Tri-Lakes Daily News

Bottom: Jim Owen; photo courtesy Branson Tri-Lakes Daily News

inventing jokes, riddles, and tales, he subtly tweaked the tourists, and everyone loved the cornball act. By the early 1930s he had built the Owen Hillbilly Theater; every day he advertised the movie bill with a new homespun saying, "Big Jim Sez…", on a chalkboard. In so doing he perfected the hillbilly alphabet and contributed to the preservation of Ozarks folklore.

Owen helped to bring the popular culture of the time to the Ozarks. He hired high-school boys to travel by mule around the countryside with a projector, setting up makeshift screens on sheets and showing his latest movies. He also engaged Steve Miller, a booking agent for top bands who had connections with radio executives in New York, to bring citified music to this rural outpost. Soon, early airwaves personalities such as Gene Autry were brought in to promote movies and the burgeoning float-fishing business. Branson became the in place for a "getting back to nature" vacation. Owen's untiring efforts paid off in major media exposure, as national publications such as *Life*, *Sports Afield*, and *Outdoor Life* reported on the fast-growing destination throughout the 1930s and early 1940s.

Branson slept for nearly two decades. But in 1959 the area's complexion changed radically once again. Table Rock Dam was constructed to alleviate the continual flooding of the White and James rivers, as well as to generate electricity. Table Rock Lake came into being, virtually destroying the communities along Lake Taneycomo, now fed by the frigid waters at the bottom of the new lake. Family resorts dependent on activities such as swimming, water skiing, and boating closed shop because of the change in water temperature; fishing resorts took their place, as it was discovered that trout thrived in the 52° waters. Warmer Table Rock attracted bass fishermen, as well as families, who flocked to new resort towns such as Kimberling City.

Also in the 1950s four visionary families began the modern era of development in and around Branson, creating businesses that cemented the area's reputation as a premier family-entertainment destination. Hugo and Mary Herschend first visited the Ozarks in 1946 and toured a local attraction known as the Marble Cave. Like Wright, they instantly fell in love with the area; a few years later they leased the cave (renamed Marvel) for

99 years and began construction on a funicular to transport tourists back to the top. Recognizing the need to entertain those waiting on line, they erected an old-time blacksmith shop, general store, doll shop, print shop, and candy store during the late 1950s. Those were the humble beginnings of Silver Dollar City, a theme park dedicated to preserving the unique artistic heritage of the Ozarks. The Silver Dollar City Corporation now owns the White Water amusement center, the Grand Village shopping center, the Grand Palace theater, the *Branson Belle* showboat, and, with Dolly Parton, Dollywood, in Pigeon Forge, Tennessee.

In 1946, the same year the Herschends first visited Branson, Dr. and Mrs. Bruce Trimble purchased the bulk of Lizzie McDaniel's estate, composed of Inspiration Point (where Harold Bell Wright camped in 1904) and the original Ross homestead (where Wright wrote his masterpiece). The Trimbles spruced up the homesite and opened a museum, restaurant, and souvenir shop on the property in the early 1950s. "Old Matt's Cabin" became the focal point of the "Shepherd of the Hills Homestead," Branson's second great theme park. In 1960 the Trimbles produced the first mammoth outdoor stage version of the novel; the wildly popular show includes donnybrooks, an old-fashioned square dance, and the torching of a log cabin, enacted by a gargantuan cast of 85 (not including more than 30 horses, a flock of sheep, 10 buggies, and assorted firearms).

The previous year saw the formation of the Baldknobbers musical group. The five Mabe brothers had made a substantial hit performing their brand of country music and hillbilly humor at Silver Dollar City. They thought the time was ripe to open a theater of their own. Their venue, on the Taneycomo lakefront downtown, was the first musical theater to open in Branson. Encouraged by the Mabes' success, the Presleys, another talented family, performed a similar show in 1963, this one way out in the "boondocks" on Route 76. Even today, paterfamilias Lloyd Presley tells stories of watching for a pair of headlights coming down the lightly trafficked road, then stopping the car and performing a funny skit to lure the potential audience. In 1967 the Presleys opened the first musical theater on what is now 76 Country Boulevard, or the Strip. Not to be outdone, the Baldknobbers followed suit in 1968. Despite the increasing number of international celebrities joining the Branson music scene, the Presleys' and Baldknobbers' shows continue to sell out, playing to capacity audiences. Perhaps it's the opportunity to watch three generations performing together in a fast-paced show that accounts for their enduring popularity.

The Baldknobbers; photo courtesy Branson Tri-Lakes Daily News.

The first artists of national repute entered the picture in 1971 when the Foggy River Boys began performing in Kimberling City. By 1974 they had opened a theater on Route 76. More musical shows, most of them in the family mode, joined the bandwagon. In 1977 Bob Mabe left the Baldknobbers to form the Bob-O-Links Country Hoedown

Roy Clark; photo courtesy Branson Tri-Lakes Daily News.

Theater, which started to attract name artists, including Mel Tillis, for short engagements. Three more theaters opened in 1981. Traffic became a problem, paving the way for the bumper-and-grind along Route 76 that greets visitors today, nicknamed by good-natured locals the "longest parking lot in America."

But Branson really came of age in 1983, when Roy Clark opened the Roy Clark Celebrity Theater. It was the first venue linked permanently to a widely known entertainer. Roy played 100 dates each year and brought in fellow celebrities such as Jim Stafford and Ray Stevens, who built their own theaters (Ray has since moved on). In 1986 the Lowe Sisters became the first Branson act to appear on the Grand Ole Opry stage, giving the fledgling entertainment mecca its first real national exposure. The following year, Boxcar Willie became the first star to buy a theater and perform on a permanent, year-round basis. And they kept coming. In 1990 Mel Tillis, Shoji Tabuchi, and Mickey Gilley opened their first Branson theaters. The following year, the city of Branson issued building permits for $84 million in new construction, including the 4,000-seat Grand Palace, whose hosts were slated to be Glen Campbell and Louise Mandrell. Glen has since built his own theater, and Louise has pursued other opportunities. Andy Williams became the first noncountry singing star to announce his intention to build a theater.

In 1991 *60 Minutes* televised its now-famous segment asking what on earth was going on here. And the rest, as they say, is history.

Essential Information

GETTING READY TO GO

VISITOR INFORMATION

The **Branson/Lakes Area Chamber of Commerce** (Box 1897, 269 W. Rte. 248 at Rte. 65, Branson 65615, tel. 417/334–4136, fax 417/334–4139) is an invaluable source of information about Ozark Mountain Country. Visitor's-center hours change seasonally; call for information.

PLANNING YOUR VISIT

Your first impressions of Branson in high season may be daunting: miles of cars lining Highway 76 (a.k.a. 76 Country Boulevard or the Strip), the crush of chattering, toe-tapping folks in theater lobbies, the constant hum of activity at hotel front desks. But the area is user-friendly, and its people are even more so. Tourism is their livelihood, yet their smiles never seem mass-produced, despite the proliferation of souvenir shops and fast-food outlets: good old-fashioned hospitality hasn't gone out of style in the Ozarks. Don't hesitate to ask for advice or information. Despite Branson's phenomenal growth, residents pride themselves on providing customized, customer-oriented service. That goes for the transplants, too.

RESERVATIONS

Branson offers a mind-boggling number of reservation specialists, many of whom can arrange your entire trip, from booking hotel rooms to acquiring tickets. The price they quote usually includes a built-in commission. Below is a partial listing of companies that can assist you with your vacation before you go; for a complete listing contact the

Branson/Lakes Area Chamber of Commerce (*see* Visitor Information, *above*). For companies that will help you with travel itineraries once you get to Branson, *see* Making Reservations in Getting Around Branson, *below*.

GENERAL BOOKINGS

Branson Bound Reservations (109 Wood Ridge Dr., Branson 65616, tel. 417/335–BEST) and **Branson Vacation Reservations** (702 S. 3rd St., Branson 65616, tel. 417/335–8747 or 800/221–5692) arrange group and individual reservations for lodgings, restaurants, shows, and theme parks. **Branson Hotline** (tel. 800/523–7589) books hotel and motel accommodations and theater reservations.

SHOWS

Attraction Tixs (Box 7193, Branson 65616, tel. 417/338–8728 or 800/884–8497), **Ozark Ticket and Travel Network** (109 N. Business Rte. 65, Branson 65616, tel. 800/233–7469), and **Tour Branson** (Box 7183, Branson 65615, tel. 417/335–6007, 800/64–TICKET, or 800/269–1376) will reserve seats for your favorite shows.

ACCOMMODATIONS

For information about bed-and-breakfasts, contact **Bed & Breakfast Inns of Missouri** (Box 775294, St. Louis 63177, tel. 314/947–7000) or **Ozark Mountain Country B&B** (Box 295, Branson 65615, tel. 417/334–4720 or 800/695–1546), which also provides information about the Branson Lakes area. Although it won't assist you with making reservations, the **Missouri Association of RV Parks and Campgrounds** (3020 S. National St., Springfield, MO 65804, tel. 314/564–7993) provides statewide listings.

RESTAURANTS

Many hotels will make dinner reservations for guests, but restaurants don't often require or accept reservations for any meal unless they are for a group of 10 or more. If you are with a group, however, calling ahead will expedite seating, and the restaurant may offer a group discount or a special menu that will get your crowd in and out faster.

SIGHTSEEING BUS TOURS

Among the sightseeing companies offering bus tours of the area are **Celebrity Tours** (Box 460, Kimberling City 65686, tel. 417/739–1313), **Branson's Unique Sightseeing** (Box 1114, Branson 65616, tel. 417/335–5881), and **Ozark Mountain Sightseeing** (Box 1167, Branson 65616, tel. 417/334–1850 or 800/925–8498). They cater to groups that want to explore the Branson Lakes area on day trips. Advance booking is recommended, especially during peak season. Individual travelers and families can occasionally tour with larger groups.

TOURS AND PACKAGES

For travelers with time and budget constraints, group package tours—invariably via bus—can be a tremendous bargain. Most tours range from 5 to 14 days in length and generally originate and conclude in a nearby large city; St. Louis, Memphis, and Little Rock are the most common hubs. The preplanned and prepaid itinerary usually includes tours, transfers, lodging, shows, and meals (most of the time) and eliminates a lot of the hassle involved in arranging your own vacation. Joining a group is a great opportunity to make friends, particularly if you're traveling alone. It's also an excellent way to hit the high points and familiarize yourself with the region.

Two drawbacks to consider: (1) although group tours cram a lot of sightseeing into a short period of time (according to the "If it's Tuesday, this must be Branson" philosophy of travel), you'll invariably miss—or race through—several potential highlights of your trip; and (2) you'll have little flexibility in where you go or stay—and probably won't be able to choose your traveling companions.

When researching your options, always ask the following questions:

• What expenses are included? Hidden costs such as meals, side excursions, service charges, taxes, gratuities, and entertainment can make a seemingly affordable option more expensive than you had expected.

• What's the cancellation policy, and how steep are the penalties?

• What are the ratings for hotels and restaurants on the itinerary, including facilities and amenities that may be important to you, such as fitness rooms or children's programs?

• Are there surcharges for single accommodations?

• Can you choose to complete only part of the tour (usually at least 50%) for a slight surcharge, if your time is limited or if part of the tour itinerary doesn't appeal to you? This must be arranged in advance, as no tour operator will refund a portion of your trip because you ended up not liking the destination.

• Does the motor coach have air-conditioning, a rest room, and other amenities?

Below is a selection of tour operators. The Branson/Lakes Area Chamber of Commerce can provide a complete list of tour guides for the immediate area.

Maupintour (Box 807, Lawrence, KS 66044, tel. 913/843–2121 or 800/255–4266) is a six-night/seven-day package beginning and ending in Little Rock, Arkansas, and including three shows in Branson as well as stops in Silver Dollar City, Eureka Springs, and the Ozark Folk Center in Mountain View, Missouri.

Tauck Tours (11 Wilton Rd., Westport, CT 06880, tel. 203/226–6911 or 800/468–2825) offers an eight-day/seven-night package that begins in Memphis,

Tennessee, and ends in St. Louis, Missouri, making a brief one-day stop (no overnight) in Branson.

For a more moderately priced package try **Mayflower Tours** (1225 Warren Ave., Downers Grove, IL 60515, tel. 708/960–3430; outside IL, 800/323–7604), a five-night/six-day round-trip vacation from St. Louis, Missouri, that includes two nights in Branson. **Domenico Tours** (751 Broadway, Bayonne, NJ 07002, tel. 800/554–8687) also prices its five- to eight-day trips through the Ozarks for the budget traveler.

Globus Gateway's (95-25 Queens Blvd., Rego Park, NY 11374, tel. 800/221–0090) first-class but affordable itinerary includes eight nights and nine days beginning in St. Louis, Missouri, and taking in Branson and Eureka Springs, among other stops, before ending in Memphis, Tennessee.

WHAT IT WILL COST

On a Branson vacation you can splurge to your heart's content or enjoy one of the most affordable trips you'll ever take. Unless you're staying at one of a few premier resorts, you won't need to pay more than $100 for a double room, and you could pay as little as $20. Dinner at the fanciest restaurants could set you back more than $60 for two, but you can also get a decent three-course meal for less than $12 per person. Show tickets are one of the best bargains in live entertainment, at $12–$20 per ticket. Here's an average jam-packed day's expenses, based on peak-season rates. Quoted costs do not include sales tax (9¼% on lodging and attractions, 7¼% on restaurants), service (figure 15% tip for waiters, $1 per bag for bellhops), or drinks.

Double room in moderately priced hotel on Strip	$ 59.95
Breakfast show for two (meals and tickets included)	$ 30.00
Lunch and full day for two at Silver Dollar City	$ 60.00
Dinner for two at moderate restaurant	$ 35.00
Two tickets for typical show	$ 35.00
TOTAL	$ 219.95
On a stricter budget? Try this typically full itinerary.	
Double room in lower-price motel on Strip	$ 39.00
Breakfast cruise for two	$ 25.90
Lunch buffet for two	$ 9.98

Admission for two to Ripley's Museum	$ 17.90
Dinner show for two	$ 61.00
TOTAL	$ 153.78

HOW TO CUT EXPENSES

Branson is a value vacation destination; two people can get by comfortably on $150 a day and still enjoy most of the local attractions. You'll often realize significant savings by joining a tour group, of course, but travelers on a budget who prefer to travel on their own have plenty of cost-efficient options. Always ask about bargain rates for children and senior citizens before you make reservations. An RV holiday costs less, since you're paying a token fee for campground use and can cook your own meals. You can also cut corners by getting motel rooms with refrigerators and kitchenettes and preparing your own meals. It pays to inquire about the lowest rates, since published rack rates are generally much higher than frequent promotions. If you don't mind a little fingernail-biting, most hotels drop their rates dramatically at the last minute if they're not full. However, we recommend this primarily in shoulder seasons—spring and late fall—when a cruise down Highway 76 reveals ever-decreasing prices on hotel signs.

In general, downtown accommodations (away from the main part of the Strip) are less expensive, more basic, and farthest from most of the theaters. Prices drop significantly during Ozark Mountain Christmas in November and December, although most theaters and attractions remain open. Check out buffets (*see* Chapter 8, Dining) offered at family dining establishments, find out about early-bird specials (usually served between 4 and 6 PM), and combine entertainment with a meal (there are two dinner theaters, lunch and dinner cruises, and several breakfast shows). There is no cut-rate or discount ticket service yet, but you can save by buying combination tickets for some attractions. For example, you can pay admission to Silver Dollar City (SDC) and Whitewater, or to SDC and a show at the Grand Palace.

WHEN TO GO

If you crave the excitement of packed theaters and buzzing crowds, go to Branson during the traditional high season, Memorial Day through Labor Day. Almost all of the headliners are in town then, although some take a one- or two-week break in July and August. The crowds (and by now legendary traffic) are at their heaviest in June, September, and October, which is also when prices soar. If you do go during peak season, early planning will be the key to a successful vacation. Although you'll receive a warm welcome whether you've made reservations or not, without them you may find yourself waiting in long lines for tickets, and you still may not get the first-row seats you'd hoped for. Moreover, many shows—and hotel rooms—sell out well in advance, thanks to busloads of tour groups. This is not to suggest that you have to adhere to a strict schedule, but you should be prepared for the occasional disappointment, inconvenience, and long line.

More and more people come to town for **Branson Country Spring** (mid-March–mid-April), a celebration that has helped extend the tourist season through specially scheduled concerts, sporting events, and festivals that celebrate everything from the blooming wildflowers to the spawning bass. Late April and early November are perhaps the best months to visit, when the stars are still around, rates are low, crowds are limited, and the weather and scenery are glorious. Early spring coaxes the delicate white and pink blossoms from the dogwoods, and autumn triggers a dazzling fireworks display of the turning oak and hickory trees.

November and December have become popular months, as well, as **Ozark Mountain Christmas** (mid-November–December) celebrates the yuletide spirit, transforming the town into a soundstage for a remake of the movie *It's a Wonderful Life*. The rest of winter is quiet and likely to remain so. There has been a concerted effort to promote Branson in January and February, but most businesses, including theaters and theme parks, still close up shop. Locals welcome this down time, though, as it gives them a chance to rest. Prices at those hotels, stores, and restaurants that remain open plummet even lower. Jim Stafford and Pump Boys and Dinettes are among the few who perform year-round, even when the temperature drops and a chill settles over the town.

OZARKS WISDOM

With so many outdoor activities available in Branson, it helps to be able to forecast the weather. You've heard of the groundhog's ability to foretell the end of winter, but did you know that if cats sneeze, rabbits romp in the road, hogs start building a nest, or sheep turn their backs to the wind, you're about to be drenched? Or that according to the old nursery rhyme, "If a cock crows when he goes to bed, he'll get up with a wet head"? On the other hand, "When the morning sun is red, the ewe and the lamb go wet to bed." Plan your day accordingly.

WEATHER

The Ozarks enjoy a generally mild climate, although they can experience extremes of heat and cold common to the Great Plains, farther north. Winter temperatures can fluctuate wildly but average in the low 50s during the day and around freezing at night. Ice storms are more prevalent than snowstorms, and driving along back roads can be hazardous. Spring and fall offer mild days and a pleasant nip in the air at night. The dogwoods of spring give way to the dog days of summer, when high temperatures usually exceed 90°, but brisk mountain breezes keep the air circulating on even the most humid days, and nighttime temperatures hover in the balmy mid-60s.

The following are average maximum and minimum daily temperatures for Branson

Jan.	40F	4C	Feb.	43F	6C	Mar.	54F	12C
	25	-4		27	-3		36	2
Apr.	65F	18C	May	76F	24C	June	85F	29C
	47	8		58	14		67	19
July	88F	31C	Aug.	88F	31C	Sept.	81F	27C
	72	22		70	21		63	17
Oct.	68F	20C	Nov.	54F	12C	Dec.	43F	6C
	50	10		38	3		29	-2

FESTIVALS AND SEASONAL EVENTS

BRANSON COUNTRY SPRING (MID-MARCH–MAY)

Branson Country Spring, initiated in 1993 to stimulate tourism during the shoulder season, is a selection of events that celebrate the region. These include Americana Branson Jam, which brings many stars—and their friends—back home for a rip-roaring jamboree in mid-March; a film festival at the larger-than-life, state-of-the-art IMAX theater, with a six-story screen; the opening of the 20-mile, self-guided Dogwood Trail, lined with blossoming trees; and the two biggest U.S. fishing tournaments, the Bass Pro Spring Fishing Classic in early March at Table Rock Lake and April's White Bass Round-Up in Forsyth.

OZARK MOUNTAIN CHRISTMAS (NOVEMBER–DECEMBER)

Christmas is a joyous time in the Ozarks. Nativity scenes replete with camels and chariots are brought to vivid, messy, smelly life, and towering, 40-foot Nativity figures glow atop rocky bluffs. Marching bands and extravagant floats take to the streets for the Adoration Parade. There's a Festival of Lights, with blazing lights illuminating the highway from Springfield to Branson. For the Enchanted Forest display, at the village of Indian Point, fanciful, multicolored lights shaped like animals and fairy-tale characters are strung around Table Rock Lake and reflected in the water. Radio City Music Hall's Rockettes come to town, too, to perform a Christmas show, and the stars tailor their acts for the season. All this adds up to Ozark Mountain Christmas, which draws more than 400,000 visitors to Branson each November and December.

OTHER NOTABLE EVENTS

Flower and Garden Festival (mid–late April) celebrates the region's profusion of wildflowers and cultivated plants; **Country Crafts Show and Sale** (July and August) is the ticket for picking up items ranging from saddles to scented candles; **National Quilt Festival** (early September) presents pieces from around the country; **National Crafts Festival** (mid-September–late October) compares regional traditions in crafts such as woodcarving, leather working, quilting, and glassblowing; and **Fall Harvest festivals** (mid-September–late October) at Silver Dollar City and Shepherd of the Hills showcase the earth's bounty with related fun and games like apple-bobbing and scarecrow-building contests.

WHAT TO PACK

Be sure to pack at least one sweater or jacket, regardless of when you travel, as nights can turn nippy even in summer. If you're an angler or hiker, bring the appropriate clothing and gear, although there are many sporting goods stores and rental shops (most notably Bass Pro, the world's largest; *see* Chapter 5, Excursions in Ozark Mountain Country) in the region. A camera is a virtual necessity to capture the area's quiet, natural beauty, your family whooping it up on a thrilling ride, even the music stars themselves, many of whom board tour buses for autographs and "photo ops." Don't worry if you run out of film; nearly every souvenir shop carries an assortment of brands and speeds, and Walmart and the new K-Mart sell it at discount prices. If you use prescription drugs, be sure to bring an adequate supply for the duration of the trip. And don't forget your eyeglasses or contact lenses: You wouldn't want to miss seeing any of the performances.

DRESS

Locals are casual and practical, dressing for the elements more than for style—after all, they still view their land as an outdoors paradise first and an entertainment center second. Although Branson's shops sell glitzy sequined and appliquéd apparel, you'll rarely see residents so attired. Even attending the theater is an informal affair, with jeans outnumbering suits. However, some visitors like to dress up for the ritzier restaurants and hottest shows, and no one will think it strange if you do so: Feel free to bring a jacket and tie, or dress.

CAR RENTALS

Rental-car reservations are recommended April through October. Rates vary depending on when you need a car, the size and type of car, and additional features, but special deals are available throughout the year.

Most major rental-car companies are represented in the Springfield area, all with airport desks, including **Avis** (tel. 417/865–6226 or 800/331–1212), **Budget** (tel. 417/831–2662 or 800/527–0700), **Hertz** (tel. 417/865–1681 or 800/654–3131), and **National** (tel. 417/865–5311 or 800/227–7368).

Agencies in Branson are **A-1** (823 Rte. 165, tel. 417/335–3932 or 417/334–0246), **Avis** (College of the Ozarks, Clark Airport, Point Lookout, tel. 417/334–4945 or 800/331–1212), and **Dollar** (1029½ W. Rte. 76, tel. 417/335–8588 or 800/800–4000).

For an unforgettable whirl, you can relive the flapper era and rent a colorful Model A replica, replete with rumble seat, from **Roadsters U-Drive** (3030 Rte. 76 W, Branson, tel. 417/335–2337). This car is available April–October at a rate of $24.95 per hour, gasoline and unlimited mileage included; the daily rate may vary.

HINTS FOR TRAVELING WITH CHILDREN

Branson is the ultimate family destination: In fact, you could liken it to one giant theme park. Children are enthusiastically welcomed everywhere, even in the theaters (indeed, many stars' kids perform in shows). You'll never lack for things to do together. Go-carts, miniature golf, and water slides are common sights along the highways. Parents and children enjoy special events held throughout the Ozarks, from craft, music, and flower festivals to old-fashioned county fairs. They are a great way to introduce your children to other cultures and lifestyles. There are no child-care centers in the Branson/Lakes area, but local baby-sitters can be contacted through the front desk of your hotel.

> OZARKS WISDOM
>
> *Hill folks joke that it's only when the kids are back in school after summer vacation that "you unnerstand jist how important book larnin' really iz."*

Family Travel Times, a newsletter published 10 times a year by *Travel with Your Children* (45 W. 18th St., 7th Floor Tower, New York, NY 10011, tel. 212/206–0688) is an invaluable resource, offering ideas for having fun with your children. A one-year subscription costs $40 and includes access to back issues and twice-weekly opportunities to call for advice.

HINTS FOR TRAVELERS WITH DISABILITIES

The Ozark region has begun to recognize its responsibility to provide access for travelers with disabilities. Unfortunately, however, that awareness seems limited to providing special parking spaces, ramps, elevators, a few wider entries, and support bars in rest rooms. The wheelchair symbol is used to indicate accessibility. The following organizations and publications help people with disabilities plan their vacations:

The **Society for the Advancement of Travel for the Handicapped** (347 5th Ave., Suite 610, New York, NY 10016, tel. 212/447–7284) publishes a list of tour operators that run tours for travelers with disabilities.

The **Information Center for Individuals with Disabilities** (Ft. Point Pl., 1st Floor, 27–43 Wormwood St., Boston, MA 02217, tel. 617/727–5540) provides problem-solving assistance, as well as a list of travel agents specializing in tours for travelers with disabilities.

Handicapped Travel Newsletter (Drawer 269, Athens, TX 75751, tel. 903/677–1260) has more than 200,000 subscribers and costs $10 per year.

Travel Industry and Disabled Exchange (5435 Donna Ave., Tarzana, CA 91356, tel. 818/368–5648) issues a quarterly newsletter and information on travel agencies for a $15 annual fee.

Mobility International USA (Box 3551, Eugene, OR 97403, tel. 503/343–1284) coordinates exchange programs for travelers with disabilities throughout the world. For a $20 annual fee, the organization offers information on accommodations and organized study programs.

Greyhound Bus Systems (tel. 800/752–4841) offers a "Helping Hand" program, which enables the traveler with disabilities and his or her companion to travel for the price of a single fare. The two nearest Greyhound stops are in Springfield, Missouri (803 St. Louis St. at National St., tel. 417/862–5097), and in Branson (1911 Main St., in front of Branson Welcome Center, tel. 417/337–9323), but the latter is not a terminal.

Amtrak (tel. 800/USA–RAIL) offers pamphlets regarding special travel arrangements. The nearest Amtrak stations are in Little Rock, Arkansas (Markham and Victory Sts., tel. 501/372–6841), 150 miles from Branson; and in Kansas City, Missouri (2200 Main St., tel. 816/421–3622), 213 miles from Branson.

The **U.S. Department of Transportation** (tel. 202/366–2220) publishes the free "Fly Rights," containing airline service information for travelers with disabilities.

Lone Star Airlines (tel. 800/877–3932) flies from Dallas and Houston, Texas, into Harrison, Arkansas, 35 miles south of Branson. Flying into Springfield, 40 miles north of Branson, are **American Eagle** (tel. 800/433–7300), **Northwest Airlink** (tel. 800/225–2525), **TWA** (tel. 800/221–2000), and **USAir** (tel. 800/428–4322). Federal law requires that all airplanes be accessible to people using wheelchairs; however, you should call the airlines to find out how each one accommodates people with disabilities.

Although they are not Branson-specific, several fine publications are also available for travelers with disabilities, among them *Fodor's Great American Vacations for People with Disabilities* ($18), published by Fodor's Travel Guides, Inc.; and *Travel for the Disabled* ($19.95), *Directory of Travel Agencies for the Disabled* ($19.95), and *Wheelchair Vagabond* ($19.95), all available from Twin Peaks Press (Box 129, Vancouver, WA 98666, tel. 206/694–2462).

HINTS FOR OLDER TRAVELERS

In Branson, many local hotels and restaurants prominently advertise discounts for senior citizens. For additional information, contact the following organizations:

The **American Association of Retired Persons** (601 E St. NW, Washington, DC 20049, tel. 202/434–2277) has two programs for independent travelers: (1) the Purchase Privilege Program, which offers discounts on hotels, airfare, car rentals, RV rentals, and sightseeing; and (2) the AARP Motoring Plan, provided by Amoco, which furnishes emergency road-service aid and trip-routing information. AARP also arranges group tours to the Ozarks at reduced rates through **AARP Travel Experience from American Express** (400 Pinnacle Way, Suite 450, Norcross, GA 30071, tel. 800/927–0111). AARP members must be 50 years of age or older. Annual dues are $8 per person or couple. For membership information, write to AARP Membership Processing Center (Box 199, Long Beach, CA 90848).

If you're using an AARP or other senior-citizen identification card to obtain a reduced hotel rate, remember to mention it at the time you make your reservation. Likewise, produce your card before being seated at participating restaurants, as menus, days, and hours of validity may vary. When renting a car, be sure to ask about special promotional rates, which may be cheaper than the published discounts.

Elderhostel (80 Boylston St., Suite 400, Boston, MA 02116, tel. 617/426–7788) is an innovative program for people age 60 or older. Participants live in dormitories on some 1,600 campuses around the world. Mornings are devoted to lectures and seminars, afternoons to sightseeing and field trips. The YMCA of the Ozarks sponsors such a program in Potosi, near St. Louis on the other side of the Ozarks Plateau, almost 200 miles from Branson; the program provides an excellent introduction to the region. The Elderhostel catalog is free if you participate in a program, or $10 annually.

Saga International Holidays (120 Boylston St., Boston, MA 02116, tel. 800/343–0273) specializes in group travel for individuals 60 years of age or older. A selection of variously priced tours lets you choose the package that interests you most. Saga tours either take in the entire Ozark region or concentrate on the Branson/Lakes area.

> **OZARKS WISDOM**
>
> *One timeless Ozark saying runs, "Better to be 80 years young than 40 years old."*

National Council of Senior Citizens (1331 F St. NW, Washington, DC 20004, tel. 202/347–8800) is a nonprofit advocacy group with about 5,000 local clubs across the country. Annual membership is $12 per person or couple. Members receive a monthly newsletter with travel information and an ID card that entitles them to reduced rates on hotels and car rentals. Contact the Missouri State Council (1520 St. Charles Rock Rd., Bridgeton 63044, tel. 314/739–7975) for information on local chapters.

Mature Outlook (6001 N. Clark St., Chicago, IL 60660, tel. 800/336–6330) is a travel club for people over age 50, offering a bimonthly newsletter and discounts at participating hotels and motels. Annual membership is $9.95 per person or couple. Several Branson properties subscribe.

Greyhound Bus Systems (803 St. Louis St. at National St., Springfield, MO, tel. 417/862–5097 or 800/752–4841; 1911 Main St., in front of Branson Welcome Center, tel. 417/337–9323) offer senior citizen fares, subject to blackout restrictions.

"Fly Rights," a free pamphlet providing information on airline services available to elderly passengers, is issued by the **U.S. Department of Transportation** (tel. 202/366–2220).

HINTS FOR SINGLE TRAVELERS

Although Branson is better known as a family destination, single travelers won't be bored or lonely thanks to the array of attractions and the warm atmosphere. Most motels offer a lower room rate for singles, and it's easy to strike up conversations with locals and visitors alike at the various venues. But there are no organized events aimed at single travelers, and if you're looking for pickups it had better be a Chevy at the local dealership. Branson just ain't a swingin' singles town. If you want action, head for Springfield, a college town with several clubs and rock venues.

HINTS FOR FOREIGN VISITORS

The Branson/Lakes Area Chamber of Commerce is starting to market itself more aggressively overseas and can help plan group trips. They'll also contact local residents or college students who speak the appropriate language to act as informal guides and interpreters. There are no multilingual tour operators in the Branson area as yet, but people are invariably helpful and can point you in the right direction if you're lost or in need of assistance.

FURTHER READING

Harold Bell Wright's classic novel of Ozark country life, *Shepherd of the Hills*, is required reading for anyone hoping to understand the enduring spirit of the area and its people. Readers respond to the heart-warming, at times harrowing, account of how an artist from the city in poor health is transformed by his encounters with hill folk. The novel interweaves reflective moments with melodrama, from barn dances to barn burnings.

Branson, Country Themes and Neon Dreams, by Crystal and Leland Payton, is the first coffee-table book on Branson. Through 282 vivid, never-before-published color photographs and rare vintage images, the book depicts the growth of the town from backwoods outpost to country-music phenomenon. To order, call 800/475-7893.

If you're interested in local folklore, *Ozark Magic and Folklore* (originally titled *Ozark Superstitions* and out of print until recently), by Vance Randolph, is a fascinating collection of tales (tall, old wives', and otherwise) and an insightful oral history. Eula Mae Stratton's booklet *Ozarks Cookery* is a delightful compilation of pioneer recipes spiced with recollections of growing up in the hills. The nonfiction book *The Land of Taney*, by Elmo Ingenthron, is a vivid portrait of the figures that have shaped Ozark Mountain Country history.

HOW TO GET TO BRANSON

BY PLANE

AIRPORTS AND AIRLINES
The closest major commercial airport is the **Springfield Regional Airport** (tel. 417/869–0300), 40 miles north of Branson. **American Eagle** (tel. 800/433–7300), **Northwest Airlink** (tel. 800/225–2525), **TWA** (tel. 800/221–2000), and **USAir** (tel. 800/428–4322) offer daily service via their respective hubs.

Regional carrier **Lone Star Airlines** (tel. 800/877–3932) offers limited service to

Harrison's tiny Boone County Airport (tel. 501/741–3433), 35 miles south of Branson on U.S. 65. There are no organized shuttles or taxi service from Harrison to Branson.

BETWEEN SPRINGFIELD AIRPORT AND BRANSON

BY TAXI   **Branson City Cab** (tel. 417/334–5678) and **A-1 Shuttle & Taxi** (tel. 417/335–4486) can arrange airport transfers from Springfield for about $60 each way. You'll need reservations for the 50- to 60-minute drive. If you're traveling with a group, find out if transfers are included in your package before you purchase them.

BY CAR   Branson is 40 miles south of Springfield along U.S. 65. It's a scenic 50- to 60-minute ride along well-maintained highway. During winter, watch for ice. For rental-car services, *see* Car Rentals in Getting Ready to Go, *above*.

BY BUS   The **Show-Me Shuttle Service** (tel. 417/883–7900 or 800/795–7555) schedules several round-trips daily for $40 per person, as well as service between Branson and Tulsa, Oklahoma. It also provides discount shuttle service for shows and shopping in Branson. **Branson Shuttle** (tel. 417/335–4466) runs regularly between the airport and Branson for $60 per person one way; group discounts are available.

BETWEEN M. GRAHAM CLARK AIRPORT AND DOWNTOWN

BY TAXI   **Branson City Cab** (tel. 417/334–5678) offers service between M. Graham Clark Airport and the downtown area and hotels along Highway 76 for about $10–$16. You must call ahead, otherwise you'll wait 5 to 20 minutes.

BY CAR   The airport is about a 10-minute drive from downtown along Route 65. For rental-car services *see* Car Rentals in Getting Ready to Go, *above*.

BY BUS

Greyhound Bus Systems (tel. 800/752–4841) runs daily service from most major North American gateways to Springfield (803 St. Louis St. at National St., tel. 417/862–5097) and Branson (1911 Main St., Branson Welcome Center, tel. 417/337–9323).

BY CAR

Branson is known as a "rubber tire" destination: The majority of visitors drive from within a 500-mile radius. The American Automobile Association (AAA) recently ranked Branson as the number-two drive destination in the country, just behind Orlando/Walt Disney World. Branson is still growing strong. Every year sees an influx of tourists from as far afield as Boston and San Francisco. For detailed driving tours, *see* Chapter 2, Driving Tours.

GETTING AROUND BRANSON

TOURIST INFORMATION

There is no end to the tourist material available in Branson. Just about every theater, restaurant, hotel, shop, and attraction prominently displays a brochure rack near the entrance. For a comprehensive assortment of material on the area, most of it free of charge (with the exception of local magazines and more detailed maps), stop by the **visitor's center** (269 W. Rte. 248 at U.S. 65, tel. 417/334–4136; hours vary seasonally; call for information). To get there from downtown, drive about ¼ mile north on Business Route 65 to the Branson Tourist Information Office, on the left. Among the most useful publications are the *Slip Away* vacation guide, *Sunny Days*, *This Week in Branson*, and the *Best Read Guide*. *Slip Away* is especially informative for up-to-date schedules and services in the Branson Lakes region; at $2.95 it's a wise investment.

SERVICES

EMERGENCIES
Dial 911 for emergency services in the Ozarks region.

POLICE **Branson Police Department** (tel. 417/334–3300), **Kimberling City Police Department** (tel. 417/739–2131), **Taney County Sheriff's Department** (tel. 417/546–2191), **Stone County Sheriff's Department** (tel. 417/357–6117).

FIRE **Branson Fire Department** (tel. 417/334–2600).

HOSPITALS AND AMBULANCES **Skaggs Community Hospital** (N. Business Rte. 65 at Skaggs Rd., Branson, tel. 417/335–7000; ambulance, 417/334–1441) has a Level III Trauma Center and 24-hour emergency service.

DENTISTS The **Branson Dental Center** (1034 W. Main St., tel. 417/334–6120) offers 24-hour emergency service.

PHARMACIES **Family Discount Drug** (650 N. Rte. 65, Branson, tel. 417/334–1390), **Master's Pharmacy** (811 S. Commercial St., Branson, tel. 417/334–6665), and **Wal-Mart** (2050 W. Rte. 76, Branson, tel. 417/334–5005) fill prescriptions daily 9–6.

BARBERS AND BEAUTY SALONS
Hair Dealers (Rtes. 76 and 165, Branson, tel. 417/334–8181), **Chick's Barber Shop** (112 Main St., Branson, tel. 417/334–2678), **Branson's Hair Place** (215 W. Pacific St., Branson, tel. 417/334–8044), **Fantasia Hair Creations and Tanning Salon** (Turkey

Creek Rd., Hollister, tel. 417/334–0300), **Squeeze and Tease Shop** (Stoneridge St., Kimberling City, tel. 417/739–5336).

CAR CARE
GAS STATIONS **E-Z Center** (W. Rte. 76, Branson, tel. 417/334–9732), **Tri-Lakes Petroleum** (E. Rte. 76, Branson, tel. 417/334–3940).

RV SERVICES **Branson Motorcoach Specialists** (Rinehart Rd., 5 mi north of Branson, tel. 417/336–5935) and **Ozark Mountain Mobile Bus Repair** (Rte. 13, Reeds Spring [17 mi from Branson], tel. 417/335–0299), offer 24-hour road service, maintenance, and repairs. Other facilities include **Music Country USA Bus Barn/Bus Wash** (Rte. 165, Branson, tel. 417/335–5060), which also offers interior and exterior cleaning, and **Fastrip-Fastlube** (Rte. 65, Hollister, tel. 417/334–3278).

EYE GLASSES
Ozark Family Vision (530 N. Business Rte. 65, tel. 417/334–7291).

GROCERY STORES
Consumers (W. Rte. 76, Branson, tel. 417/334–6024), **Country Mart** (I–65, Hollister, tel. 417/334–3383), **Hart's Supermarket** (Branson Heights Shopping Ctr., tel. 417/334–2101), and **Kimberling Supermarket** (Rte. 13, Kimberling City [15 mi from Branson], tel. 417/739–2544) are four of the largest in the Tri-Lakes area.

HEALTH CLUB
Club Roark (405 N. Business Rte. 65, Branson, tel. 417/334–8090) is the only game in town, but it should suit all your workout needs, with an indoor pool, two hot tubs, wet and dry saunas, Nautilus equipment, free weights, a cardiovascular room with treadmills and StairMasters, a basketball court, an aerobics room with classes, tanning beds, and massage therapy. You must purchase a $10 day pass.

RADIO STATIONS
KCOZ FM (College of the Ozarks, Point Lookout) airs National Public Radio. **KHOZ 103 FM** (Harrison) is pure country. **KLFC 103.5 FM** (Branson) is country. **KLTQ 96.5 FM** (Springfield) features the Top-40 and adult contemporary sounds. **KOMC 1220 AM** and **KZRK 106.3 FM** (Branson) plays a mix of country and golden oldies such as big band music, as well as local news and gossip. **KRLK F100.1 FM** (Eureka Springs) has a primarily country play list. **KTTS 94.7 FM** (Springfield) is the area's number-one station, offering mostly country. **KTXR 101.3 FM** (Springfield) plays big band, jazz, and classical favorites. **KWTO 560 AM** (Springfield) is all news and talk, with Paul Harvey and Rush Limbaugh among the commentators. **KGBX 105.9 FM** (Springfield) offers adult contemporary music. **KXUS 97.3 FM** (Springfield) offers the latest rock. **KGMY 100.5 FM** (Branson) showcases young, hip country stars.

RELIGIOUS SERVICES
There are nearly 100 churches of various denominations within a 10-mile radius of the

Branson Lakes area. The following is an abbreviated list concentrating on Branson itself. For more information, consult the chamber of commerce or the *Slip Away* guide. The nearest synagogue, **United Hebrew Congregation** (931 S. Kickapoo St., tel. 417/866–4760), is in Springfield.

Assembly of God (600 W. Main St., Branson, tel. 417/334–3803), **Branson Bible Church** (N. Business Rte. 65, Branson, tel. 417/334–3678), **Branson Christian Fellowship** (Rte. 65, Branson, tel. 417/335–4856), **Catholic Church–Our Lady of the Lake** (Rte. 76, 2 blocks west of Rte. 65, Branson, tel. 417/334–2928), **Church of Christ** (307 7th St., Branson, tel. 417/334–3866), **Church of Jesus Christ Latter Day Saints** (401 Pine St., Branson, tel. 417/335–6833), **First Baptist Church** (400 S. Sunshine St., Branson, tel. 417/224–7437), **First Presbyterian Church** (420 W. Main St., Branson, tel. 417/334–3468), **Kingdom Hall of Jehovah Witnesses** (Rte. 65-70 N, Branson, tel. 417/334–5507), **Nazarene Church of Branson** (3rd and Hensley Sts., Branson, tel. 417/334–4308), **Revival Fires Ministries** (Notch Village, Hwy. 76 W, Branson West, tel. 417/338–2422), **St. Paul's Lutheran Church—St. Paul's** (Parnell Dr. at Malone St., Branson, tel. 417/334–2469), **Seventh-Day Adventist Church** (Joe Bald Rd., Kimberling City, tel. 417/334–7950), **Shepherd of the Hills Episcopal Church** (Walnut and Highland Sts., Branson, tel. 417/334–3968), **United Methodist Church** (Rte. 76 W, Branson, tel. 417/334–3423).

MAKING RESERVATIONS

Several companies specialize in creating group tours (escorted or independent) once you're in Branson. Among the biggest are: **All Services TNT** (1316 W. Rte. 76, Branson 65616, tel. 417/336–2316 or 800/737–TNTT) and **Casey's Branson Connection** (Box 1064, Branson 65616, tel. 417/335–5933 or 800/766–3738). Both are experienced in dealing with RV groups.

It's recommended that you reserve theater seats before you arrive in Branson. *See* Making Reservations in Getting Ready to Go, *above,* to do so. If you need seats once you arrive, contact individual theaters. The advantage of calling ahead or stopping by before the show is seat selection: Although theaters usually reserve blocks of good seats for regular tour groups, remaining seats are doled out on a first-come, first-served basis, so the sooner you can get tickets, the better. Remember, however, that people sometimes return tickets, in which case you may luck out and get excellent seats at the last minute.

GETTING ORIENTED

It's hard to get lost in Branson proper. All activity radiates from Highway 76, which becomes Main Street downtown. Downtown, with its handsome stone-and-brick edifices, seems to have been transported from the 1930s and is an excellent place to browse through stores and eat a leisurely meal. The Strip, on the other hand, is all neon glitz, with its constant stream of traffic and an excitement all its own. If you're here for the shows, the Strip is where you'll spend your time. It's Branson's heartbeat, although newer theaters such as Glen Campbell's, Lawrence Welk's, and Charley Pride's sit along back roads a mile or two off the main drag. Routes to other attractions such as Silver Dollar City and Table Rock Lake are clearly marked.

Hot Tip

Are your favorite stars' performances sold out? One of Branson's secrets is the cancellation line: Anywhere from one to two hours before curtain, tickets that haven't been picked up are released to the general public.

TRAFFIC SURVIVAL KIT

Locals laugh about Highway 76 being "the longest parking lot in America," and for many it's become a way of life, but it's no joke when you're late to a show, particularly if you purchased the tickets months ago. Mindful of the problem, the municipal, county, and state governments have teamed up on a series of road-improvement and expansion programs.

Among the literally groundbreaking developments are the widening of U.S. 65 to four lanes in the most congested areas; the widening of Route 248 to five lanes by late 1995, between U.S. 65 and Shepherd of the Hills Expressway; and construction of an alternate loop road, the Ozark Mountain Highroad, which will take several years to complete. These improvements will help redirect the flow of traffic into Branson.

Within the town itself, a 1991 bond issue allocated $10 million to improve the infrastructure and is already paying dividends. There are three designated, color-coded "Time Saver" routes to help you avoid traffic along the Strip. Each parallels the 5-mile length of Highway 76. More than 180 "Guitar Logo" signs in red, yellow, and blue are matched with arrows at major intersections to point you in the right direction. Shepherd of the Hills Expressway (red) feeds into the western end of the Strip, near Shepherd of the Hills, Mutton Hollow, and the Country Tonite Theater and provides easier direct access to outlying venues like the Glen Campbell and Mel Tillis theaters. The blue route, along Gretna and Forsythe roads, leads to the heart of the Strip. The yellow route along Wildwood Street and Fall Creek Road allows easy access to downtown and sights around Lake Taneycomo.

Traffic is heaviest around lunchtime (11:30–2), at dinner time (5–7:45), and right after the shows let out (9:15–11). You'll save time if you plan to eat in the neighborhood of the theater you're going to (you can even leave your car in the restaurant parking lot). In general you should leave your hotel by 11:30 for a leisurely lunch before a matinee (2–3) and by 5 to ensure plenty of time for dinner before evening performances (7–8). Of course, if you're staying in a hotel centrally located on the Strip you may be able to walk to some restaurants and theaters. Whenever possible, pick up your tickets in advance or have them mailed to you to avoid waiting in line before the show.

CHARGE IT!

Major credit cards (American Express, Diners Club, Discover, MasterCard, and Visa) are common currency at all theaters and major hotels and restaurants. It's a good idea, though, to call ahead to make sure they accept your card of choice.

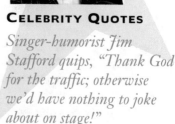

CELEBRITY QUOTES

Singer-humorist Jim Stafford quips, "Thank God for the traffic; otherwise we'd have nothing to joke about on stage!"

WHERE TO GET MONEY

ATMs (automated teller machines) dispense cash at conveniently located machines throughout the Branson area. There are also seven banks, open weekdays 9–3, that can handle most transactions: **Boatmen's Bank** (510 N. Business Rte. 65, Branson, tel. 417/336–6363), **Capital Bank** (203 N. Commercial St., Branson, tel. 417/334–2191), **Commerce Bank** (2210 W. Rte. 76, Branson, tel. 417/335–5684), **First Community Bank of Taney Co.** (121 S. Commercial St., Branson, tel. 417/336–6310), **Great Southern Savings Bank** (110 W. Hensley, Branson, tel. 417/334–6422), **Ozark Mountain Bank** (400 S. Commercial St., tel. 417/334–4125), and **United Savings and Loan** (520 W. Main St., Branson, tel. 417/335–2122).

Western Union (tel. 800/325–6000) charges a 5%–10% fee for transactions; money sent from the United States and Canada is usually available within minutes. There is an office at **Mailboxes Etc.** (200 E. College St., Branson, tel. 417/336–5776).

PARKING

Parking usually isn't a problem. Theaters, hotels, restaurants, and shopping malls have their own lots, all with ample space (a building-code requirement). Parking is free; validation is unnecessary. In addition, a new multilevel parking facility opened downtown in late 1994 on Sycamore Street just east of Commercial Street. It was not determined at press time if there would be a fee.

TAXIS

A-1 Shuttle & Taxi (tel. 417/335–6001) and **Branson City Cab** (tel. 417/334–5678) offer 24-hour service throughout the Branson Lakes region and are usually prompt. The drivers know the back routes. There is no meter; fixed fares to various points on the

Strip generally run $8 and $10, up to $15 to outlying destinations like Shepherd of the Hills Homestead and Silver Dollar City. There's no posted list of fares, but cabbies are reliable, and the dispatcher will quote your fare when you call.

WALKING

The town of Branson is relatively level, making walking a good bet for those seeking exercise. Bear in mind, however, that downtown is somewhat hillier, and the sidewalk along the length of the Strip is inconsistently paved. Your destination could be more than 6 miles away, but if you're going only a short distance, you'll save time by walking and avoiding the usual traffic jams and the search for parking spaces close to theater entrances. The Strip from downtown Branson to the last major theater, the Country Tonite Theater, is roughly 5 miles. But most of the theaters, restaurants, and shops are within 2 miles of one another. (Watch out for heavy two-way traffic while crossing Highway 76 and Shepherd of the Hills Expressway.) Attractions such as Silver Dollar City, Shepherd of the Hills, Mutton Hollow, College of the Ozarks, and Table Rock Lake are miles away and reachable only by car or taxi.

CRUISES

In the 1930s, Hollywood stars such as Gary Cooper and Gene Autry escaped to Branson for R&R, chartering fishing-float expeditions down the White River (subsequently dammed to form the troika of sparkling lakes that still attract fishermen from all over the country). Lake excursions are still a great way to experience the area. The **Lake Queen** stern-wheeler (downtown Branson, tel. 417/334–3015; admission $12.95 adults, $7.50 children under 12 for breakfast; $16.95 adults, $8 children under 12 for dinner; $6.95 adults, $4.50 children under 12 for sightseeing) plies the waters of Lake Taneycomo, offering 9 AM breakfast and 5 PM dinner cruises with entertainment, as well as four narrated sightseeing cruises daily. A **Festival of Lights Cruise** (Nov. 5–Dec. 19) is offered nightly at the same evening prices.

The *Princess* (tel. 417/335–4144; admission $22.95 adults, $10.95 children under 12) offers five cruises daily on Lake Taneycomo: an afternoon sightseeing trip and breakfast, lunch, and two dinner cruises. Prices range from $7 to $19.50. The *Princess* steams through winter (Nov.–Mar.) on a limited schedule. The ***Polynesian Princess*** re-creates the South Seas with Hawaiian-luau and Tahitian-style dances, and when the sun sets a laser show flashes across Table Rock Lake. A later dinner show and sightseeing cruise are also available.

The ***Showboat Branson Belle*** (tel. 417/336–7100) at White River Landing is Branson's newest lake attraction. A joint project developed by Silver Dollar City and Kenny Rogers, this glorious 1,000-passenger paddle-wheel riverboat will begin cruising Table Rock Lake in April 1995. After the food and entertainment, you'll be able to shop or enjoy a drink by the water at the new White River Landing complex.

Ride the Ducks (amphibious World War II vehicles converted into land-sea sightseeing vehicles) and **Sammy Lane Pirate Cruises** (*see* Chapter 4, Other Fun Things to Do in and Around Branson) are popular attractions for kids of all ages. Duck tours originate on the Strip; the Pirates set sail on Lake Taneycomo at the downtown dock.

Driving Routes to Branson

Millions of people make the pilgrimage to Branson by car each year. The Ozarks are centrally located within a full day's drive of most major cities in the Midwest and mid-South. If you're driving to Branson from the Heartland or the mid-South, you might want to consider adding a couple of days to your itinerary so you can see some sights along the way. "The Scenic Route" itineraries below are not the most direct drives from the major cities but will lead you to towns and attractions that will add spice to your trip. If you don't have time to meander, follow "The Straight Shot" route, usually a faster journey to Branson, that still includes highlights of the towns along the way.

FROM HOUSTON VIA DALLAS AND LITTLE ROCK

TOURIST INFORMATION
Dallas Convention & Visitors Bureau (1201 Elm St., Dallas, TX 75270, tel. 214/746–6677), **Fort Worth Convention & Visitors Bureau** (100 E. 15th St., Suite 400, Fort Worth, TX 76102, tel. 817/336–8791), **Houston Convention and Visitors Council** (3300 S. Main St., Houston, TX 77002, tel. 713/523–5050 or 800/231–7799), **Little Rock Convention and Visitors Bureau** (Statehouse Center, Markham and Main Sts., Box 3232, Little Rock, AR 72203, tel. 501/376–4781 or 800/844–4781).

THE SCENIC ROUTE
Houston is 621 miles away, roughly a 12-hour drive from Branson; Dallas is 440 miles, or about eight hours away; and Little Rock is 177 miles (3½ hours away. If you combine all three cities on one tour you'll get a good overview of the wonders of East Texas and the Arkansas Ozarks. Far from the classic image of cattle ranches and tumbleweeds dotting the vast plains of Texas, the eastern portion of the state, composing a third of its total land mass, offers rolling hills, fragrant pine forests, and a rollicking coastline. You'll find oil derricks here, too, as well as bird sanctuaries and wildlife preserves.

Sprawling Houston is one of America's great cities, a futuristic tribute to the oil and aerospace industries. Downtown resembles a series of gleaming glass-and-chrome canyons: Be sure to see I.M. Pei's **Texas Commerce Tower** (600 Travis St., no phone; admission free; open weekdays 8–6) and the **Smith-Louisiana corridor,** where you can wander among pieces of outdoor sculpture, including works by some of the century's greatest artists (Jean Dubuffet, Claes Oldenburg, Joan Miró, and Louise Nevelson), reflected in the glinting skyscrapers that line the mall. Weaving ribbons of green through downtown's urban canyons are cool oases such as **Sam Houston** and **Tranquillity parks.** Two blocks apart along Bagby Street downtown, they offer a taste of Houston's future and past. Several historic structures are preserved on Sam Houston's rolling green, including the 1847 Kellum-Noble House, the oldest brick structure in the city; the 1850 Nichols-Rice-Cherry House, home of the founder of Rice University; and the 1891 St. John's Church. Call the Heritage Society (tel. 713/655–1912; admission $6 adults, $4 senior citizens, students, children; tours Mon.–Sat. on the hour 10–3) for information on guided tours. The adjacent **Gallery of Texas History** (admission free; open Mon.–Sat. 10–4, Sun. 1–5) showcases artifacts dating from 1519. An intricate walk-through fountain with waterfalls and reflecting pools is the heart of Tranquillity. A tribute to the *Apollo* flights, it includes bronze plaques relating the story of American manned flight in 15 languages, and grassy knolls shaped to represent lunar mounds, the earth, and other celestial bodies. Recreational activities are limited in these parks; for information on other parks contact the **Houston Parks and Recreation Department** (2999 S. Wayside Ave., Houston, TX 77023, tel. 713/845–1000).

While in this great city, don't miss Houston's three cultural pearls: the **Menil Collection** (1515 Sul Ross St., tel. 713/525–9400; admission free; open Wed.–Sun. 11–7), which displays African tribal art and the work of early modernists such as Pablo Picasso and Fernand Léger; the **Contemporary Arts Museum** (5216 Montrose St., tel. 713/526–3129; admission free; open Tues.–Sat. 10–5, Sun. noon–6), whose avant-garde exterior, resembling a trapezoid constructed of aluminium foil, offers a taste of the creative works housed within; and the byzantine warren of galleries in the **Museum of Fine Arts** (1001 Bissonnet St., tel. 713/526–1361; admission free; open Tues., Wed., Fri., and Sat. 10–5; Thur. 10–9; Sun. noon–6), showcasing magnificent Renaissance and impressionist collections; significant African, pre-Columbian and Oriental holdings; and modern masters such as Picasso and Jackson Pollock.

Shoot down to **Space Center Houston** (NASA Rd. 1 off I-25, tel. 713/244–2105; admission free; open daily 9–4), 25 miles south along I-25, and NASA's adjacent **Johnson Space Center** (including Mission Control when it's not in use), where *Gemini* and *Apollo* junkies can gaze at rockets like the towering four-stage *Saturn V*; study samples brought back from the moon; and tour a dramatic mock-up of a space station. (Sorry, helmets and free-floating rides are not included. But just looking will impart a sense of the technology used and the vast spaces left to conquer.) May the G-force be with you.

Crew of STS-45 inside the KC-135 zero-g aircraft. Astronauts use the aircraft in space flight to experience a brief period of weightlessness; photo courtesy Lyndon B. Johnson Space Center.

Before leaving the Houston area you may want to make a pilgrimage to the chic stores of the **Galleria** (near intersection of Westheimer Rd. and I-610), located near the opulent mansions of River Oaks. Also consider taking a detour to the lazy historic coastal towns of Galveston and Port Arthur before heading four hours up I-45 to the Big D (Dallas), the city that's become synonymous with Texan success and excess.

Your first stop, 69 miles north of Houston, might be **Huntsville,** which abuts the pristine wilderness of the **Sam Houston National Forest,** and also offers the **Sam Houston Memorial Museum Complex** (1836 Sam Houston Ave., tel. 409/295–7824; admission free; open Tues.–Sun. 9–5), eight buildings that once belonged to the first president of Texas (and its first U.S. senator), including two impeccably restored homes, and replicas of the original blacksmith shop and gazebo.

The next stop of note, an hour shy of Dallas, is **Corsicana,** a small town famed for the **Collin Street Bakery** (401 W. 7th St., tel. 903/872–8111; open Mon.–Thurs. 7–5:30, Fri. and Sat. 7–6, Sun. noon–6), where you can nibble on what some consider the best fruitcake in the world. Other special places here are the **Gaston C. Gooch Library** (Navarro College, Rte. 31, tel. 903/654–4810; admission free; open Mon.–Thurs. 8–5), where you can enjoy a treasure trove of Native American arts and crafts, historical journals, and books, and **Pioneer Village** (912 W. Park Ave., no phone; admission free; open Mon.–Sat. 9–5), a restored community of frontier homes and businesses dating from the 1830s.

Soon you'll approach the gleaming city of **Dallas,** a virtual monument to oil (and the

Dallas Cowboys football team) that has assiduously erased all traces of its cow-town past. For many, Dallas is inextricably linked with John F. Kennedy's assassination; a moving exhibit in the Texas School Book Depository called **The Sixth Floor** (411 Elm St., tel. 214/653–6666; admission $4 adults, $3 senior citizens, $2 children 6–18, under 6 free; open Sun.–Fri. 10–6, Sat. 10–7; closed Christmas) documents the tumultuous early '60s. You'll also want to spend time in the restored turn-of-the-century West End warehouse district, whose centerpiece is the five-story **West End Market Place** (603 Mungre Ave., tel. 214/954–4350; open daily 8 AM–midnight), a bustling complex of restaurants and boutiques.

The Big D has size and swagger, but neighboring **Fort Worth** (20 miles west), proud of its humble cattle-and-stockyard roots, retains a greater sense of history and thrives in its big sister's shadow. Downtown is an elegant mélange of brick Victorians reflected in glass-and-steel monoliths. The **Stockyards Historic District** includes the **Stockyards Museum** (131 E. Exchange Ave., tel. 817/625–5087; admission free; open Mon.–Sat. 10–5), housed in the old Livestock Exchange Building, **Cowtown Coliseum** (121 E. Exchange Ave., tel. 817/625–1025), home of Saturday-night rodeos, and **Billy Bob's Texas** (2520 Rodeo Plaza, tel. 817/624–7117), the "world's largest honky-tonk bar." Fort Worth's cattlemen polished their rough-hewn image by amassing extraordinary art collections, today proudly displayed in three museums. The **Modern Art Museum** (1309 Montgomery St., tel. 817/738–9215; admission free; open Tues.–Sat. 10–5, Sun. 1–5) houses fine examples of most major 20th-century schools, including works by artists as diverse as Picasso and Robert Rauschenberg. The **Amon G. Carter Museum** (3501 Camp Bowie Blvd., tel. 817/738–1933; admission free; open Tues.–Sat. 10–5, Sun. 1–5:30), designed by architect Philip Johnson, specializes in American artwork, including paintings by those pioneers of the Western mythos Frederic Remington and Charles Russell. The **Kimbell Art Museum** (3333 Camp Bowie Blvd., tel. 817/332–8451; admission free; open Tues.–Sat. 10–5, Sun. 11–5) has a stunningly eclectic collection of the work of old and modern masters, including Francisco Goya's provocative *The Matador Pedro Romero* and Edvard Munch's haunting *Girls on a Jetty*. The building, designed by Louis Kahn, is a work of art in itself; its large, airy galleries silvered with sunlight are considered a model for creative, accessible exhibition space.

Kids of all ages will want to make the pilgrimage to **Arlington,** between the two mega-lopolises on I-30, where the gigantic theme parks **Six Flags over Texas** (2201 Road to Six Flags, tel. 817/530–6000; admission $25.95 adults, senior citizens over 54 and anyone under 48″ $19.95; open Apr., May, and Labor Day–Oct., weekends 10–6, and June–Labor Day, daily 10–10) and **Wet 'N' Wild** (across from Six Flags, tel. 817/265–3356; open May and Sept., weekends 10–6, and June–Aug., daily 10–9) tantalize speed-and-thrill demons with dips, dives, and climbs galore on roller coasters, water slides, parachute drops, and waterboggans. Bring a change of clothes (including your best tapping shoes for the shows), a camera, and a healthy appetite for the many eateries.

Two interstates travel east from Dallas. Interstate 30, the quicker route, crosses the Arkansas border at Texarkana, and I-20 meanders through piney woodlands and bogs to Shreveport, Louisiana (where U.S. 71 whisks you 70 miles north to Texarkana). Interstate 30 cuts through cattle country, a land of vast grassy plains and weather-beaten pickups side by side with sleek Cadillacs. **Sulphur Springs,** halfway to the border, is home to the charming **Southwest Dairy Center** (1210 Houston St., tel. 903/439–6455; admission free; open Tues.–Sat. 9–4), where you can churn butter in a typical 1930s kitchen and order a milk shake at an old-fashioned soda fountain. Visit **Texarkana** to pay homage to the king of ragtime, Scott Joplin, who was born here. Colorful murals splashed along Main Street tell the life story of the composer of "The Entertainer" and the "Maple Leaf Rag." Those carefree, prosperous days are also recalled by the neo-Baroque, royal-blue and gold-gilt **Perot Theater** (3rd and Main Sts., tel. 903/792–4992), renamed for the billionaire politician manqué who financed its restoration (it now hosts touring performance artists and Broadway shows), and by the opulent, 22-sided **Ace of Clubs House** (420 Pine St., tel. 903/793–7108; admission $3; open Wed.–Fri. 10–4, weekends 1–4), built in the shape of that suit and lavishly decorated in Victorian-Italianate fashion.

Interstate 20 meanders between pine-carpeted hills, passing through historic towns such as **Marshall** (*see* Straight Shot from Houston, *below*), once an important Confederate commercial center that produced saddles, clothing, gunpowder, and ammunition for the troops; when Vicksburg fell, Marshall became the seat of civil authority west of the Mississippi. You can make a quick detour 20 miles north on U.S. 59, to one of the state's loveliest hamlets, **Jefferson,** a showcase of Victoriana; then wander among cypress trees and swamplands abutting the Louisiana border, the haunt of steamboats trundling down-river through Big Cypress Bayou, Caddo Lake, and other waterways. **Caddo** is a mecca for water-sports enthusiasts, especially bass battlers and boaters, who can follow a 40-mile maze of water "roads" under lush canopies of Spanish moss, which gives the lake a primeval jungle aura. Call **Caddo Lake State Park** (tel. 903/679–3351) for information. Iron engine fans will love clattering down the tracks of the **Jefferson and Cypress Bayou Railroad** (E. Austin St. Depot, tel. 903/665–8400; $7.95 adults, $4.95 children under 12; tours Fri. 1:30 and 3:30, Sat. 1:30, 3:30, and 5, Sun. 12:30), which wind between gracious Victorian homes and the lazy Big Cypress River.

President Bill Clinton's birthplace, **Hope,** is just up the interstate a piece, about 30 miles from Texarkana. The current owners of his childhood home open it on a limited basis for tours; call the **Hope Chamber of Commerce** (tel. 501/777–6701) for information. Hope is also well known in these parts as the home of the world's largest watermelons, averaging up to 50 pounds. A drive 8 miles northwest along Route 4 brings you to the **Old Washington Historic State Park** (tel. 501/983–2684; admission free; open daily 9–5), a century-old village caught in a time warp, with gracious antebellum homes, a working cotton gin, and museums devoted to weaponry, printing, and African-American history. Outside town is the world's only public diamond mine in **Crater of Diamonds State Park** (2 mi SE of town on Rte. 301, tel. 501/285–3113; admission $3.50; open daily 8–5). You keep what you find at the eighth-largest-known deposit on the planet. The biggest discovery was the "Uncle Sam," at 40.23 carats, followed by the "Star of Murfreesboro," weighing in at 34.5 carats. Geologic forces continually push diamonds up through the surface, making this a potentially felicitous spot for a family picnic.

The Route 7 detour leads to **Hot Springs** and the **Hot Springs National Park** (visitor's center, Rte. 7, tel. 501/623–1433; open daily 8–5), with one of the country's leading turn-of-the-century spas. The spa is still awash in period elegance and fringed with fragrant magnolias along Bath House Row and the Grand Promenade. Everyone from Hernando de Soto (in 1541) to Al Capone (in the Roaring '20s, when Hot Springs was a hotbed for bathtub gin, gambling, flappers, and floozies) took the cure here. Nothing beats luxuriating in the thermal springs after a brisk hike through the Ouachita Mountains. Then browse the antiques shops along Central Avenue, take in dinner and a jazz performance at the grand old Arlington and Majestic hotels, and retire to one of the town's many quaint B&Bs.

Bowie knife

Then it's back on I-30 to **Little Rock,** capital of Arkansas, immortalized by Carol "Diamonds are a Girl's Best Friend" Channing as Lorelei Lee, "just a little girl from Little Rock" in *Gentlemen Prefer Blondes*. Perched on hills overlooking the scenic Arkansas River, Little Rock is a pleasing blend of contemporary and quaint. Its vital downtown historic district includes the Italianate and Greek Revival Quapaw Quarter and rustic **Arkansas Territorial Restoration** (Scott and 3rd Sts., tel. 501/324–9351; admission $2 adults, $1 senior citizens, 50¢ children under 17; open Mon.–Sat. 9–5, Sun. 1–5; tours hourly except noon), a collection of 14 buildings from the 1820s to 1840s that re-create the hardships of pioneer life. The sturdy frontier buildings also house old-fashioned crafts shops and decidedly modern art exhibitions, providing a vivid sense of how the surroundings have influenced locals over many years.

From the capital take I-40 to **Conway.** If you're fortunate enough to be here in May, you'll be able to attend the (in)famous "Toad Suck Daze." It's one of those weird community-sponsored festivities revolving around such toad-related games as jumping-frog competitions. The town does a brisk trade in bulbous-eyed souvenirs year-round. No one's saying, but the name may pay tribute to that particular species of toad whose sweat

is a hallucinogen. From here, follow signs for U.S. 65, which will lead you 170 miles straight through the Arkansas Ozarks to Branson. En route, be sure to stop off at the bevy of natural and man-made attractions outside **Harrison,** 35 miles south of Branson on U.S. 65. The area is known for its dazzling system of sinkholes and caverns, including the delicate crystal gardens and rich fossil beds of the **Hurricane River Cave** (U.S. 65, Pindall, tel. 501/429–6200; admission $6.50 adults, $4 children 4–12, under 4 free; open Mar.–Oct., daily 9–4), whose entrance is guarded by a shimmering 45-foot cascade, and **Mystic Caverns** (Rte. 7, 8 miles south of Harrison, tel. 501/743–1739; admission $6.50 adults, $4 children 4–12, under 4 free; open May–Nov., daily 9–5).

Plum Bayou Log House at Arkansas Territorial Restoration; photo courtesy Arkansas Territorial Restoration.

South of Harrison on Route 7 is **Dogpatch USA** (call Harrison Chamber of Commerce, tel. 501/741–2659 for information; admission free; open Apr.–Nov., daily 9–6), which commemorates the cartoon antics of L'il Abner in a series of rides and shows. At press time it was uncertain whether or not Dogpatch would reopen for 1994–95.

THE STRAIGHT SHOT FROM THE BIG D TO THE BIG B

The direct route from Dallas to Branson takes you through the lake-and-hill country of Oklahoma, along U.S. 75 (which becomes Oklahoma Route 69). Your first major stop will be the twin cities of **Sherman** and **Denison,** south of the Texas-Oklahoma border. Both towns are rich in the drama and history of the early railroads, and both offer a variety of recreational facilities. Denison is the birthplace of President Dwight D. Eisenhower, whose modest, two-story, white frame home is now a **museum** (208 E. Day St., tel. 903/465–8908; admission $2 adults, $1 children 6–12, under 6 free; open daily 10–4). You'll also find the **Grayson County Frontier Village** (Loy Park off U.S. 75, Frontage Rd., Denison, tel. 903/463–2487; admission free; open mid-May–Oct.,

Wed.–Sat. 1–5, Sun. 1–6), with 13 rustic buildings dating from 1840 to 1900, including a log schoolhouse and a portable jail.

In Sherman you'll find several elegant, turn-of-the-century mansions. The two cities serve as gateway to giant **Lake Texoma,** which straddles the Texas-Oklahoma border and is a favorite spot for anglers to battle black bass, crappie, and lunker catfish. Call the Dallas Parks and Recreation Department (tel. 214/670–4100) or the Fort Worth Department of the U.S. Army Corps of Engineers (tel. 817/334–2150) for information, or stop by the visitor center at the south end of the lake on U.S. 75A.

Another three hours north on U.S. 75/Rte. 69 will take you to Muskogee, whose origin as a trading post in Indian Territory (Oklahoma's name before it achieved statehood) is recounted in nearby **Fort Gibson Military Park** (1 mi north of Fort Gibson on Rte. 80, tel. 918/478–2669; admission free; open Mon.–Sat. 9–5, Sun. 1–5) and the sobering **Five**

Civilized Tribes Museum (Honor Heights Dr., tel. 918/683–1701; admission $2 adults, $1 children under 12; open Mon.–Sat. 10–5, Sun. 1–5), which features artwork and artifacts of the Cherokee, Choctaw, Chickasaw, Seminole, and Creek tribes. A quick detour along U.S. 62 through dense forest skirting crystalline lakes will bring you to **Tahlequah,** home to the Cherokee Nation, where a **museum** (Willis Rd., tel. 928/456–6007; admission $2.75 adults, $1.50 children under 12; open Memorial Day–Labor Day, Mon.–Sat. 10–8, Sun. 1–5; Labor Day–Memorial Day, Mon.–Sat. 10–5, Sun. 1–5) re-creates a typical 16th-century tribal village. Each night in summer, volunteers from the heritage center perform the epic drama *The Trail of Tears,* recounting the mammoth forced migration of the tribes from their southeastern homes.

More history is on tap at the **Har-Ber Village** (Har-Ber Rd., tel. 918/786–6446; admission free; open Mar.–Nov., daily 9–6), northeast along U.S. 69, 3½ miles west of Grove. At this complex you can explore nearly 100 cabins, each re-creating a typical room from the last century, including a prairie church, schoolhouse, and jail. In about an hour you'll reach the junction with I-44, which takes you past Joplin (*see* From Oklahoma City, *below*) and into Springfield.

THE STRAIGHT SHOT FROM HOUSTON TO BRANSON

The direct route from Houston will take you up Route 59 to Texarkana (where you can follow the Little Rock itinerary to Branson). The route slices across the heart of Texas timber country, through towns such as Lufkin, which produces more than a million board feet of saw lumber annually from thick stands of pine, cypress, hickory, oak, gum, and magnolia trees in the Angelina and Davy Crockett national forests. In the **Texas Forestry Museum** (1905 Atkinson Dr., tel. 409/632–8733; admission free; open daily 1–4:30) you can learn about regional flora and fauna and see early logging equipment and antique railroad and sawmill steam engines.

Some 25 miles north of Lufkin lies one of the state's most historic cities, **Nacogdoches.** Walk along North Street, the oldest public thoroughfare in the United States, once used by Native Americans to connect the powerful local community with outlying "suburbs," and tour the 1779 **Spanish Colonial Old Stone Fort** (Stephen F. Austin State University, tel. 409/568–2011; admission free; open Tues.–Sat. 9–5, Sun. 1–5) and **Millard's Crossing** (6020 North St., tel. 409/569–6631; admission free; open Mon.–Sat. 9–4, Sun. 1–4), a cluster of 19th-century pioneer buildings jammed with antiques and memorabilia.

U.S. 59 heads to **Carthage,** best known as the birthplace of two country-music legends, Jim Reeves and Tex Ritter. The **Tex Ritter Museum** (300 W. Panola St.; call Carthage Chamber of Commerce for details, tel.

Tex Ritter; photo courtesy Tex Ritter Museum.

903/693–6634; admission free; open weekdays 8–5) features assorted memorabilia of the cowboy singer who was one of the first members of the Grand Ole Opry. Three miles south on U.S. 79 is the life-size **Reeves Memorial statue,** a tribute to the local Country Music Hall of Famer, who died in a tragic 1964 plane crash at the height of his career. Your next stop before hooking up with the previous itinerary should be **Marshall,** another lovingly restored frontier town. The three-square-block **Ginocchio National Historic District** showcases superlative examples of Victorian architecture—a reminder that Texas is a southern state as well as a western one.

Jim Reeves Memorial

FROM KANSAS CITY, MISSOURI

TOURIST INFORMATION

Greater Kansas City Convention & Visitors Bureau (10 Main St., Suite 2550, tel. 816/221–5242 or 800/767–7700).

Kansas City is 220 miles from Branson, a four-hour drive down U.S. 71, which skirts Joplin (*see* From Oklahoma City, *below*), or the more scenic state Route 13, which heads directly to Springfield.

Kansas City is world famous for its steaks, its hundreds of fountains, and its bluesy jazz. Straddling two states along the Missouri River, it has always been a strategic trade center and river port, where scouts, trappers, and other intrepid pioneers would outfit them-selves for the arduous journey ahead on the Oregon or Santa Fe trails; today everything's still "up to date" (as the famous *Oklahoma* song claimed) in **Westport** (Broadway and Westport Rd., tel. 816/931–3400), the original outpost, now thoroughly renovated and housing trendy shops and eateries. Other dining and shopping meccas include **Country Club Plaza** (47th and Main Sts., tel. 816/753–0100) and **Crown Center** (Grand Ave. at Pershing Rd., tel. 816/274–8444), the latter home to Hallmark Greeting Cards and its **Visitor's Center and Museum** (tel. 816/274–3613; admission free; open weekdays 9–5, Sat. 9:30–4:30). Tours of the facility are self-guided; no freebies.

The most notable stop along U.S. 71, two hours south of Kansas City, is **Lamar**, birth-place of President Harry S. Truman, who epitomized Missouri's no-nonsense "Show Me" attitude and endearing mulishness. Twenty miles farther south, where U.S. 71 intersects I-44 east into Springfield, is **Carthage.** The town's distinction is the popular **Precious Moments Chapel and Museum** (480 Chapel Rd., tel. 800/543–7975; admis-sion free; open daily 9–7), famed for the delicate figurines called Precious Moments that have been crafted by local artist Sam Butcher, as well as his impressive series of religious murals. Originals and reproductions of his work are for sale in the adjoining gallery.

Route 13 weaves through western Missouri's lake country, a fertile agricultural area whose products are bountifully displayed in general stores throughout the region. The aromatic **Osceola Cheese Factory** (Rte. 13 N, tel. 417/646–8131; open daily 7:30-6:30), in Osceola, has produced and sold some 50 varieties for more than a half-century, as well as homemade preserves and cured ham—the perfect makings of a picnic on the shores of Truman Reservoir, part of a series of man-made lakes culminating in the state's largest, Lake of the Ozarks. You can no longer tour the factory; the cheese is now processed elsewhere and shipped.

Candy lovers should continue south along Route 13 for 26 miles to its intersection with Route 32. Drive southwest on Route 32 to **Stockton,** where the aroma of black-walnut caramels permeates the **Missouri Dandy Pantry** (212 Hammonds Dr., tel. 417/276–5121; admission free; open weekdays 8–5, Sat. 9–4). Factory tours are free.

FROM NASHVILLE

TOURIST INFORMATION

Nashville Area Chamber of Commerce (161 4th Ave. N, Nashville, TN 37219, tel. 615/259–4755).

Nashville lies 486 miles from rival Branson, about nine hours by car. Frankly, Nashville tries to dismiss the competition, yet there's no question that the defection of many top artists associated with the city has unnerved the powers-that-be enough to create more live-music venues outside Opryland. Still, Nashville is the undisputed center of the recording industry. Start your Nashville tour with a visit to venerable **Ryman Auditorium and Museum** (116 5th Ave. N, tel. 615/254–1445; admission $2.50 adults, $1 children under 12; open daily 8:30–4:30), home of the Grand Ole Opry from 1943 to 1974. The imposing 3,000-seat Union Gospel Tabernacle that served as auditorium was built by riverboat captain Thomas Ryman, replete with wooden pews and stained-glass windows—no wonder it's called the "Mother Church of Country Music." Then stroll down Music Row to the nearby **Country Music Hall of Fame and Museum** (4 Music Sq. E, tel. 615/256–1639; admission $7.50 adults, $2 children under 12; open June–Aug., Mon.–Sat. 8–7, Sun. 9–5, and Sept.–May, daily 9–5), a repository of memorabilia from the greats who've strutted on the Grand Ole Opry stage. Admission to the legendary **RCA Studio B**, a few blocks away, where folks from Elvis to Dolly have recorded, is included. Next head for **Opryland USA** (2802 Opryland Dr., tel. 615/889–6600; admission $24.84 adults, $14.02 children under 12; open late Mar.–May, Sept., and Oct., weekdays 10–8; June–Aug., daily 10–9), where you could spend a full day taking in the 22 rides, museums honoring Roy Acuff and Minnie Pearl, and the *General Jackson* showboat, or choosing among 15 live-music shows, including America's longest continuously running radio show, where country music's top artists perform on weekends.

Although most people's first association with Nashville is country music, this is far from the capital's only attribute. Nashville, the "Athens of the South," is rich in Greek Revival architecture, including the imposing **Hermitage** (4580 Rachel's La., tel. 615/889–2941; admission $7 adults, $3.50 children 6–18, under 6 free; open daily 9–5; closed Thanksgiving, Christmas, and 3rd week of Jan.), residence of Andrew Jackson, our seventh president. The formal gardens are a delightful place to stroll, and the gracious colonnaded edifice stands in intriguing counterpoint to the log cabins—former smokehouses and outhouses—that dot the grounds. Nashville also earns its nickname because of its august center of higher education, **Vanderbilt University,** and the city's exact replica of the **Greek Parthenon** (West End and 25th Aves., tel. 615/862–8431; admission $2.50, $1.25 senior citizens and children under 12; open Apr.–Sept., Tues.–Sat. 9–4:30, Sun. 12:30–4:30, and Oct.–Mar., Tues.–Sat. 9–4:30), constructed for the 1897 Tennessee Centennial Exposition. *Athena,* one of the world's tallest sculptures, stands at 41 feet, 10 inches. Today the Parthenon houses rotating exhibits, as well as the city's permanent art collection. Free classical concerts are given here several evenings a week between May and October.

Northwest of Tennessee's capital, along I-24, is **Clarksville.** The 200-year-old **Cumberland RiverWalk** (Riverside Dr., tel. 615/645–7444; open daily) is a wide waterfront promenade dotted with flowering trees. From here you can take an excursion on a paddleboat or walk through downtown, which is listed on the National Register of Historic Places for its imposing churches, whose vaulting spires seem to bisect the stylish town houses. Clarksville also serves as gateway to the **Land Between the Lakes recreational area** (tel. 502/924–5602), which straddles the Tennessee-Kentucky border. You can fish and hike here, enjoy the living-history farm, and view the planetarium.

Interstate 24 continues to Paducah, Kentucky, home of the **Museum of the American Quilters Society** (215 Jefferson St., tel. 502/442–8856; admission $4 adults, $3 students, children under 12 free; open Tues.–Sat. 10–5, Apr.–Oct., also Sun. 1–5). Anyone who loves quilts will enjoy the more than 200 antique coverlets displayed. Continue 100 miles along Route U60 to Cairo, where you'll ford the Ohio and Mississippi rivers via two vaulting bridges, then arrive in Missouri.

Stay on Route U60 for approximately 125 miles to **Van Buren,** unofficial eastern border of Ozark country and jumping-off point for the Ozark National Scenic Riverways. This series of waterways is preserved by the National Parks Service as "wild and scenic." Their deep emerald color contrasts with the pine and hardwood forests and the eternal bluish mist that filters through the hills. Write to the **Outdoor Library of the Missouri Department of Conservation** (Box 180, Jefferson City, MO 65102) for information on float trips through this pristine wilderness.

Drive another hour and you'll reach **Mansfield,** hometown of Laura Ingalls Wilder, author of the beloved *Little House on the Prairie* series. Her residence has been transformed into the **Wilder Home and Museum** (Road A, tel. 417/924–3626; admission $5 adults, $4 senior citizens, $3 children 12–18, under 12 free; open Mar. 15–Oct. 15, Mon.–Sat. 9–5, Sun. 12:30–5:30, and Oct. 15–Nov. 16, Mon.–Sat. 9–4, Sun. 12:30–4:30), where exhibits and documents bring to life her touching stories of families carving out a life on the harsh frontier. The simple whitewashed house contains several items avid readers will recognize, such as Mary's None-Patch quilt and Braille slate, Pa's fiddle, and the glass bread plate from Almanzo and Laura's first Christmas together. There are also rare original manuscripts and first editions. It's another 90 minutes to Springfield and the Branson turnoff.

FROM NEW ORLEANS VIA MEMPHIS

TOURIST INFORMATION

Jackson Visitor Information Center (1150 Lakeland Dr., Jackson, MS 39215, tel. 601/960–1800), **Memphis Convention and Visitors Bureau** (47 Union Ave. Memphis, TN 38103, tel. 901/543–5300), **Greater New Orleans Tourist and Convention Commission** (529 St. Ann St., New Orleans, LA 70112, tel. 504/566–5068).

THE SCENIC ROUTE

New Orleans is 595 miles (11 hours) from Branson, but you can break up your trek by stopping in Memphis, 292 miles (5½ hours) into your trip. The compelling rhythms of Dixieland and the blues will keep things humming for you en route. If time doesn't permit, eliminate the plantation and Faulkner-country detours recommended below (they add four hours of driving), and take I-10 straight to I-55 through Mississippi and western Tennessee.

It isn't hard to understand why New Orleans is called the Big Easy. No other American city is quite as sensual, even hedonistic. The name conjures up the aroma of coffee and beignets mingled with last night's gumbo; the smoky strains of jazz wafting down the street; the flamboyant, often tasteless extravaganza that is Mardi Gras. To fully appreciate New Orleans you must let it sweep you along, sitting on a stoop chatting with a local one minute, marching in line with a sassy jazz funeral the next. Many of the sights are concentrated in the famed French Quarter, or Vieux Carré, whose quaint Creole houses are trimmed with lacy gingerbread, adorned with flower boxes and intricate wrought-iron balconies, and daubed in vivid pastels.

The best way to sop up the jambalaya of sights, sounds, and smells is to explore the Quarter by foot. Start in **Jackson Square,** admiring the exquisite symmetry of St. Louis Cathedral, the oldest active cathedral in America; the adjacent Pontalbo Apartments (built in the 1840s by a Spanish baroness); and the Spanish Colonial Cabildo and Presbytere, two former seats of government during the Spanish occupation. The Presbytere was the original courthouse. The Cabildo was the city hall where the 1803 Louisiana Purchase was signed. Today they are run as part of the **Louisiana State Museum Complex** (Jackson Sq., tel. 504/568–6968; admission $3 adults, $1.50 senior citizens, children under 12 free; open Tues.–Sun. 10–5), housing permanent exhibits on local history. Open from sunrise to dusk, the square is jam-packed with jugglers, fire-eaters, tap dancers, caricaturists, zydeco (a Cajun variety of accordion music) players, and mimes: a fun, free taste of everything New Orleans has to offer.

Also visit the superlative Mardi Gras and jazz collections at the stately old **Mint** (400 Esplanade, tel. 504/568–6968; admission $3 adults, children under 12 free; open daily 10–4), run as part of the Louisiana State Museum Complex; typical 19th-century homes such as the **Beauregard-Keyes House** (1113 Chartres, tel. 504/523–7257; admission $4 adults, $1.50 children under 12; open Mon.–Sat. 10–3) and quintessential N'Awlins odd-ities such as the **Voodoo Museum** (724 Dumaine St., tel. 504/523–7685; admission $5 adults, $4 senior citizens, $3 children under 12; open Mon.–Sat. 10–6, Sun. 10–5), whose tiny rooms are crammed with grisly artifacts and whose gift shop sells gris-gris potions for casting spells and voodoo dolls.

When night falls, check out such fabled jazz haunts as the dark, cramped **Preservation Hall** (726 St. Peter St., tel. 504/523–8939) and **Jelly Roll's** (501 Bourbon St., tel. 504/568–0501). Or simply experience the living theater of Bourbon Street: a nonstop parade of tap-dancing kids, hawkers, college boys on the prowl, and revelers on balconies hailing anyone who looks interesting. If you're hungry, you can get a good "air sand-wich" just strolling past such refined Creole eateries as the legendary **Arnaud's, Galatoire's,** and **Brennan's,** or try the fiery Cajun specialties at **K-Paul's** and **Alex Patout's.**

Outside the Quarter, the state-of-the-art **Aquarium of the Americas** (Riverfront, tel. 504/861–2537; admission $8.75 adults, $3.50 children under 12; open daily 9–5) features marvelous exhibits on the Amazon Rain Forest, Caribbean Reef, Mississippi Delta, and Gulf of Mexico, as well as hands-on displays and video corners that delight children, whatever their age. Take a leisurely cruise on the free ferry to Algiers and see **Blaine Kern's Mardi Gras World** (233 Newton St., tel. 504/361–7821; admission $4.50 adults, $2.50 age 20 and under; open daily 10–5), where the extravagant floats are made and stored—an eerie echo of the day after the revelry. Wander the upscale **Garden District** to see the whimsical turrets and gaudy mullioned windows of the antebellum houses. Take a walking tour of the "Cities of the Dead," New Orleans's unique, hauntingly beautiful above-ground cemeteries. Mausoleums mark the graves: because the city is below sea level, anyone buried below ground would be washed out to sea. Kids and adults love viewing animals in their natural habitat at the outstanding **Audubon Zoological Park** (Audubon Park, tel. 504/861–2537; admission $7.50 adults, $3.50 children under 12; open daily 9–5), and if you have the time, the Big Easy also makes a fine base for exploring bayou country. Contact the Tourist and Convention Commission for a list of tour operators.

Exit New Orleans via I-10 W. Our route from New Orleans west and north to Branson traverses some of the South's most glorious plantation country and heads toward the state capital of Baton Rouge and along the sweet-smelling "Magnolia Trail" between Natchez and Vicksburg. As the saying goes, "Take time to smell the flowers."

Among the magnificent antebellum mansions you'll pass traveling west through plantation country are **Destrehan** (9999 River Rd., tel. 504/764–9315; admission $5 adults, $3 children 13–17, $2 under 13; open daily 9–4:30; closed major holidays), **San Francisco** (Rte. 44 near Reserve St., tel. 504/535–2341; admission $6.50 adults, $3.75 children 13–17, $22.50 under 13; open daily 10–4; closed major holidays), **Houmas House** (Rte. 942, ½ mi off Rte. 44 near Burnside, tel. 504/473–7841; admission $7 adults, $5 children 13–17, $3.50 children 6–12; open Feb.–Oct., daily 10–5, and Nov.–Jan., daily 10–4; closed major holidays), where *Hush Hush Sweet Charlotte* was filmed; and **Nottoway** (2 mi north of White Castle, tel. 504/545–2730; admission $8 adults, $3 children under 12; open daily 9–5; closed Christmas), the South's largest plantation home.

When you reach Baton Rouge, curl north onto U.S. 61, which flirts with the mighty Mississippi, yielding spectacular views of golden bluffs that line your way to **Natchez.** Considered of little strategic significance, Natchez was spared destruction during the Civil War, and its elegant plantation homes and opulent town houses have been carefully restored. Among the best are the grandiose **Stanton Hall** (400 High St., tel. 601/442–6282; admission $4 adults, $2 children; open daily 9–5) and **Rosalie** (100 Orleans St., tel. 601/445–4555; admission $4 adults, $2 children; open daily 9–5).

Driving north from Natchez toward Vicksburg, you'll pass through **Port Gibson,** one of the most exquisite antebellum towns in the South, which Ulysses S. Grant reputedly called "too beautiful to burn." Whereas Natchez escaped the War between the States relatively unscathed, Vicksburg (considered the key to the Mississippi trade—and Confederate solvency—that Lincoln wanted to unlock) was viciously contested during a lengthy bombardment and siege. These are vividly commemorated in the **National Military Park** (U.S. 80, 1 mi from I-20 Exit 4B, tel. 601/636–0583; admission $3 per car; open daily 10–5; closed Christmas), which rivals Gettysburg in beauty and importance.

Interstate 20 travels east from Vicksburg to **Jackson,** the state capital, whose downtown contains the **1857 Gothic Revival Manship House** (420 E. Fortification St., tel. 601/961–4724; admission free; open Tues.–Sun.; tours Tues.–Fri. hourly 9–4, weekends hourly 1–4), noted for its hand-painted wood graining, the **Governor's Mansion** (300 E. Capitol St., tel. 601/359–3175; admission free; tours Tues.–Fri. 9:30, 11:30), built in Greek Revival style in 1841, and the splendidly ornate 1903 Beaux Arts **New Capitol** (400 High St., tel. 601/359–3114; admission free; tours weekdays 9, 10, 11, 1:30, 2:30, 3:30), whose dome is crowned by a gold-plated copper eagle with a wingspan of 15 feet.

It's a lazy three-hour drive to the sophisticated college town of **Oxford** in Lafayette County, at the junction of I-20 and Route 6 E. Native son William Faulkner immortalized this hamlet as Jefferson, Yoknapatawpha County, in novels such as *Light in August* and *The Sound and the Fury.* Literary associations abound here, including Faulkner's home, the 1844 white-frame **Rowan Oak** (Old Taylor Rd., tel. 601/234–4651; admis-

Rowan Oak, home of William Faulkner; photo courtesy Rowan Oak

sion free; open Tues.–Sat. 10–noon and 2–4, Sun. 2–4), a National Historic Landmark run by the University of Mississippi. The study is particularly fascinating; Faulkner's presence is meticulously evoked by his bed, typewriter, and desk, along with such personal items as an ink bottle, a can of dog repellent, a Colgate shave-stick refill, and his sunglasses.

If historic architecture is your interest, drive 29 miles north on Route 7 to **Holly Springs,** a town that contains more than 300 buildings on the National Register of Historic Places. Among them is the 1858 **Montrose Mansion** (307 E. Salem Ave., tel. 601/252–2943; admission $3 adults, children under 12 free; open by appointment). Its elaborate design includes fanciful cornices and plaster ceiling medallions, as well as a sinuous spiral staircase. From Holly Springs, take U.S. 78 northwest 35 miles to Memphis.

Memphis is just as steeped in music and tradition as New Orleans. But unlike the Big Easy's raucous Dixieland, the rhythms of Memphis are more reflective, with the soulful blues of such giants as W.C. Handy, "Father of the Blues." And, of course there's the music of Elvis Presley, the King. Memphis's lifeblood has always been Ol' Man River, and its influence is celebrated on the inauspiciously named **Mud Island** (entrance at 125 Front St., tel. 901/576–7212; admission to grounds $2 adults, $1 children; admission to grounds and all attractions $6 adults, $4 children under 12; open Apr.–Nov., Tues.–Sun.; hours vary, so call ahead). A monorail and footbridge cross the mighty Mississippi to this 52-acre theme park, where a five-block-long scale model River Walk duplicates the river in miniature, sandbars and all, from Cairo, Illinois, to New Orleans. The **Mississippi River Museum** offers an intriguing assortment of river arcana and paraphernalia such as scale-model riverboats and full-size animated river characters like Mark Twain; also on park grounds is the famed World War II B-17 bomber, the *Memphis Belle.*

The Million-Dollar Quartet: Jerry Lee Lewis, Carl Perkins, Elvis Presley, and Johnny Cash; photo courtesy Sun Studio.

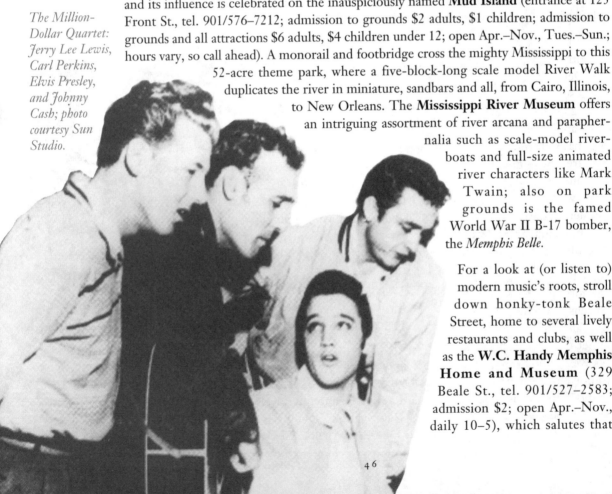

For a look at (or listen to) modern music's roots, stroll down honky-tonk Beale Street, home to several lively restaurants and clubs, as well as the **W.C. Handy Memphis Home and Museum** (329 Beale St., tel. 901/527–2583; admission $2; open Apr.–Nov., daily 10–5), which salutes that innovative musician. Nearby is **Sun Studio** (706 Union Ave., tel. 901/521–0664; admission $7 adults, $4 children 4–12, under 4 free; tours Memorial Day-Labor Day, daily 9–7; Labor Day-Memorial Day, daily 10-6), lionized by many as the birthplace of rock and roll. Elvis, B.B. King, Jerry Lee Lewis, and Roy Orbison are among the greats who got their recording starts here. Of course, no trip to Memphis is complete without a stop at **Graceland** (3717 Elvis Presley Blvd., tel. 901/332–3322; admission: $7.95 adults, $4.75 children 4–12, under 4 free; open Memorial Day–Labor Day, Wed.–Mon. 8–6; Labor Day–Memorial Day, Wed.–Mon. 9–5), the elaborate Colonial-style home and burial site of Elvis Presley, where you can admire his gold-sequined costume and gold-gilt piano, among other personal items. For a sobering look at another side of the city's history, stop by the **National Civil Rights Museum** (450 Mulberry St., tel. 901/521–9699; admission $5 adults, $4 senior citizens and students, $3 children 6–12, free Mon. 3–5; open Mon. and Wed.–Sat. 10–5, Sun. 1–6), converted from the motel where Martin Luther King, Jr., was assassinated in 1968.

Cross the river along I-55 W to Arkansas and U.S. 63, and take a detour through Delta Country, an area rich in musical as well as agricultural history. This is the birthplace of the Delta Blues sound pioneered by legends like John Lee Hooker from **Helena** (50 miles south of Memphis on U.S. 61) and Roosevelt Sykes from **Clarksdale,** across the river 25 miles south on Route 1 in Mississippi. (Among the other talented musicians born and raised in Clarksdale are Sam Cooke, Ike Turner, and Muddy Waters.) Visit Helena's Delta Cultural Center (Natchez and Missouri Sts., tel. 501/338–8919; admission free; open daily 9–5) for a fascinating glimpse of Delta life, from roadhouses where the blues sound was forged to "river rats" (a term used both for the rodents that plagued those who lived on the Mississippi and the itinerant workers who plied its waters). Then wander the streets of this well-preserved antebellum town, once one of the richest in the South. Its onetime preeminence as a port and logging center is richly reflected in the magnificent Victorian architecture.

Over the next 100 miles along U.S. 63, loamy fields gradually give way to the foothills and forests of the Ozarks. **Hardy** is a fetching village and a haven for antiquers and crafts mavens, little changed since its 1920s heyday, when it was a popular retreat for fishermen and artists. A few miles north along the Missouri border is **Mammoth Spring,** the outlet of a subterranean river that flows at an astounding 10 million gallons per hour. Native American lore relates that it was formed when a great chief dug a grave for his son, who was searching for water during a drought. A half-hour farther along U.S. 63 brings you to West Plains, Missouri, where you turn east on I-60 for a bumpy two-hour drive to Branson.

FROM OKLAHOMA CITY

TOURIST INFORMATION

Oklahoma City Convention and Visitors Bureau (1 Santa Fe Pl., Oklahoma City, OK 73102, tel. 405/278–8900 or 800/225–5652), **Tulsa Visitor Information Center and Chamber of Commerce** (616 Boston St., Tulsa, OK 74119, tel. 918/585–1201).

THE SCENIC ROUTE

Oklahoma City, 302 miles from Branson, or just under six hours by car, is the mythic Old West: the land of oil and cattle barons, cowboys and Indians, pioneers and gunslingers. They've left their imprint on dusty roads where, in places, you can still spy the faint ruts of wagon wheels.

Oklahoma City is the only place in America where you'll find oil wells pumping on the grounds of the **State Capitol** (N.E. 23rd St. and Lincoln Blvd., tel. 405/521–3356; admission free; open daily 9–5). The derricks are an odd counterpoint to the limestone Corinthian columns of the capitol. Oil is the theme of Oklahoma's present and future, but the state's Western roots get equal play in the **National Cowboy Hall of Fame and Western Heritage Center** (1700 N.E. 63rd St., tel. 405/478–2250; admission $6 adults, $5 senior citizens, $4 children under 12; open daily 9–5; closed major holidays), among whose extensive holdings you'll find John Wayne's kachina-doll collection. The **Kirkpatrick Center** (2100 N.E. 52nd St., tel. 405/427–5461; admission $6 adults, $4.50 senior citizens, $3.50 children under 12; open Memorial Day–Labor Day, Mon.–Sat. 9–6, Sun. noon–6, and Labor Day–Memorial Day, weekdays 9:30–5, Sat. 9–6, Sun. noon–6) documents the state's vibrant ethnic communities. Here you'll find the Native American Museum, African and Oriental galleries, as well as the International Photography Hall of Fame, a gallery devoted to Oklahoma artists, an aerospace museum and planetarium, and several other institutions.

Take I-44 out of Oklahoma City. It parallels two routes of somber historic significance: the old Route 66, the road Okies followed west from the Dust Bowl during the 1930s; and the infamous Trail of Tears, along which thousands of Cherokee were herded a century earlier when they were forcibly resettled from their southeastern homes.

Your first stop, just under two hours from the state capital, is **Tulsa**, an appealing blend of Old West and Art Deco, the latter courtesy of the oil money that flowed liberally during the 1920s. Images of the Old West are on rich display at the **Gilcrease Museum** (1400 Gilcrease Museum Rd., tel. 918/582–3122; suggested donation $3 adults, $5 families; open Mon.–Sat. 9–5, Sun. and holidays 1–5; closed Christmas), which is devoted to Americana—from paintings by Remington and James Whistler to quilts, saddles, and Native American artifacts. The Art Deco style is evidenced by the flourishes adorning more than a dozen downtown buildings, which are part of a walking tour sponsored by the **chamber of commerce** (*see* Tourist Information, *above*). During the salad days when oil wells gushed, magnates vied with each other to erect stunning homes such as the building that is now the **Philbrook Museum** (2727 S. Rockford Rd., tel. 918/749–7941; admission $3 adults, $1.50 senior citizens and college students, children under 18 free; open Tues.–Sat. 10–5, Sun. 1–5). This radiant Venetian-style palazzo surrounded by lushly landscaped gardens houses an eclectic, top-flight art collection strong in Italian Renaissance works.

Bartlesville, 45 miles north on U.S. 75, is the site of two first-class attractions. Families with children will appreciate the first highlight, the **Woolaroc Museum** (Rte. 123, 14 mi southwest of Bartlesville, tel. 918/336–0307; admission free; open Memorial Day–Labor Day, daily 10–8, and Labor Day–Memorial Day, Tues.–Sun. 10–5), a drive-through wildlife preserve where buffalo (as well as coyotes, gophers, and assorted prairie critters) roam. The main building has vast holdings of Native American artifacts and Western crafts, including Teddy Roosevelt's saddle. Frank Lloyd Wright fans will want to drive into Bartlesville proper to see the 19-story **Price Tower and Bartlesville Museum** (6th and Dewey Sts., tel. 918/336–8708; admission free; guided tours on ½-hour Thurs. 1–2), designed by the great architect in 1956 as a "tower in a country town." Cantilevered and decorated with copper plating and gold-tinted glass, it is a Baroque dream in a rural setting.

If you have time for another detour, drive 40 miles southeast on Routes 60 then on 169 from Bartlesville (or 25 miles on Routes 88 and 169 northwest from Tulsa) to **Will Rogers's home** (Rte. 88, Oologah, tel. 918/275–4201; admission free; open daily 8–5). The public is invited to tour the log-and-clapboard house in Oologah where Will grew up. One mile west on Route 88 is the **Will Rogers Memorial** (tel. 918/341–0719; admission free; open daily 8–5), where the legendary humorist and his family are buried. The staff continuously runs old movies and newsreels starring the beloved figure who never met a man he didn't like (but whose tart tongue and sharp mind didn't suffer fools gladly). From here you can explore the Cherokee Nation region to the southeast (*see* The Straight Shot from the Big D to the Big B, *above*) or return to I-44 and cruise northeast past the turnoff for Grove.

The first sizable settlement along I-44 in Missouri is the town of **Joplin,** perched precariously atop a catacomb of water-filled lead-mine shafts. The **Dorothea Hoover**

Historical Museum (4th St. and Schifferdecker Ave., tel. 417/623–1180; admission free; open May–Oct., Tues.–Sat. 10–4:30, Sun. 1–4) displays a large doll collection, a miniature "animated" circus replete with calliope and braying animals, and a 19th-century pioneer dwelling. A few miles south on U.S. 71 is the **George Washington Carver National Monument** (2 mi west of Diamond, tel. 417/325–4151; admission $1 adults, senior citizens and children under 18 free; open daily 8:30–6), a museum devoted to the life and work of the great botanist and educator. Springfield is about an hour away, Branson barely 90 minutes.

FROM ST. LOUIS

St. Louis is 250 miles—less than five hours by car—from Branson. One of the most unforgettable portals to the West is St. Louis's famed silver **Gateway Arch** (Market St. at waterfront, tel. 314/425–4465; admission $2 adults, $4 family, $1 children under 12; tram ride $2.50 adults, $1.50 children 3–12, under 3 free; various rates for theater presentations; open year-round, daily except major holidays; hours vary depending on presentation), a national monument that soars 630 feet above the Mississippi. For breathtaking panoramas of the mighty river take a tram up either leg of the arch to the Observation Room. Authentic paddle-wheeler steamboats like the *Huck Finn*, *Tom Sawyer*, and *Becky Thatcher* chug along the river, packed with sightseers. Beneath the arch is the underground **Museum of Westward Expansion**, a tribute to the pioneer spirit that forged this country.

Plan to visit the downtown area at lunchtime. Across Washington Street (from the north end of the national monument park) is **Laclede's Landing**, a charming cobblestone quarter of 19th-century warehouses, now home to delightful shops and restaurants. St. Louis is known for the **Anheuser-Busch Brewery** (12th and Lynch Sts., tel. 314/577–2626; admission free; tours Mon.–Sat. on ½-hour 9–4) and Budweiser's Clydesdale horses, whose stables are on the grounds. Take a tour of the brewery that insists "This Bud's for you," and enjoy free samples in the tasting room (complimentary soft drinks and Eagle snacks for those under 21).

Photo courtesy Anheuser-Busch.

From St. Louis I-44 W rolls into Springfield, 210 miles away. **Eureka,** 30 miles west of St. Louis on I-44, is an attraction in itself, with more than 100 music shows, rides, and attractions at **Six Flags over Mid-America** (I-44 and Allentown Rd., tel. 314/938–4800; admission $23.95 adults, $12 senior citizens over 54, $18.95 children 3–12, under 3 free; open Memorial Day–Labor Day, Mon.–Sat. 10–10, Sun. 10–8, and Labor Day–Memorial Day, Fri. and Sat. 10–10, Sun. 10–8).

If Daniel Boone was your childhood hero, detour via Routes 100 and 47 to quaint

Augusta on the Missouri River, home of the pioneer immortalized with shrines throughout the area. Today the primary attractions in the region, however, are the wineries that grace the bluffs overlooking the river. **Mount Pleasant Vineyards** (5634 High St., tel. 314/228–4419; admission free; tours and tastings daily 10–6) has the distinction of being awarded the first Viticultural Area designation in the United States, meaning that grapes used in its wines could only be grown within that region. Here and at neighboring **Montelle Winery** (Rte. 94 at Osage Ridge, tel. 314/228–4464; admission free; tours and tastings daily 10–6), you can sample fresh, fruity hybrid white wines such as Vignoles and Vidal Blanc.

Caves pock the region. At **Meramec Caverns** (I-44 Exit 230, tel. 314/468–3166; admission $9 adults, $4.50 children 5–11, under 5 free; open Mar. and Oct., daily 10–5; Apr. and Sept., daily 9–6; May and June, daily 9–7; July–Labor Day 8:30–7:30; Nov.–Feb. hours vary, so call ahead; closed Thanksgiving and Christmas) in Stanton you'll find the world's largest single cave formation. The cavern served as a Civil War munitions factory and as a hideout for Jesse and Frank James. Hour-long tours explore only a fraction of the labyrinthine system. From here it's 2½ hours to Springfield and the Branson turnoff.

A Little Bit of Country: America's Music

It doesn't matter if you're in New York or Nashville, the Ozark Mountains or the Hollywood Hills: Country has become America's music, the indisputable king of the airwaves. In the last 15 years alone, the number of country music radio stations has doubled; today one out of every four stations plays a country format. In 1991, 35 country albums went platinum (sales of more than 1 million), another 33 went gold (more than 500,000 sold), proving its broad-based appeal. Everyone from blue-collar workers to baby-boomer yuppies has embraced the country phenomenon.

Sure, country singers have crossed over onto the pop charts before: Hank Williams and Patsy Cline in the '50s; Mel Tillis, Johnny Cash, Tammy Wynette, Loretta Lynn, and Glen Campbell in the '60s and '70s; Kenny Rogers, Dolly Parton, and Willie Nelson in the '80s. But no group has achieved the superstar, sex-symbol status of the current crop, which includes Garth Brooks, Bonnie Raitt, Clint Black, Reba McEntire, Alan Jackson, Wynonna Judd, David Allan Coe, Randy Travis, George Strait, Travis Tritt, Mary Chapin Carpenter, Lorrie Morgan, Dwight Yoakum, and Vince Gill.

"Sailing the Ocean" by Luke Highnight and His Ozark Strutters; photo courtesy New York Public Library Picture Collection

More than ever, country music strikes a responsive chord in almost everyone who listens: The territory is reassuringly familiar, with unabashed, emotional lyrics that might be lugubrious and self-pitying but are always honest and heartfelt. They tell of hard lives and hard lessons. Recession. Divorce. Losing a lover, losing a job. They're songs about the Big Hurt. Maybe that more than anything accounts for their newfound popularity with the baby-boomer generation, which has grown up and encountered the problems of adulthood.

The author would like to acknowledge his invaluable primary sources, the Ralph Foster Museum and Country Music USA *(University of Texas Press), by Bill C. Malone.*

Then there are the voices, themselves—smoky and sonorous, resonating with experience. Even the smoothest country crooners, from Glen Campbell to Garth Brooks, seem to have a catch in their throat. They're the voices of the ramblin' men who've done rail time and jail time, of the women who keep the home fires burning. And that's another thing about country. The men sound like men, the women sound like women. (They look their parts, too.) Think about those lyrics again. The men suffer. They learn from their mistakes, displaying a hard-won sensitivity. And Tammy Wynette might have spelled out her complaints while threatening "D-I-V-O-R-C-E," but you knew she believed in the end you should "Stand by Your Man."

When the songs aren't salvos—or truces—in the battle of the sexes, they seem to voice the mood of America. They teach pride in country and pride in self, championing the underdog and glorifying the common man as far back as Woody Guthrie with his brand of social protest during the Depression. Country is the ordinary Joe thumbing his nose at the big shots, as when the aptly named Johnny Paycheck told the boss to "Take This Job and Shove It" or Garth Brooks celebrated "the hardhat/Gunrack, achin' back/Overtaxed, flag-wavin', fun-lovin' . . . American Honky Tonk Bar Association." (Bryan Kennedy and Jim Rushing [EMI April Music, Inc./The Old Professor's Music/ASCAP]).

Earl Johnson (center), one of Georgia's best "breakdown" fiddlers, with his brothers, Albert and Ester; photo courtesy New York Public Library Picture Collection.

It may seem hard to believe, but today's country music traces its roots to British and Irish ballads of the 16th through 18th centuries. (Is it really so far from the gentle plaint of "Greensleeves"—"Alas, my love, you do me wrong to treat me so discourteously"—to Linda Ronstadt pleading "Please, Mister, please, don't play B-17, it was our song, it was his song, now it's over" and Hank Williams bemoaning "Your Cheatin' Heart" or "I'm So Lonesome I Could Cry"?) Seventeenth and 18th-century Anglo-Celtic immigrants brought their folk traditions—and the fiddle—across the Atlantic, settling first in the fertile Virginia tidewater and Carolina piedmont, then gradually moving south and west into Appalachia, the Ozarks, the Deep South, and Texas. Although many of the melodies and rhythms remained the same, over time the subject matter changed to reflect the immigrants' daily experience: instead of lionizing King Arthur, Lancelot, and Guinevere, for example, they might celebrate the exploits of American folk heroes like Daniel Boone, the rugged frontiersman.

As the North became increasingly industrialized and urbanized, attracting a melting pot of European immigrants seeking jobs, the more homogeneous South clung to its agricultural tradition, with slavery providing the economic base. While other ethnic groups (notably the French and Spanish along the Mississippi and Gulf of Mexico) influenced the emerging southern musical culture, the most significant contributions were made by the slaves. Low-down dirty blues and ragtime were taken up in honky-tonks, the uplifting African-American spirituals in churches. The banjo—originally four strings stretched tautly across a gourd, and today so closely identified with hillbilly music—was brought from Africa on slave ships.

Even though the rural South stubbornly resisted change, popular urban musical styles and tastes gradually influenced folk culture. Long before television and radio, the traveling tent show and its cousin, the medicine show, entertained the masses. The tent show took many forms. Most popular was the circus, usually a one-ring fleabag affair that nonetheless had a brass band tooting the latest tunes from Tin Pan Alley. There was also the tent repertory, a small-scale vaudeville operation that brought in a dazzling array of acts from magicians to minstrels in blackface.

Even more pervasive were the medicine shows, whose "doctors" would hawk patent nostrums, liniments, and elixirs guaranteed to "cure what ails you." To lure potential customers, they usually prefaced their smooth talk with an entertainer who, in keeping with the up-to-date medical advances, regaled his rapt audience with the latest big-city jokes or tunes. The heritage of these traveling snake-oil salesmen is echoed by the aggressive but charming hucksterism in Branson, as stars admonish audiences with almost evangelical fervor to check out the gift shops at intermission.

Another act taken on the road was the revival meeting. Religion played a vital role in southerners' daily lives; many of them learned to sing in church by "lining" hymns. This meant that the congregation either repeated the lines sung to them or answered the preacher. To make it even easier on (and perhaps more compelling to) the flock, established texts were often reset to popular tunes. This was the origin of gospel music, which remains a mainstay of the country canon. Gospel, borrowing from a rich source of traditional hymns, folk songs, and spirituals, was used by evangelists at revival meetings to work the crowd into a frenzy. The advent in the 1870s of the Pentecostal movement, a reaction by Methodists who sought to reinvigorate their church with passion, signaled a further liberation of musical forms. The worshipers drew from secular styles like blues and jazz to give full-throated vent to their feelings and introduced other instruments, such as the tambourine and trumpet, into their services. "When the Saints Go Marching In," that quintessential Dixieland ditty, debuted in church.

Many of the pious regarded these new offerings as the Devil's music (British folk tradition had long painted the fiddle as Satan's instrument), but the joyous, insistent rhythm could not be denied. The conflict still exists. Only in the South, it seems, could the same family produce two such flamboyant yet diametrically opposed figures as cousins Jimmy Swaggart, the hellfire-and-brimstone fundamentalist preacher, and Jerry Lee Lewis, the hell-raising "Great Balls of Fire" singer. This dichotomy is eloquently expressed in southern music, which borrows from mournful ballads and bawdy Elizabethan drinking songs.

The roots for southern music's enduring regional popularity were already in place by the turn of the century, but it needed a catalyst to gain more widespread acceptance. This proved a problem. Urban interests controlled the music industry, which at the time was composed of live vaudeville, sheet-music companies, and phonograph concerns. Cities boasted not only a higher but a generally more affluent population, and a prejudice existed toward simpler, "backward" southern melodies, which were stripped of complex chords for often illiterate audiences that learned music orally rather than from sheet music. The style produced what some music pros felt was a harsher, flatter sound. As a result, very few southern artists could cash in on the record craze that swept the nation during World War I.

OKeh label featuring Fiddlin' John Carson, 1923; photo courtesy New York Public Library Picture Collection

Southern music had to wait for the invention of radio to broaden its demographic base. In 1922 radio sales totaled $60 million; by 1929 they had grown to more than $800 million. Conversely, record sales dwindled from more than 100 million units to fewer than 5 million during the same period. The clearer broadcast tone was favored to scratchy recordings. Southern and midwestern radio stations immediately began showcasing live local talent, led by Atlanta's WSB, which began broadcasting on March 16, 1922. Shortly thereafter, Fort Worth's WBAP arguably produced the first so-called barn dances. The most famous of these were the "National Barn Dance" on Chicago's WLS and, of course, Nashville's "Grand Ole Opry," both of which began their fabled runs during the mid-1920s.

The local public clamored for more. Shrewd record executives began to see an untapped gold mine in what was then called "hill country," "old-time" or "hillbilly" music. Experts are uncertain about the first country recording artist (evidence leans toward two champion fiddlers named Eck Robertson and Henry Gilliland), the first indisputable commercial hit was scored by Fiddlin' John Carson on the OKeh label in 1923. Soon other record companies were sending agents and talent scouts to scour the South for fresh talent. They snapped up such seminal artists as Carson Robison, Dick Burnett, Charlie Poole and the North Carolina Ramblers, the Skillet Lickers, Bradley Kincaid, and Buell Kazee. The most influential of the early recording artists was probably Vernon Dalhart, whose rendition of "The Prisoner's

Song" eclipsed the 1 million mark in sales and introduced hillbilly music to an international audience.

The '20s screamed to a close with the introduction of two country legends: the Carter Family and Jimmie Rodgers. The Carters, led by A.P. and his sister-in-law Maybelle (whose daughter June went on to a substantial career of her own and to marry Johnny Cash), never had a million seller, but their inexhaustible efforts led to the preservation of much genuine folk music. Their music ran to nostalgic paeans to home and family, representing one end of the country music spectrum.

Jimmie Rodgers, often called the "Father of Country Music," may be the single most influential country performer of all time. Rodgers helped popularize the predominant singing style of the 1920s–'50s, as well as two enduring images: the hard-living, hard-drinking, wandering railroad man and the singing cowboy. Musically, he synthesized most of the major southern influences, from swing to blues, adding a distinctive yodel that was copied ad nauseam for decades (late-night TV addicts may recall commercials for Slim Whitman, one of Rodgers's major imitators). One of his nicknames was "The Singing Brakeman," evoking the powerful longing to travel and discover the world, footloose and fancy free, felt by many restless youths of rural America. Even today the railroad assumes almost mythic proportions in country music: a romantic vehicle of escape from the dreary daily routine of farm life, the train's shrill, lonely whistle echoed in the keening scrape of a fiddle.

Jimmie Rodgers, 1927; photo courtesy New York Public Library Picture Collection

Although others (most notably Carl Sprague) hit the charts with cowboy songs, Rodgers's inimitable, twangy renditions of songs like "The Yodeling Cowboy" and "When the Cactus Is in Bloom" forever associated hillbilly music with the West, paving the way for the country-and-western (C&W) tag. From now on, southwestern influences, predominantly from Texas (where Rodgers settled), played upon the classic American myth of the Wild West and that uniquely American hero, the outlaw. It remains a potent image, the renegade beholden to nothing and nobody: Witness the number of today's stars sporting a trademark black hat.

In 1933, at the age of 35 and at the height of his popularity, Rodgers died of tuberculosis. During the 1930s one of his most ardent imitators, Gene Autry, catapulted to fame as "the Singing Cowboy" in a series of B-movies that helped disseminate hillbilly music to a larger, more appreciative audience than ever before. Indeed, "Western" came to supplant "hillbilly" as the most common descriptive term for all southern and southwestern music. The Western persona also helped Patsy Montana score the first major country music hit by a woman soloist, "I Want to Be a Cowboy's Sweetheart," in 1935. Other top stars to emerge during the Depression and early war years were Tex Ritter, Ernest Tubb, and Bob Wills (along with his Texas Playboys), whose fusion of jazz and country defined Texas swing. All of them began their careers in the ubiquitous roadside honky-tonks, a fertile training ground for performers where ranchers and oil riggers went to blow off steam. Perhaps as a response to the rough-and-tumble atmosphere, song lyrics, many of them describing relations between the sexes with increasing frankness, became more free-spirited, indeed downright raunchy.

Stars such as Bing Crosby and the Andrews Sisters habitually "covered" country songs, bringing them to an even wider audience. With the help of these and other mainstream artists, the whole nation was humming and dancing to country songs like 1941's "You Are My Sunshine" and 1943's "Pistol-Packin' Mama." In 1942 *Billboard*, the music-industry bible, finally began compiling lists of country smashes, albeit under catchall titles like "Western and Race" or "American Folk Classics," which embraced everything from Ernest Tubb to Duke Ellington. Meanwhile, thanks to host Roy Acuff (a visionary who, along with Fred Rose, organized Rose-Acuff, the most important country music publishing firm) and comedienne Minnie Pearl, the *Grand Ole Opry* soared in popularity throughout World War II, eclipsing its biggest rival, Chicago's *WLS National Barn Dance*, and helping establish Nashville as the center of the country music universe.

In the immediate postwar years, California and Nashville attracted all of the top talent. Young singers such as Lefty Frizzell, Merle Travis, and Buck Owens flocked to the West Coast, which was developing a reputation for electrical amplification with firms like Fender. The unique sound that emerged was sharper and more syncopated than that emanating from the old acoustic guitars. Other innovative stylists like Chet Atkins head-ed for Nashville and the Opry. Roy Acuff and Fred Rose saw to it that their burgeoning publishing house signed up the hottest young talent and got them recording contracts (by now far more lucrative than sheet music). But it wasn't until Patti Page's 1950 cover of the almost-forgotten "The Tennessee Waltz," which sold nearly 5 million copies, that Rose-Acuff challenged the big boys in New York, Chicago, and Los Angeles.

The late '40s and early '50s consolidated country music's crossover appeal, as new talent like Hank Thompson, Eddy Arnold, Hank Snow, Slim Whitman, and Kitty Wells (the first female country superstar) produced hit after hit. But no performer loomed larger than Hank Williams. Though his period of success lasted less than five years—from his appearances on the popular *Louisiana Hayride* radio show out of Shreveport, Louisiana, in 1948 to his tragic early death (from a heart attack) on New Year's Day, 1953—only Jimmie Rodgers could rival him in influence, and Rodgers never matched his prodigious commercial success. Like Rodgers, Williams had a versatile voice that could curl around almost any kind of tune, from sassy swing to a melancholy love song. Also like Rodgers,

Williams entranced the public with his lavish, freewheeling lifestyle, including several highly publicized bouts with drinking.

Williams's sound was about as pure and sincere as music could get. Then an explosion occurred that rocked not only the music industry but the entire world. Trend-setting disc jockey Alan Freed called it rock and roll back in 1951, but the new musical form truly took off in 1954 when Bill Haley and the Comets rocketed to stardom with "Rock around the Clock." This led to a new fusion, dubbed rockabilly, mating country with rhythm and blues as exemplified by Elvis Presley. Several great singers followed in his footsteps (and swiveling hips), each with his or her own unique style, yet perhaps unfairly lumped together under the rockabilly tag: Buddy Holly, Roy Orbison, Jerry Lee Lewis, the Everly Brothers, Charlie Rich, Conway Twitty, Janis Martin, and Brenda Lee. These and other musicians had a tremendous impact on country music, inching it even closer to the mainstream.

The reaction in the country establishment against rock (and rockabilly) ironically caused a further dilution of "pure" country in favor of what became known as the "Nashville sound," a marriage between country and other pop trends that sought to soften the harsh, twangy edge of mountain music for urban listeners. Among the foremost practitioners of the new sound were Johnny Cash, Chet Atkins, Marty Robbins, Don Gibson, Jim Reeves, and Patsy Cline—all superlative musicians who could easily slip into purer country cadences and phrasings and often did.

Country was now officially mainstream, a fact reflected by the number of network and nationally syndicated TV shows. First and foremost was probably the *Ozark Jubilee*, a radio show that moved to TV as early as 1946, finally winning a national network contract in 1956. Another wildly popular offering was the *Porter Wagoner Show*, which went on the air in 1960 and introduced Dolly Parton to television audiences in 1967. *The Beverly Hillbillies* skyrocketed to the top of the Nielsen heap in 1963, taking Flatt and Scruggs's *The Ballad of Jed Clampett* along with it, introducing the folksy, high-pitched bluegrass sound to a national audience. The decade ended with three major network hits that premiered in 1969: *The Glen Campbell Show*, *The Johnny Cash Show*, and the hardy-har-har perennial *Hee Haw*, which is still in syndication. Of course, Glen, Johnny, and Roy Clark can all be found today in Branson.

In keeping with the social foment, the '60s and early '70s also saw "minority" performers gain increasing acceptance. Female artists rivaled their male counterparts for chart-topping success, as Tammy Wynette, Loretta Lynn, Dolly Parton, and others entered the country firmament. Charley Pride opted for the country sound over the rhythm-and-blues influence of his native Mississippi Delta and opened doors not only for African-Americans but other ethnic groups as well. Freddy Fender and Johnny Rodriguez became the first Mexican-Americans to place high on the country charts. Even Kinky Friedman and the Jewish Cowboys gained a cult following with their progressive riffs.

The '60s also saw the emergence of a strong group of singer-songwriters who advanced the craft of country music with their sensitive work: Johnny Cash, Mel Tillis, Merle Haggard, Ray Price, George Jones, Roger Miller, Kris Kristofferson, and Willie Nelson among them.

Country achieved even greater exposure in the '70s and early '80s, as Hollywood came calling again, whether to debunk it (Robert Altman's *Nashville*) or glorify it (*Urban Cowboy*). The next country superstar was Kenny Rogers, whose enormous crossover success led to a series of TV movies based on his megahit, *The Gambler*. The lives of Loretta Lynn and Patsy Cline, respectively, were dramatized in *Coal Miner's Daughter* (for which Sissy Spacek won an Oscar) and *Sweet Dreams*. Dolly Parton put her best foot forward in *Nine to Five* and *Best Little Whorehouse in Texas*. Willie Nelson displayed a winning screen presence in *Electric Horseman*, *Barbarosa*, and *Honeysuckle Rose*. Horton Foote's penetrating study of a down-on-his-luck country singer in *Tender Mercies* won an Academy Award for him for best screenplay and one for Robert Duvall as best actor. Good ol' boys like Mel Tillis and Jerry Reed also became movie stars as sidekicks to Clint Eastwood (*Any Which Way but Loose*) and Burt Reynolds (*Smokey and the Bandit*).

The 1980s saw the emergence of supergroups, including the Oak Ridge Boys and Alabama, and a new generation of stars, many of them (notably George Strait, Alan Jackson, Garth Brooks, Randy Travis, Clint Black, and Mark Chesnutt) returning to their country roots, leading critics to dub them the "New Traditionalists." All of them will gladly trace their influences back to the heart-hurtin' songs of George Jones, the somber, sentimental ballads of Roy Acuff, and the infectious Western swing of Bob Wills. They've overseen country music's rise to the top of the charts yet again.

Barbara Mandrell, a frequent and popular guest in Branson, once sang, "I Was Country When Country Wasn't Cool." Today country's hotter than ever, and Branson is leading the parade.

The Theaters
and the Stars

The entertainment scene in Branson is volatile, to say the least. Although many performers live here year-round, the theaters where they perform change hands overnight, as established stars build bigger, better facilities. The morning and matinee acts move almost as frequently, shifting allegiance from one theater to another. Keeping track of these changes can be like keeping notes on a soap opera. The scene is that tangled. Rest assured that, even if you're stuck in traffic, things are moving briskly somewhere in town.

Stars usually overhaul their acts every year, although their greatest hits are always prominently featured. Around Christmas, seasonal songs take center stage, and many performers bring their families on to perform carols and spirituals. Most stars remain in Branson for the traditional tourist season *Boxcar Willie* (May through October), and many others extend their schedule into Ozark Mountain *Theater* Christmas (mid-November through late December). Many take a vacation, usually for a couple of weeks in July and August. Don't worry, though: They usually bring in some of their friends as replacements. Most audiences would gladly welcome Ronnie Milsap or Johnny Cash as a stand-in.

At press time the acts and theaters reviewed below were firmly in place, but schedules and venues may change in 1995. For example, soon after this book reaches the shelves, the Osmonds may be ensconced in their new, state-of-the-art, 3,500-seat theater in the Branson Meadows development (*see* Chapter 4, Other Fun Things to Do in and Around Branson). Who knows what legendary performer might take over the current Osmond Family Theater? Or maybe a matinee artist will go big-time here, as John Davidson did when he claimed Jim Stafford's theater in 1993, after Jim remodeled his new, larger facility in the same handsome, art-deco style. You can call the chamber of commerce or individual theaters for the latest update. Please note: the phone numbers listed in this chapter are for the acts themselves, not necessarily the theaters. Dates and show times may change, so call ahead. Although theaters may be closed one or two days a week, box offices are usually open daily for reservations and ticket pickup.

Branson's theaters are state-of-the-art venues designed with the audience's comfort in mind: Most provide superb sight lines and acoustics from all seats. Thanks to fierce competition, even the older theaters have been overhauled with updated sound and lighting systems, and many have reworked the seating arrangements to improve sight lines. Theaters range in size from the tiny 500-seat 76 Music Hall to the mammoth 4,000-seat Grand Palace. The larger theaters incorporate enormous video screens to ensure that those sitting in back don't miss a minute of the action. Each theater has at least one refreshment concession and gift shop, many selling souvenirs, crafts, and personalized memorabilia, such as Shoji Tabuchi fishing rods.

Most theaters present morning, matinee, and evening shows. Headliners usually perform in the evening, leaving the earlier shows for lesser-known, up-and-coming talent. Below you'll find information about the shows, indicated by ▐▌▌▐▌▌ and beginning with the featured performer; a behind-the-scenes look at the headliners follows, indicated by 👢. Unlike most performing venues around the world, theaters here allow flash pictures, and you'll have plenty of opportunities to play paparazzo: In laid-back Branson, many stars travel into the audience during the show and afterward sign autographs and pose for photos in the lobby (Shoji poses before his show, while playing pool in the gentlemen's rest room). Some even board tour buses for an up-close and personal moment.

Unless otherwise noted, box office hours are 9–9, reservations (you can usually guarantee them with a credit card) are accepted, and show lengths vary from 90 minutes to two hours, including intermission. Prices quoted below may be subject to change. Many theaters offer children's discounts, which usually apply to kids under 12. Prices rarely vary with the season; with a few exceptions, stars' performances (whether matinee, weekend, or evening) cost the same. For more reservation information, *see* Getting Around Branson in Chapter 1, Essential Information.

What has made so many stars flock to Branson? The wholesome family atmosphere, the beautiful scenery, and most of all the fact that they don't have to strike out on tour, leaving their families behind for half the year. (An exception is rambunctious rolling stone Willie Nelson, who left Branson singing "On the Road Again" after one season.) For Charley Pride, Glen Campbell, and Mel Tillis, it's Branson's recreational opportunities. Every chance they get, Glen and Charley hit the tees, while Mel hangs up a sign, GONE FISHIN'.

What makes a star a star? Everyone has his or her personal favorites, of course. Crowd appeal, record sales, and visibility all play a part. We list those performers who make a commitment to Branson for a good portion of the year. Many stars appear here regularly, but for only one or two weeks each year: There's Johnny Cash, who usually comes to town three or four times a season, and the Ozark Jubilee Theater brings in the likes of Eddie Rabbitt and Tom T. Hall. Grand Palace engagements have included Bill Cosby, Lorrie Morgan, Reba McEntire, Vince Gill, Tanya Tucker, Ricky Van Shelton, Neil Sedaka, the Smothers Brothers, and the Oak Ridge Boys.

ENTERTAINMENT

AMERICANA THEATER

2905 W. Rte. 76, tel. 417/335–8176. 950 seats. Admission for both shows: $17 adults, children free. Moe Bandy: Apr. 2–15, June 3–Sept. 16, and Nov. 3–Dec. 16, Mon.–Sat. at 2; Apr. 17–June 2 and Sept. 17–Oct. 28, Mon., Thur., and Fri. at 7, and Tues., Wed., and Sat. at 2 and 7. Jennifer Wilson: admission $14 adults, children free; Apr. 2–15, June 3–Sept. 16, and Nov. 3–Dec. 16, Mon.–Sat. at 9:30; Apr. 17–June 2 and Sept. 17–Oct. 28, Mon., Thur., and Fri. at 9:30 and 2, and Tues., Wed., and Sat. at 9:30. Please call to confirm holiday schedules.

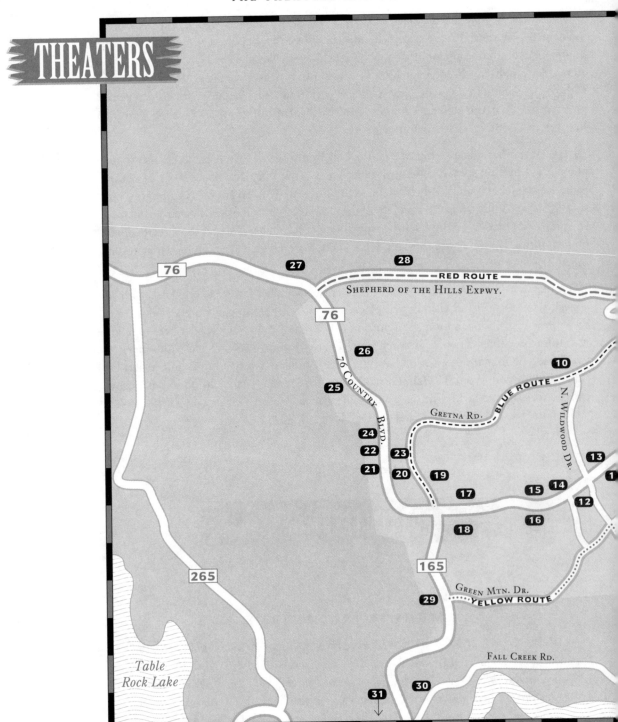

THEATERS

76

27   28

━━ RED ROUTE ━━
Shepherd of the Hills Expwy.

76

26

25

10

Gretna Rd.   BLUE ROUTE

N. Wildwood Dr.

24

22   23

21   20   19

17   15   14   13

16   12   1

18

165

Green Mtn. Dr.
29   YELLOW ROUTE

265

Fall Creek Rd.

Table
Rock Lake

31   30

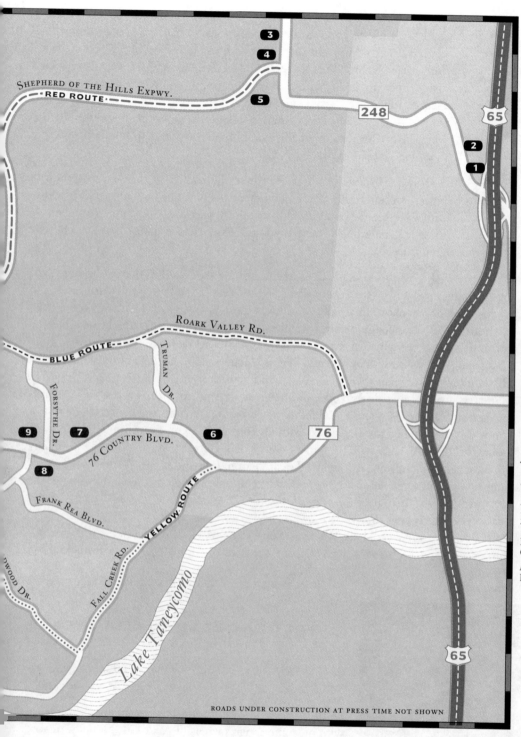

Americana, **15**

Baldknobbers Jamboree, **14**

Boxcar Willie, **24**

Branson Mall Music Theater, **8**

Braschler Music Show, **19**

Glen Campbell's Goodtime, **1**

Roy Clark Celebrity, **20**

Country Tonite, **27**

John Davidson, **22**

Dixie Stampede, **6**

Five Star, **26**

Gettysburg, **4**

Mickey Gilley, **23**

The Grand Palace, **12**

Cristy Lane, **25**

Tony Orlando Yellow Ribbon, **30**

Osmond Family, **18**

Ozark Jubilee, **17**

Presleys' Jubilee, **16**

Charley Pride, **10**

Pump Boys and Dinettes, **29**

Will Rogers, **2**

76 Music Hall, **7**

Shenandoah South, **5**

Jim Stafford, **21**

Shoji Tabuchi, **28**

Thunderbird, **9**

Mel Tillis, **3**

Bobby Vinton's Blue Velvet, **13**

Lawrence Welk Champagne, **31**

Andy Williams' Moon River, **11**

ROADS UNDER CONSTRUCTION AT PRESS TIME NOT SHOWN

Moe Bandy's evening shows are a crackling blend of music and comedy, with Moe singing hits such as "Bandy the Rodeo Clown," "Americana," and "Till I'm Too Old to Die Young." He and his backups also do comic, eerily authentic impersonations of other greats such as George Jones and Patsy Cline. It's just Moe, the band, and his crackerjack singers—no special effects, splashy costumes, or big dance numbers. But you'll be crying for mo' of this good ol' boy as you help him belt out "We Got Our Mojo Workin'."

Star-in-the-making Jennifer Wilson is the feature of the morning show, a power-packed production to jump-start the day. She's a whirlwind of energy with a big blonde mane and bigger smile, who does everything from belting to ballet, including a rambunctious Missouri clog dance that she choreographed.

Moe Bandy is one performer who knows whereof he sings. His music about small-town America and the Wild West That Was rings with truth and strikes a responsive chord in anyone who loves those open spaces. His lyrics come from the heart: Moe was a genuine cowboy and rodeo star who specialized in bronco busting and bull riding before forming his first band, the Mavericks. Born in Meridian, Mississippi, and raised in San Antonio, Texas, Moe came by his love of music naturally: His mother played piano while his dad strummed the guitar. Since he and his wife, Margaret, invested their life savings (pawning their furniture in the process) in a recording session back in 1974 and a Columbia executive signed him to a contract (an almost unheard-of occurrence for any singer without contacts), Moe has won four Academy of Country Music Awards and a Country Music Association Award. But he's probably proudest of his friendship with fellow Texan George Bush, who used "Americana" as his campaign theme song. After performing at several rallies, Moe was invited to sing at the 1988 presidential inauguration. ***Popular songs:*** *"I Just Started Hatin' Cheatin' Songs Today" (1974), "It Was Always So Easy" (1974), "Just Good 'Ol Boys" (1979), "Americana" (1988).* ***Popular albums:*** Hank Williams You Wrote My Life *(Columbia)*, Just Good 'Ol Boys *(Columbia/CBS)*, You Haven't Heard the Last of Me *(MCA)*, Live from Branson *(Laserlight)*.

BALDKNOBBERS JAMBOREE THEATER

2845 W. Rte. 76, tel. 417/334–4528. 1,700 seats. Admission: $14.50 adults, $6 children. May–mid-Dec., Mon.–Sat. 8 PM.

At 7:15, Ragtime Joe warms up the audience with old-time songs such as "I Ain't Got Nobody" before the rest of the Baldknobbers join in for a nonstop barrage of music and comedy, with everything from Droopy Drawers's hillbilly humor to searing renditions of such favorites as "I Can't Stop Loving You."

The Mabe Brothers took their name from the infamous vigilante group called the Baldknobbers, who first protected, then terrorized the Branson area during the 1880s and whom Bill, Jim, Lyle, and Bob Mabe portrayed in the original *Shepherd of the Hills* outdoor drama back in the late 1950s. The Mabes were also the first street band (and street gunfighters) to perform at Silver Dollar City, and in 1959 they opened the first show in Branson, in an old skating rink downtown; they moved to their present location in 1976. Today three generations—Jim and Bill, Jim's son Tim and Bill's son Dennis, and granddaughter Joy—share the stage with assorted performers. They blend fast and furious hillbilly humor, country songs, and stirring gospel, demonstrating their wizardry with all sorts of instruments, including the traditional five-string banjo and dulcimer. ***Popular albums:*** The Ultimate Baldknobbers *(Bransounds)*.

BOXCAR WILLIE THEATER

3454 W. Rte. 76, tel. 417/334–8696. 901 seats. Boxcar Willie: admission $15 adults, $7 children; late Apr.–late Oct., Mon. and Wed.–Sat. 8 PM, Tues. 2 PM.

Boxcar opens his act with his trademark train-whistle sound, which rises in his throat like a—well, a train's whistle. He then launches into a mix of old railroad songs and country favorites by the masters—Hank Williams, Sr., Jimmy Rodgers, Roger Miller (Box does another definitive "King of the Road"), and Ernest Tubb, with plenty of time out for great fiddling and hilarious, sometimes ruthless impersonations of other country stars. As a tribute to his father, who was a train engineer, Box adorned his theater with a series of vivid Iron Engine–theme murals. The real treasures lie next door in the **Boxcar Willie Museum** (admission:

$3, $1.50 with ticket stub), joyously crammed with seemingly everything Box picked up while on the road. He's cataloged all of his obsessions, including railroad, airplane, and recording memorabilia; Roy Rogers paraphernalia; Elvis's rocking chair; even the cockpit of the KC97 World War II fighter plane around which the building was constructed.

Boxcar Willie was born deep in the heart of Texas as Lecil Travis Martin, the son of a train foreman, from whom he inherited his enduring love of railroads and country music. Today he's "the World's Favorite Hobo," but things weren't always that easy. After 22 years in the Air Force, and playing everything from honky-tonks to church socials, Box was discovered in 1979 by Wesley Rose of Rose-Acuff Publishing at the Wembley International Country Music Festival in England. Rose told his partner, the legendary Roy Acuff, that Box *had* to appear on the Grand Ole Opry stage. In little more than 10 years Box had earned 15 gold and 4 platinum albums and a bronze star imbedded in the Country Music Hall of Fame Walkway of the Stars. He was inducted as the 60th member of the Opry. In 1987 he opened his Branson theater. In addition to collecting accolades, Box is the proud owner of what may be the largest private collection of specialty Jim Beam bottles in existence (but he *never* indulges). ***Popular songs:*** *"King of the Road" (1980), "Train Medley" (1980).* ***Popular albums:*** King of the Road *(Prism),* Daddy Was a Railway Man *(Big R),* Live in Concert *(Pickwick).*

BRANSON MALL MUSIC THEATER

Branson Mall, 2200 W. Rte. 76, tel. 417/335–3500 or 800/337–7469. 500 seats. Admission: $13 adults, $12 senior citizens. Showtimes (please call to confirm): Mar. 3–Dec., Wed.–Sun. 9:30 AM.

Magician-comedian Bob Nichol entertains in the morning, rousingly backed up by more of Branson's top talent.

BRASCHLER MUSIC SHOW THEATER

Gretna Rd. 2 blocks north of intersection of Rtes. 76 and 165, tel. 417/334–4363. 720 seats. Admission to both shows: $12 adults, children free. The Braschlers: May–Oct., Sat.–Thurs. 2 and 8:30 PM; limited schedule Nov. and Dec. The Sons: May–Oct., Mon.–Sat. 10 AM; limited schedule Nov. and Dec.

In their show the Braschlers sing all of your favorites, including "Amazing Grace" and "Down by the River," throwing in a good measure of cornball humor, courtesy of Homer Lee. Look for hilarious segments, such as a parody of Joan Rivers, and tributes to country greats like Patsy Cline and Buck Owens.

Taking over the morning with their patented blend of old-fashioned Western swing, the **Sons of the Pioneers** play heart-hurtin' road songs such as "Tumbling Tumbleweed" and "Cool Water."

GLEN CAMPBELL'S GOODTIME THEATER

Rtes. 248 and 65, tel. 417/336–1220. 2,200 seats. Admission: $18 adults, $9 children. May–early Dec., Tues.–Thurs. and Sat. 3 and 8, Fri. and Sun. 8.

Drawing from his entire repertoire, Glen crafts an evening of ballads and up-tempo musical favorites. He's surrounded himself with top-notch singers, dancers, and comedians, including versatile ventriloquist Jim Barber and his 6-foot singing-dummy sidekick Seville. In addition to this live entertainment are video duets with other great stars. The Oak Ridge Boys fill in for Glen several weeks during the season. Of note in Glen's new $7 million theater is the majestic 64-foot-by-20-foot curtain depicting Ozarks life and culture. The image was computer-generated onto the curtain from a painting commissioned from artist John Rush and evokes the origins and lore of country music while celebrating the vitality of the region. The lobby is home to a Will Rogers Museum, with memorabilia of and about the great comedian who never met a man he didn't like (Glen's credo, too).

Glen Campbell grew up just down the road from Branson, in Delight, Arkansas. When Glen was four his father bought him a $5 guitar from the Sears-Roebuck catalog. He was so precocious that at 14 he left home, starting a band with his uncle that toured the

Southwest. After working several years as a session guitarist in Los Angeles, where he proved his musical versatility by backing such stars as Nat King Cole, Frank Sinatra, Elvis Presley, and the Beach Boys, Glen took a shot at a solo career. He was soon snatched up by Capitol Records and started scoring hits, from "Gentle on my Mind" to "Galveston." Along the way his easygoing manner won him starring roles in *True Grit* and *Norwood* and eventually his own TV variety show. After a year cohosting for the Grand Palace, Glen began to build his own theater, which opened in June 1994. ***Popular songs:*** *"Turn Around, Look At Me" (1961), "Gentle on my Mind" (1967), "By the Time I Get to Phoenix" (1967), "Rhinestone Cowboy" (1978), "Wichita Lineman" (1968), "Faithless Love" (1984), "She's Gone, Gone, Gone" (1989).* ***Popular albums:*** I Remember Hank Williams *(Capitol)*, Rhinestone Cowboy *(Capitol)*, It's Just a Matter of Time *(Atlantic-America)*, Unconditional Love *(Capitol)*.

ROY CLARK
CELEBRITY THEATER

3425 W. Rte. 76, tel. 417/334–0076. 1,000 seats. Roy Clark: admission $17 adults, $5 children for matinee and evening shows; late Mar.–Nov., Wed.–Sun. 3 and 7. $25,000 Game Show: group rate $14 per person; mid-Apr.–mid-Dec., Mon.–Sat. 9:30 AM.

Roy and his band take over the stage in the evening, playing up a storm with such hits as "Oh Lonesome Me," "Tips of My Fingers," and "Thank God and Greyhound You're Gone." Roy's voice has thickened a bit over the years, but his pickin' and wit are as nimble as ever. The second half of the show is mostly given over to several hilarious, musical *Hee Haw* routines led by Roy himself. For a special evening, sit up in Roy's Loft, a cozy aerie overlooking the stage where you can order a succulent prime rib dinner while taking in the show. If you sit in the first row of the loft you'll have the best view (since the balcony is somewhat far back), but no matter where you end up it's a convivial setting. After the show everyone is invited to stay for drinks and dancing to top local bands.

Early risers can participate in the *$25,000 Game Show*, an actual win-prizes-and-loot game show that combines such American TV classics as *The Price Is Right*, *Wheel of Fortune*, *Family Feud*, *Let's Make a Deal*, *Truth or Consequences*, and *Card Sharks* in a fast, funny 90 minutes. The list of masters of ceremony includes Bob Eubanks, Dick Van Patten, Dennis James, and Peter Marshall, who host the show on a rotating basis. As many as 100 contestants are selected daily at random from the audience to compete for prizes worth up to $25,000.

Roy Clark was the first nationally known recording and TV star to set up shop in Branson, in 1983, and can be credited with starting the recent Branson boom. But Roy's impeccable credentials go back to before he hosted TV's ever-popular *Hee Haw*, which ran for a quarter century. He's won numerous country music awards, a Grammy, and Entertainer of the Year, Instrumentalist of the Year, and Comedy Act of the Year from the Academy of Country Music and the Country Music Association. Talk about virtuosity! And all from a performer who started pickin' on a cigar box that his mother rigged with a ukulele neck and four strings. A pioneer and pacesetter, he was the first country artist to be inducted into the Las Vegas Entertainer Hall of Fame and one of the first to cross over into jazz, as well as to break through as a guest on prime-time network television, on shows such as *Ed Sullivan, Merv Griffin* and specials by Dean Martin and Tom Jones. He was also the first country artist to guest host *The Tonight Show* for Johnny Carson. But Roy's talents go beyond performing—one of his proudest achievements was being named first National Ambassador to UNICEF. His other interests include an addiction to flight "as bad as the Wright brothers," in his words. He owns two classic flyers, a Stearman biplane and a Piper Tri-Pacer. When he was 12, he and his cousin fashioned their own glider: "It was solid oak, covered with bed sheets. If it had ever gotten off the ground, it would have killed us." ***Popular songs:*** *"Tips of My Fingers"* (1963), *"Thank God and Greyhound You're Gone"* (1970), *"Come Live with Me"* (1973), *"If I Had to Do It All Over Again"* (1976), *"God Didn't Make Little Green Apples"* (1972). ***Popular albums:*** My Music and Me *(DOT),* Roy Clark Sings Gospel *(Word),* The Entertainer *(DOT/Ember),* 20 Golden Pieces *(Bulldog),* Makin Music *(MCA).*

COUNTRY TONITE THEATER

3815 W. Rte. 76, tel. 417/334–2422. 2,011 seats. Admission: $18.50 adults, $9.25 children 4–11; mid-Mar.–mid-Dec., Mon.–Sat. 3 PM and 8 PM.

When Country Tonite premiered in Vegas, it was an instant smash, with audiences hailing it as the best country show west of Branson. An energetic cast, most of them from Vegas, Broadway, Nashville, and Hollywood, and ranging in age from 9 to 49, delivers your favorite top-100 country hits in rousing style. Past performers include Kimberley Caldwell, a five-time *Star Search* Female Song Artists winner, and the Moffett Brothers from TNN. One of the most popular segments includes cowboys doing rope tricks and displaying their marksmanship.

JOHN DAVIDSON THEATER

3446 W. Rte. 76, tel. 417/334–0773. 874 seats. Admission: $16 adults, $8 children. Mid-Mar.–mid-Dec., Tues.–Sat. 3.

John's is the most intimate show in Branson: With a minimum of glitz, he works up a sweat singing his heart out. You'll feel you're getting to know him as he gracefully weaves his life story into the act, with poignant tributes to his loving, religious parents and comic riffs on breaking into show biz. He excels at crafting medleys, evoking nostalgia, and treating every song as a mini-relationship. His mellifluous tenor has roughened over the years, for the better, investing his music with the feeling and weight of experience. The showstopper is his Jolson medley, but you'll love the human jukebox routine, as he and the band serenade those in the audience who are celebrating an anniversary with smash love songs from that year—whether it's 1920 or 1990.

John Davidson is one of Branson's most versatile entertainers. The son of ordained Baptist ministers, John started singing in church like so many other Branson stars. At first he resisted theater, thinking it was "namby-pamby," but as a pretheological student at Denison University he was advised to get some people skills and switched to a theater major in order to become a better preacher. The acting bug bit: John reasoned he could best lift people's spirits by performing. He launched his career in Broadway musicals like *Fiddler on the Roof* and played the romantic lead in the Disney movie *The Happiest Millionaire* before gaining TV stardom in *The Girl with Something Extra* (with Sally Field) and as host of *That's Incredible, The New $100,000 Pyramid,* and his own talk-variety series, *The John Davidson Show.* All the while he continued to tour in musicals such as *The Music Man, Oklahoma,* and *Paint Your Wagon.* He came to Branson in 1992 as the matinee performer for Jim Stafford before taking over Jim's theater in 1993. Branson is his home year-round. When he isn't performing, there's a good chance Davidson is spending time near the water. An avid yachtsman, scuba diver, and admitted beachcomber, John has sailed around the United States, Mexico, and through the Panama Canal with his family on his 96-foot yacht *Principia*, and he dreams of sailing around the world. ***Popular albums:*** From Branson with Love: John Davidson (*Bransounds*).

DIXIE STAMPEDE DINNER THEATER

1527 W. Rte. 76, tel. 800/520–5544. 1,000 seats. Admission: $26.35 adults, $15.35 children 4–11, children under 4 free if they sit on parent's lap. Apr. and May, Tues. and Sun.; June–Aug., daily; Sept., Mon.; Nov. and Dec., Mon. and Tues. 5:30 PM for all shows.

Formerly the Copper Penny Restaurant, this completely remodeled venue is now owned by Dolly Parton's production company, which plans to have the theater up and running by May 1995. Dolly won't be on hand herself, but she promises the 90-minute shows will provide a "horse-racing, whip-cracking, wagon-busting good time: northerners, southerners, the Western prairie, 30 sensational horses, beautiful girls, tough-as-nails heroes, and all the galloping glory of the wild 1800s, plus a fantastic, more-than-you-can-eat, sit-down feast!" Fun begins with a festive musicale in the "Carriage Room Saloon" (no alcohol will be served) and continues with the main event, which re-creates the honor and chivalry of the Old South, with a friendly, spirited competition between cast members representing the Blue and the Gray. Instead of using guns, they compete in riding and doing rope tricks, with the audience cheering them on. Every night ends differently.

FIVE STAR THEATER

3701 W. Rte. 76, tel. 417/336–6220. 2,000 seats. Admission: $19 adults, $13 children. Mar.–Nov., Wed.–Mon. 2 and 8.

Kirby and Philip (illusionist and comedian, respectively) are featured in one of Branson's glitzier productions, with lots of energetic choreography and costume and scenery changes that take you around the world to Egypt and Japan. The dance numbers will let you catch your breath after laughing at Wellford's routines (including hilariously inept juggling and fire-eating and an outrageous, wisecracking retelling of the Garden of Eden story) and gasping at Kirby's astonishing tricks, including escapes reminiscent of Houdini and sly twists on familiar routines like sawing a lady in half.

Kirby Van Burch has found a way to combine the two great loves of his childhood: magic and animals. He spent his teen years in Houston, shuttling between two jobs, working in a magic shop after school and on weekends helping his uncle, an exotic-animal trainer. For Kirby's 16th birthday his uncle rewarded his diligence with a Bengal tiger, which he added to a magic act that already featured a menagerie of reptiles and birds. Within a few years he had conquered Reno and Las Vegas, then took his act on tour through Europe and Asia. Kirby is noted for his efforts on behalf of animal rights and the environment and for his crusade to preserve the historic illusions of such illustrious predecessors as Harry Houdini and Doug Henning.

Philip Wellford was raised in Sarasota, Florida, winter home of the world-famous Ringling Brothers, Barnum and Bailey Circus. The influence certainly shines

through in his routine of comic juggling, a talent he used to support himself through seminary school in Berkeley, California. The two loves of his life dovetailed soon after, when he was asked to travel for a year with the Royal Liechtenstein Circus, which was run by a Jesuit priest. He then worked as a chaplain in Hawaii and moonlighted as a comedian but soon realized "I juggle better than I preach." A Las Vegas producer caught his act in a Waikiki club and featured him in his cabaret revue at Harrah's Las Vegas. From there, he opened for such headliners as Johnny Mathis, Dionne Warwick, Jay Leno, and Phyllis Diller and also appeared on syndicated TV comedy shows. His rendition of the story of Adam and Eve netted him a 1985 Emmy on the *Comedy Tonight* show, hosted by Whoopi Goldberg.

GETTYSBURG THEATER

2211 Rte. 248, tel. 417/334–8400. 922 seats. Admission: $17 adults, $8 children 6–12. Mar., Tues.–Fri. 8 PM, Sat. 2 and 8 PM, Sun. 2 PM. Apr.–Oct., Tues. 8 PM, Wed.–Sat. 2 and 8 PM, Sun. 2 PM.

It's 1863, and a Pennsylvania farm family finds itself swept up in the Civil War in this dramatic musical extravaganza. Their faith, love, and courage help see them through the legendary battle of Gettysburg. The Gettysburg Theater Orchestra plays rousing renditions of period music, from romantic ballads to stirring anthems, while the talented young cast acts, sings, and dances up a storm, abetted by lavish sets and costumes and Surround Sound that thrusts the audience right into the action.

MICKEY GILLEY THEATER

3455 W. Rte. 76, tel. 417/334–3210. 950 seats. Admission: $17 adults, $8 children. May–Oct., daily 2 and 8; Apr. and Nov.–early Dec., weekends 2 and 8.

From boogie to blues to ballads, Mickey delivers a powerhouse show, with help from his superb band and backup singers (listen for the sassy repartee between Mickey and the musicians). The original Urban Cowboy lets loose on hits like "Don't the Girls All Get Prettier at Closin' Time," turns soulful on ballads like "Roomful of Roses," "Talk to Me," and "Put Your Dreams Away." In between, he shows off the foot-stomping piano-playing that is his family's hallmark and lets the audience in on family secrets, including what it was like to be the first cousin of Jerry Lee Lewis ("Great Balls of Fire," "A Whole Lotta Shakin' Goin' On"), and second cousin of televangelist Jimmy Swaggart.

Mickey Gilley soared into national prominence when the 1980 film *Urban Cowboy* became a hit in movie theaters, showcasing Gilley's rowdy, rambunctious honky-tonk—called Gilley's, what else?—in Pasadena, Texas. But country music fans recognized Mickey's talents long before that, with his string of number-one smash hits, including "Roomful of Roses" and "Don't the Girls All Get Prettier at Closin' Time?" Born in Mississippi and bred in Ferriday, Louisiana, Mickey grew up exposed to a broad range of musical influences and later fused blues, jazz, gospel, and pure country to craft tender ballads and honky-tonk with equal authority. He's parlayed his musical success into an acting career, with appearances on

Murder, She Wrote; Dukes of Hazard; and *Fantasy Island.* He is one of the few country singers to have a star emblazoned on the Hollywood Walk of Fame. In Branson, Mickey has demonstrated amazing fortitude: The lobby of his original theater was virtually destroyed by fire in 1993 (the only things left intact were a Reese's candy bar and a St. Jude medal), but Mickey continued to perform in old friend Boxcar Willie's theater. A spanking new theater rose from the ashes, and Mickey was back on his own stage in April 1994. ***Popular songs:*** *"Lonely Wine" (1964), "That's All That Matters" (1971), "Stand by Me" (1971), "Roomful of Roses" (1974), "I Overlooked an Orchid" (1975), "Don't the Girls All Get Prettier at Closin' Time?" (1976), "Doo-Wah Days" (1986).* ***Popular albums:*** At His Best *(Paula),* Welcome to Gilley's *(Playboy),* Gilley's Smokin' *(Epic),* From Pasadena with Love *(Sundown).*

THE GRAND PALACE

2700 W. Rte. 76, tel. 417/334–7263 or 800/5– PALACE. 4,000 seats. Admission: $12 (upper balcony), $28 (orchestra) adults, $5–$12 children. Patsy Cline tribute: Apr. 14–Oct., 2 shows daily (times to be announced; please call for information). Yakov Smirnoff: Apr. 3–Dec. 23, most days (days to be announced; please call for information) 9 AM. Christmas show: late Nov.–late Dec., Wed.–Sun. 8 PM.

The Grand Palace lives up to its name with lavish spectacles and crowd-pleasing special effects. All that glitz would mean nothing, however, without glamorous star power to light up the stage. Whether the headliners are guest artists such as Bill Cosby, Reba McEntire, Neil Sedaka, or co-owner Kenny Rogers, you can count on powerhouse entertainment. The featured show for 1995 will be "Patsy Plays the Palace," a tribute to the late Patsy Cline, which will open in April. Famed Russian comedian Yakov "What a Country" Smirnoff holds sway in the morning, beginning in April 1995. His stage persona has undergone a transformation: He's no longer the wide-eyed immigrant, mangling English, questioning the difference between perfume and toilet water. Instead, he shares his experiences in becoming an American, a husband ("You know the difference between in-laws and outlaws? Outlaws are wanted"), and a father. No one sees the humor inherent in the English language better than Yakov: He encourages the audience to visualize what it means literally to quit smoking cold turkey or to learn to play the guitar—no strings? At the end of the show he often leads an uproarious, no-holds-barred Q & A session with the audience.

Kenny Rogers's show is intimate: just Kenny and the band. You'll feel as if he's singing ballads like "You Decorated My Life," "Lady," "Through the Years," and "She Believes in Me" just for you. At press time, his schedule had yet to be announced.

Christmas is a special time at the Grand Palace, with high-kicking, energy-packed performances by the Radio City Music Hall Rockettes. Few people know that the famed group started life in 1925 in St. Louis as the Missouri Rockets. They've finally come home in a Christmas spectacular that sees them kick up their heels in classics such as "Christmas in New York," along with the moving "Living Nativity" pageant and the lively "Parade of the Wooden Soldiers."

Kenny Rogers was raised with seven siblings in a public housing project in Houston. His inspiring rags-to-riches story made him the first entertainer to receive the prestigious Horatio Alger Award. Of course, his audiences treasure him as the 3-time Grammy, 11-time People's Choice, 8-time Academy of Country Music, and 5-time Country Music Association awards winner. Hits such as "Lucille," "The Gambler," "Lady," and "She Believes in Me" led *Billboard* magazine to bestow on him the Decade's Hottest Crossover Star Award. He has starred in many movies and TV miniseries, including *The Gambler*, and his other interests include photography. He codesigned a line of Western wear that bears his name. ***Popular songs:*** "Lucille" (1977), "The Gambler" (1979), "She Believes in Me" (1979), "You Decorated My Life" (1979), "Lady" (1980), "We've Got Tonight" (1983), "Love Is Strange" (1989), "Islands in the Stream" (1988). ***Popular albums:*** The Gambler (UA), Duets (EMI/American), Back Home Again (Reprise), Eyes That See in the Dark (RCA), If Only My Heart Had a Voice (Giant).

CELEBRITY QUOTE

Kenny on Branson (as quoted in "All Roads Lead to Branson"): "An interesting statistic is that, in 1993, about 4½ million people will go to the south rim of the Grand Canyon, which is one of the eight wonders of the world, and more than 5 million will come to Branson." And the traffic: "The traffic jam is part of the glory, part of the glamour. People love it—it's kind of like what they do on Van Nuys Boulevard in California, where they call it cruising. They drive along and look at each other and look at the stores—and that's what people do in Branson. Part of the excitement is getting from Point A to Point B."

Yakov Smirnoff honed his craft at comedy clubs in Moscow and on cruise ships plying the Black Sea. In 1976 he and his parents received exit visas, and his love for America began immediately. "It started in the airport. You see, *yep* means *sex* in Russian. Really. So I heard all these people walking around going, 'Yep.' I thought, 'What a country!'" He tried many trades at first, including tending bar, where he claims he picked up much of his English. "Unfortunately, people don't make much sense after a few drinks." He worked the comedy-club circuit with his immigrant act, getting his first major national exposure in *Moscow on the Hudson*, the heartwarming comedy film with Robin Williams. Since then, he's headlined in Vegas and became instantly recognizable as TV spokesperson for Days Inn. Yakov is just as zany and lovable in real life: Every year on their anniversary he and his wife Linda renew their vows in a different way. Most memorably, it was in full wedding regalia on skis at Utah's posh Deer Valley for their first anniversary and in astronaut uniforms at NASA for their fifth. He'll entertain almost any suggestions, but bungee-jumping is out of the question.

CRISTY LANE THEATER

3600 W. Rte. 76, tel. 417/335–5111. 1,300 seats. Evening show: $18 adults, $10 children; Feb.–Dec., Fri.–Wed. 7:30 PM (Sun. with Ferlin Husky); morning show and matinee admission $15 adults, $10 children; Feb.–Dec., Ferlin Husky weekdays 10 AM and Sun. 7:30 PM with Cristy; Feb.–Dec., daily 2 PM (Love Rides the Rails).

Opening for Cristy's show is 6-foot, 6-inch Dan Willis, a tall presence with an impressive, booming voice to match. Cristy comes on as the main attraction, her pure soprano voice soaring in inspirational hits such as "One Day at a Time" and "Simple Little Words" and her expert covers of mellow country favorites, including "Midnight Blue."

Other shows throughout the day include Ferlin Husky, ruling the morning hours with a heaping helping of down-home comedy and uplifting songs such as his classic "On the Wings of a Dove." In the afternoon, "Love Rides the Rails," a rip-roaring, old-fashioned, melodramatic musical matinee is performed, replete with beautiful damsels in distress, dashing heros, and hissable, mustache-twirling villains.

Cristy Lane's song "One Day at a Time" has been called the most-requested song in music history, and it could be Cristy's motto: She almost died twice in Vietnam as a U.S.O. entertainer. Cristy comes from humble beginnings in East Peoria, Illinois. Husband Lee Stoller heard her singing while she was doing the dishes at their home. Recognizing her talent, he produced a tape that got her invited onto the prestigious WGN/Chicago National Barn Dance radio show in 1966. Since then Cristy has risen to the top of her profession, winning the 1979 Academy of Country Music New Vocalist Award for "Simple Little Words" and named number-one international artist, recording more than 50 gold and platinum albums. Her inspirational life story is cataloged in her biography, *One Day at a Time*, which has sold more than 5 million copies. ***Popular songs:*** *"One Day at a Time," "Tryin' to Forget You," "Let Me Down Easy."*

TONY ORLANDO YELLOW RIBBON MUSIC THEATER

Rte. 165 at 3220 Falls Pkwy., tel. 417/335–8669. 2,000 seats. $19 adults, $7 children. Mid-Mar.–early Dec., Fri.–Wed. 2 and 8.

The band cooks and Tony sizzles at this powerful show. In a town that is energy personified, Tony seems to reinvent it as he prowls the stage, blasting out favorites such as "Candida," "Knock Three Times," "Sweet Gypsy Rose," and, of course, the evergreen "Tie a Yellow Ribbon" (it won't leave a dry eye in the house). Tony loves the chance Branson provides him to flex his acting muscles. In a unique twist, the second act is a musical he wrote, incorporating pop and rock standards by various arists, called *Jukebox Dreams.* Whether you find it hokey or inspirational, the production offers simple lessons of life and dazzling dream sequences (imagine Elvis and Roy Orbison together in concert).

Tony Orlando achieved stardom more than 20 years ago with such smash hits as "Candida" and "Knock Three Times" before recruiting the duo Dawn to complement his act. The trio took off with their inspiring, unforgettable song of hope and homecoming for Vietnam vets and their families, "Tie a Yellow Ribbon 'round the Old Oak Tree." Nearly two decades later, yellow ribbons fluttered around millions of American homes as our troops marched off to the Persian Gulf. Thanks to that song, Tony has shaken the hands of five presidents, coming a long way from his childhood in New York City. Even then, he knew what he wanted to do. His junior high school chose him to interview visiting stars like Andy Williams for a children's radio show on WNYC when he was just 13 years old. He dropped out of school after the eighth grade to pursue his dream, scoring his first hit in 1961 at the tender age of 16 with the haunting *Halfway to Paradise*, written by Carole King. Since then, Tony has triumphed in every aspect of the industry: He hosted his own variety show for four years and has starred in dramatic made-for-TV films, including *300 Miles for Stephanie* and *The Rosemary Clooney Story* (as Jose Ferrer). He charmed Broadway audiences as Barnum in the musical of the same name and in 1990 starred in a national tour of *The Boys Next Door*, a heart-warming play about mentally challenged friends. Tony and his family now live in Branson year-round. ***Popular songs:*** *"Tie a Yellow Ribbon 'round the Old Oak Tree" (1973), "Gypsy Rose" (1970), "He Don't Love You," "Knock Three Times" (1971).*

OSMOND FAMILY THEATER

3216 W. Rte. 76, tel. 417/336–6100. 1,700 seats. Admission: $17.50 adults, $6 children; Apr.–June and Aug.–mid-Dec., Mon., Tues., and Thurs.–Sat. 2 and 8.

The Osmond Brothers keep things hopping during matinees and evenings. Merrill's the gray-fox lead singer. Jay's the drummer. Jimmy's the youngest and the entrepreneur of the family. Alan's the MC. Wayne's the, well, nut: "What do you call a cow who's just had a calf? Decaffeinated." They all play several instruments, show clips of themselves as youngsters on the *Andy Williams Show*, then perform a beautiful barbershop-quartet harmony. In between they sing such hits as "One Bad Apple" and their signature "He Ain't Heavy, He's My Brother." The second act is stolen by the second generation (as Merrill says, "When we moved to Branson, we doubled the school district with all our children."). There isn't a bad apple in the bunch, as they tap, rap, and sing up a storm. The theater is decorated with portraits of the greats and near greats the Osmonds have worked with and by a cement block (à la Mann's Chinese Theater) in which stars have left their handprints. Among those who have waved howdy are: Johnny Cash, Debbie Reynolds, Andy Williams, Loretta Lynn, and Jim Nabors.

The Osmonds have more than 35 gold and platinum albums, after performing together as a family for more than 30 years. Like so many other Branson greats, the four oldest Osmond brothers—Alan, Wayne, Merrill, and Jay—got their start singing in the church choir (theirs in Ogden, Utah). Walt Disney gave them their first break on TV's *Disneyland after Dark*, which set off their meteoric rise and attracted Andy Williams's attention. He signed them as regulars on his weekly variety show. Brother Jimmy usually joins in the fun. Even Donny and Marie have been known to get into the act when they're in town. "The Osmonds—The Second Generation" are wowing old fans and winning new ones with their razzle-dazzle, hip-hop variation on the traditional barbershop quartet. ***Popular songs:*** *"One Bad Apple," "He Ain't Heavy, He's My Brother."*

● ● ● ● ● ● ● ● ●

CELEBRITY QUOTE

Is anyone missing from the Branson firmament? Wayne claims, "Elvis really is dead. He'd have to be. He's the only one not building a theater!"

OZARK JUBILEE THEATER

3115 W. Rte. 76, tel. 417/334–6400 or 800/365–5833. 698 seats. Evening show: admission $14.50 adults, children under 18 free with adult; mid-Apr.–Nov., Thurs.–Tues. 8 PM. Matinee: admission $12.80 adults, children free; Thurs.–Tues. 2.

The evening shows occasionally bring out the headliners, including such stars as Eddie Rabbitt in no-frills concert formats. "Jubilee," a show patterned after such successful homegrown singing and comedic talent as the Presleys and Baldknobbers, takes center stage for matinees and most evening performances.

PRESLEYS' JUBILEE THEATER

2920 W. Rte. 76, tel. 417/334–4874. 2,000 seats. $14.62 adults, $6.46 children. Apr.–Oct., Mon.–Sat. 8 PM; Nov.–mid-Dec., limited schedule.

On stage the Presleys offer fast-paced entertainment laced with sly hillbilly humor reminiscent of the slapstick vaudeville days and led by comedian Gary Presley, son of Lloyd, the group's founder. There's also an eclectic collection of music, from ballads to furious fiddling presented by three generations of Presleys.

The Presleys are one of the families responsible for starting the tourism industry in Branson. Their 30 years of singing, dancing, and clowning for audiences have made them as big a hit here as any other Nashville star. They offer a savvy combination of mountain melodies and country corn, represented by Herkimer and his inimitable brand of Ozarks wisdom. Dad Lloyd is still around, as are sons Gary and Steve and *their* broods, the next generation, which includes Scott, Greg, Eric, and Nick. No, they're not related to Elvis. ***Popular albums:*** Presleys Jubilee *(Branson Records).*

CHARLEY PRIDE THEATER

Wildwood Dr. and Gretna Rd., tel. 417/337–7433 or 800/CHARLEY. 1,974 seats. Admission: $17.50 adults, $7.50 children; mid-Apr.–Aug. and Nov.–mid-Dec., Wed.–Sat. 3 and 8; Sept. and Oct., Tues.–Sat. 3 and 8.

"Just . . . old friends, down-home folks without ego" is how Charley describes the star acts at his theater: He and Don Williams share the spotlight during the matinee and evening shows. Sunday morning is a sensational singing religious service. Don and Charley keep the hits rolling with memorable titles such as "Kiss an Angel Good Morning" and "I Believe in You." Guests come for the music, but the stunning $12 million venue is an attraction in itself. There are lush gardens and fountains on the grounds, and rustic finishings and contemporary adobe tile set the tone inside. Charley's memorabilia, such as gold records and other awards, are proudly displayed in the lobby. Early construction of the theater was delayed when contractors discovered small caves on the site, but the foundation was relocated to sturdier ground and the theater opened as scheduled in 1994.

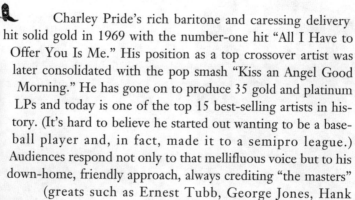

Charley Pride's rich baritone and caressing delivery hit solid gold in 1969 with the number-one hit "All I Have to Offer You Is Me." His position as a top crossover artist was later consolidated with the pop smash "Kiss an Angel Good Morning." He has gone on to produce 35 gold and platinum LPs and today is one of the top 15 best-selling artists in history. (It's hard to believe he started out wanting to be a baseball player and, in fact, made it to a semipro league.) Audiences respond not only to that mellifluous voice but to his down-home, friendly approach, always crediting "the masters" (greats such as Ernest Tubb, George Jones, Hank Williams, B.B. King, and Sam Cooke) with helping him discover his inimitable style. You can read about Charley's life in his recent autobiography, *Pride: The Charley Pride Story*, co-authored with writer Jim Henderson. In the book Charley recounts the difficulty of getting started as a black country singer. (He was once asked by Jack Johnson, a talent scout for Cedarwood Music Publishing, to change his name to George Washington W. Jones III.) After scoring a major Branson success in 1993, Charley returns this year in his own spanking-new theater. Charley will do anything to get to the links, even fib to his wife, Rozene. When she asked him to help her buy furniture for their Branson home, he played sick, played hooky, and hitched a ride (Rozene took the car) to the Pointe Royale golf course. He got caught. ***Popular songs:*** *"I'm So Afraid of Losing You" (1969), "I Can't Believe That You've Stopped Loving Me" (1970), "She's Too Good to Be True" (1972), "Hope You're Feelin' Me" (1975), "Someone Loves You Honey" (1978), "My Jamaica" (1979), "Mountain of Love" (1981), "Night Games" (1983).* ***Popular albums:*** Charley Pride *(RCA),* Classics with Pride *(16th Avenue/Ritz),* There's a Little Bit of Hank in Me *(RCA).*

Don Williams (no relation to Andy) has gained a reputation as a songwriter's singer for his impeccable phrasing and sensitive interpretation of lyrics. Maybe it's because he's a respected singer's songwriter himself, striking a chord in audiences with songs that speak of love, loss, and survival. Born in Floydada, Texas, he's come a long way since winning first prize (an alarm clock) in a local Texas talent show at age three and his first paying job in music, when he played for the grand opening of the Billings Service Station in Taft, Texas. He first achieved success as a member of the Pozo Seco Singers, and when the trio broke up Don pursued a career as a songwriter and soloist. Since then he's produced five gold records and nearly 30 top-10 country hits. Don's trademark Stetson hat was created for his costarring role (with Burt Reynolds) in *W.W. and the Dixie Dance Kings.* The hat was shaped by soaking it in beer, but Don prefers coffee, to tone down the gold of the braided hatband. ***Popular songs:*** *"The Shelter of Your Eyes" (1972), "We Should Be Together" (1972), "Love Me Tonight" (1975), "I'm Just a Country Boy" (1977), "I Believe in You" (1980), "Stay Young" (1984), "One Good Well" (1989).* ***Popular albums:*** *True Love (RCA), Portrait (MCA), Traces (Capitol), It's Gotta Be Magic (Pickwick).*

PUMP BOYS AND DINETTES THEATER

Rte. 165 at Green Mountain Dr., tel. 417/336–4319. 600 seats. Pump Boys and Dinettes: admission $16.38 adults, $8.19 children under 12; Jan. 18–Mar., Wed.–Sat. 4:30; Apr.–Dec. 16, Wed.–Sun. 12:45 and 7:30. Buck Trent: $18.95 adults, $9.50 children (both including 8 AM breakfast); Mar. 10–25, Fri. and Sat. 9; Mar. 29–31, daily 9; Apr.–Sept., Mon.–Sat. 9;

Oct., daily 9; Nov. 2–30, Thurs.–Sat. 9; Dec. 1, 2, 6–9, and 14–16 at 9; closed holidays.

 The musical *Pump Boys and Dinettes* has enjoyed long runs everywhere from Broadway to Los Angeles, but nowhere does it seem more at home and homier than in Branson. The show's waitresses and gas station attendants sing and dance their way through life at a roadside gas station/greasy spoon in a small southern town. The dinner-theater setting adds authenticity to the performance, as waitresses sling hash and insults at the men in their lives, in a series of sassy country-and-western tunes.

Morning performances (including breakfast) by Buck Trent are a winning combination of toe-tapping music and thigh-slapping comedy. He's a banjo picker extraordinaire—and wait until you see him ham it up for photos.

WILL ROGERS THEATER

Rte. 248, tel. 417/336–1333 or 800/994–9455. 2,100 seats. Admission: $16.75 adults, $9.75 children. Christmas show: Nov.–mid.–Dec., daily 8 PM.

 In November and December, world-renowned pianist Dino Kartsonakis—called the new Liberace—helps bring yuletide cheer with the wildly popular *Magical Journey of Christmas,* an extravaganza that includes three onstage grand pianos, 200 sparkling costumes, and a cast of more than 40. Dino's talented wife, Cheryl, a fine gospel singer, rounds out the show. At press time, plans for a featured show during the months of January through October had not been finalized.

The lobby of the theater houses a $750,000 mini-museum of Will Rogers memorabilia, including the silver-filigree saddle he gave his son Jim, a pair of Will's chaps, some lariats he used, old posters from his vaudeville and movie days, and family photos.

76 MUSIC HALL

1919 W. Rte. 76, tel. 417/335–2484. 500 seats. $12.75 adults, children free. Brumley Show: Mar.–early Nov., Mon.–Sat. 10 AM. Down Home Country: Mar.–early Dec., Mon.–Sat. 1:30. Texas Gold Miners: Mar.–early Dec., Mon.–Thurs. and Sat. 4, Sun. 8 PM. Memory Makers: Mon.–Sat. 8 PM. Sunday Gospel Jubilee: Mar.–early Nov., Sun. 2.

Five equally entertaining yet very different shows take turns lighting up the stage at this intimate theater. Don't expect much in the way of sets and costumes, just top-notch local performers strutting their stuff. The Brumley Show will get you smiling in the morning with a joyous combination of old-time gospel, contemporary country, and hillbilly humor. Down Home Country chimes in next with hot fiddling and Western swing. The Texas Gold Miners rope in the crowds with their youthful energy (they're all teenagers) and winning mix of country and gospel music and clogging. The Memory Makers conjure memories of big bands and sock hops, as they give a guided musical tour from the 1940s to the present. At the Sunday Gospel Jubilee the Bacon family sings your gospel favorites in an inspiring celebration of the Lord's Day.

Before you leave 76 Music Hall take a look around the complex: There's an entertainment center with a shopping mall (more than 20 stores), a motel, the country's busiest Bonanza restaurant, a video arcade, a 36-hole miniature golf course, and a 3-D movie theater showing 15-minute action shorts (admission $3 per person per ½ hour; daily 10–10 on ½ hour).

SHENANDOAH SOUTH THEATER

Rte. 248 and Shepherd of the Hills Expressway, tel. 417/336–3986. 3,000 seats. Anita Bryant: $14.50 adults, $9.50 children. Apr.–early Dec., Tues.–Sun. 9:30 AM. Matinee and evening shows: $22 adults, $12 children. Apr.–early Dec., dates and times vary.

▐▐▐▐▐▐▐ Anita Bryant starts your day off with a memorable mix of pop standards ("Paper Rose," "Little Things Mean a Lot"), Broadway showstoppers ("As Long as He Needs Me," "You'll Never Walk Alone"), and gospel standbys ("How Great Thou Art," "Mine Eyes Have Seen the Glory," "Bless This House") that will have you on your feet. *Note:* At press time, it was undetermined whether or not Anita Bryant would return for the 1995 season.

During matinee and evening performances you'll see stars who shine bright enough to rival those at the Grand Palace. Troupers as varied as Mel Torme, Neil Sedaka, Ronnie Milsap, and Dorothy Hamill (along with her Icecapades crew, a Branson first) strut their stuff, often backed by stunning production numbers. All of this entertainment is presented in an exquisite neoclassical Virginia building decorated with unique touches, courtesy of former headliner Wayne Newton. Three larger-than-life-size bronze Arabian horses, crafted in New Mexico at a cost of $1 million, are mounted in a pool in the front.

🥾 Anita Bryant made her stage debut singing "Jesus Loves Me" at the First Baptist Church in Barnsdale, Oklahoma. At 18 she was already a seasoned trouper, waltzing off with second-runner-up honors in the Miss America pageant. That same year she struck gold for the first of three times with "Till There Was You." She has recorded more than 30 albums, her versatile soprano spanning pop, patriotic, and sacred music. She has also authored 10 best-selling books, including *Bless this Food/The Anita Bryant Family Cookbook, Raising Gods' Children,* and the autobiographical *Mine Eyes Have Seen the Glory* (coauthor Charlotte Hale) and toured for seven years with Bob Hope, entertaining troops overseas. Millions know her as spokesperson for the Florida Citrus Growers (her commercials and personal appearances helped double sales, but her antigay crusade led to her dismissal) and, currently, for Coca-Cola. For these and other accomplishments she was voted Entertainer of the Year by her peers and Most Admired Woman in America according to a *Good Housekeeping* poll three years running during the 1970s. ***Popular songs:*** *"Till There Was You" (1957), "Paper Roses," "My Little Corner of the World."* ***Popular albums:*** As Long as He Needs Me *(Columbia),* Do You Hear What I Hear? *(Columbia),* In My Little Corner of the World *(Carlton),* Anita with Love— Volumes I *and* II *(gospel) and* Volume III *(pop) (Anita Bryant, Inc.).*

JIM STAFFORD THEATER

3444 W. Rte. 76, tel. 417/335–8080. 1,100 seats. Jim Stafford: admission $17 adults, $7.50 children; mid-Jan.–mid-Apr., Thurs.–Sun. 2 and 8; mid-Apr.–mid-Dec., Tues.–Sun. 2 and 8. Doug Gabriel: admission $12.50 adults, $6 children; Apr.–Dec., Mon.–Sat. 9 AM.

Matinees and evenings Jim takes over the stage, proving again and again to be one of Branson's funniest men. He's a comic tornado and a real pro, whose show adroitly blends his trademark music and comedy. You have to hear for yourself the Chihuahua jokes and the reading of audience-comment cards ("Jim, my most embarrassing moment was when I went to Reno, won $10,000, and wet my pants." Jim's response? "Well, it coulda been worse. You mighta won $20,000") and watch the soft-shoe routines and physical comedy. Then, of course, there are Jim's hits, such as "Cow Patti," which pokes fun at the country-western genre. If anyone can reach the child in us all, Jim can. This inimitable sense of humor extends even to the theater's rest rooms, which are decorated with 3-D posters (unfocus your eyes, and suddenly spaceships and dinosaurs will pop out).

In the morning, catch Doug Gabriel's powerful, soulful voice as he dazzles with renditions of pop, country, and gospel favorites, as well as his original songs. He's backed by several capable performers, including his wife, Cheryl, and impressionist Jeff Brandt.

Jim Stafford is a multitalented performer, specializing in a unique blend of country-tinged tunes and jokes he dubs "musicomedy." He was born in Winterhaven, Florida, and wanted to be a preacher until he began playing guitar at 13 (he's also taught himself to play the fiddle, banjo, harmonica, organ, and piano).

He recalls being fascinated even then by the theatricality of the church service. His first chart single came in 1974, when boyhood friend Kent "Lobo" LaVoie produced "The Swamp Witch"; Jim then scored huge hits with "Spiders and Snakes" and "My Girl Bill." His success led to TV stardom on the *Smothers Brothers Comedy Show*, for which he also served as head writer; *Those Incredible Animals*; and *The Jim Stafford Show*. Jim and his family have lived in Branson since 1990, and he's so enthusiastic about their new hometown that he serves on the chamber of commerce board of directors and organizes several charitable events here annually. ***Popular songs:*** *"The Swamp Witch" (1974), "Spiders and Snakes" (1976), "Cow Patti" (1980).* ***Popular albums:*** New Deal *(Bransounds).*

SHOJI TABUCHI THEATER

3260 Shepherd of the Hills Expressway, tel. 417/334–7469. 2,000 seats. $22 adults, $14 children. Apr.–Dec., Mon.–Sat. 3 and 8.

Perhaps the flashiest show in Branson, this lavish display incorporates neon, stage fog, a bevy of dancing girls, and elaborate choreography by Shoji's wife, Dorothy, a mean pop singer (wait'll you hear her start the evening with "I'm So Excited!"). Their charming daughter Christina joins in the huge production numbers. But the focal point is Shoji, fiddlin' up a storm, from "Turkey in the Straw" and "Orange Blossom Special" to Mozart, always with a dash of self-deprecating humor (he pulls off some of the worst jokes you'll ever hear, with ineffable charm). He says he's improved his English on fishing trips with

M-M-Mel Tillis. The man's amazing, segueing smoothly from Cajun to classical to calypso, big band to blues to bluegrass without missing a beat. He even raps, then does bird calls and train-whistle impressions on his violin. Perhaps as awesome as the performer himself is Shoji's theater—an art-deco extravaganza, a riot of jade, cream, imperial purple, lavender, mauve, and magenta. There are three gift shops, including Christina's, a children's clothing store named for his daughter; and Dorothy's Boutique de la Reve, stocked with sequined jackets and appliquéd gowns. The bathrooms are theatrical visions in marble, brass, and walnut. The Victorian-style men's room includes gold lion's-head fixtures, black leather armchairs, candelabra, and a $38,000 pool table, where Shoji often holds court between shows. The ladies' room is no less opulent: wallpaper with delicate angels, huge vases brimming with white and purple orchids, attendants dispensing perfumes and lotions from a towering display, and a magnificent lilac crystal-teardrop chandelier.

Shoji Tabuchi is Branson's first incontestable, incandescent, homegrown star. He was born in 1946 in Osaka, Japan, and trained as a classical violinist. His life changed in college when he saw Roy Acuff on tour in Japan, working wonders with his fiddle. Acuff took a shine to the eager Tabuchi; years later, when Shoji was working as a sideman in Kansas City bands, Acuff gave him a shot at the Grand Ole Opry. The notoriously discriminating audience had never seen anything like this dynamo, and Shoji has been back many times since. But it wasn't until his first Branson gig, at the Starlite Theater, that Shoji knew he'd found his calling—and home. ***Popular albums:*** Fiddlin' Around (*Bransounds*), Live from Branson (*Bransounds*).

THUNDERBIRD THEATER

2215 W. Rte. 76, tel. 417/336–2542. 700 seats. Blackwoods: admission $13.11 adults, $12.01 senior citizens, children under 15 free; Apr., Nov., and Dec., Fri.–Sun. 10 AM and May–Oct., daily 10 AM. Ragtime Lil and Banjo Banjo: admission $16.93 adults, $15.84 senior citizens, $8.46 children under 12; Apr.–Nov., Tues.–Sun. 2:30 and 7:30 PM. Thunderbird Band: admission $10.92 adults, $8.74 children 15–18 (7:30 show) and $8.74 adults, $6.55 children and senior citizens (11 PM show); Apr.–Nov., Mon. 7:30 PM, Tues.–Sat. 11 PM.

The Thunderbirds host different shows daily, all produced with minimum production values but maximum entertainment value. The Blackwood Quartet, a family act, sings its gospel hits and enduring standards such as "How Great Thou Art" and "Turn Your Radio On." Ragtime Lil and Banjo Banjo is a group of musicians and vocalists delivering the inimitable New Orleans sound, from ragtime to Dixieland jazz. The Thunderbird Band offers a nostalgic trip to the '50s, doing such old rock-and-roll standbys as "Rock around the Clock" and "Blueberry Hill."

MEL TILLIS THEATER

Rte. 248, tel. 417/335–6635. 2,672 seats. Admission: $18.50 adults, $5 children. Apr.–Dec., Tues.–Sun. 2 and 8.

The consummate professional, Mel strides his enormous stage twice daily. He's in great voice, gliding effortlessly from bluegrass to honky-tonk to soulful ballads. The famous stutter milks plenty of laughs (listen for the one about why he started stuttering as a child), but you won't notice the impediment when his creamy tenor curls around hits such as "Ruby, Don't Take Your Love to Town" (which he wrote for Kenny Rogers), "Detroit City," "Time Has Treated You Well," and "Coca-Cola Cowboy." It's a family affair at Mel's when singing-star daughter Pam Tillis joins Dad for duets; daughter Connie Lynn performs every show with Mel, and seven-year-old Hannah—a star in the making—occasionally stops by, too, now that she's over her stage fright.

Mel Tillis has been a Branson fixture since 1992, the year he was named Entertainer of the Year in a national vacationers' poll. He started his career in the early 1950s with a group called the Westerners while serving in the U.S. Air Force as a baker, stationed in Okinawa. He achieved chart-topping success as a songwriter with Webb Pierce's rendition of the soulful "I'm Tired." Since then, artists as varied as Kenny Rogers, Brenda Lee, Ray Price, Charley Pride, and the Oak Ridge Boys have recorded his work. His authoritative baritone has also brought him great success: He burst on the national scene with a string of honky-tonk hits, such as the rollicking "Heart over Mind." His 60 albums have spawned nine number-one smashes and 34 top-10 titles, leading to a slew of awards, including 1976 Country Music Association Entertainer of the Year Award and an induction into the Nashville Songwriters Hall of Fame. He reached a new audience costarring in good ol' boy movies such as *Smokey and the Bandit*, *Cannonball Run* (both with Burt Reynolds), and *Every Which Way but Loose* (with Clint Eastwood and Clyde, the orangutan). Mel has big plans for Branson's performing-arts industry and for his new theater. When the venue is finally complete, in late 1995, it will house production offices, an underground recording studio, and a 156,000-square-foot TV and motion-picture soundstage that should lure even more artists to Branson. Mel's complex is cavernous, and it's a good thing: When asked how he prepares for performances Mel explained that he walks up and down the tunnel beneath his theater—belting out my songs and listening to the echoes ricochet off the walls." ***Popular songs:** "Wine" (1965),*

"Who's Julie?" (1968), "Good Woman" (1976), "In the Middle of the Night" (1983). **Popular albums:** I Believe in You *(MCA)*, American Originals *(Columbia)*, New Patches *(MCA)*.

BOBBY VINTON'S BLUE VELVET THEATER

2701 W. Rte. 76, tel. 417/334–2500 or 800/US–BOBBY. 2,000 seats. $18 adults, $9 children. Apr.–Oct., Thurs.–Tues. 2 and 7; Nov.–mid Dec., weekends 2 and 7.

No need for dancing girls or flashy stage effects here, not when you have the world-renowned Glenn Miller Orchestra backing up Bobby Vinton. It would take several shows for Bobby to sing all of his smashes, but how's this for starters—"Melody of Love," "Roses Are Red," "Blue on Blue," "Blue Velvet," "Mr. Lonely," "Sealed with a Kiss," "I Love How I Love You." Like so many other Branson performers, Bobby's a virtuoso on several instruments, and he displays his versatility on the oboe, trumpet, saxophone, clarinet, drums, and piano (playing—what else?—"Rhapsody in Blue"). There's even some time left over for Bobby's mother, Dorothy, and daughters, Kristin and Jennifer, to perform (son Chris acts behind the scenes as his dad's theater manager). The orchestra kicks in with classics such as "In the Mood," and the audience is encouraged to come up and dance on stage at the beginning of the second act. In his theater Bobby wanted to duplicate the look and feel of the grand old Hollywood movie palaces like Grauman's (now Mann's) Chinese, the Pantages, and the Egyptian. Murals of angels adorn the ceiling, imparting an Italian Renaissance elegance. Since so many of his hits have the word *blue* in their titles, it's appropriate that his theater be a fantasy in various shades of the color. The lobby's tile floor was hand dyed blue. The carpeting inside the theater is likewise blue, stamped with gold records bearing the initials "BV." And the stage curtain was custom made with hundreds of yards of blue velvet drapery, edged with a band of fabric fashioned with 14-carat-gold threads.

Bobby Vinton has been dubbed by *Billboard* magazine "the all-time most successful love singer of the Rock Era (1956–66)." During the first 10 years, Vinton had more number-one hits than any other male vocalist, including Elvis Presley and Frank Sinatra. He's sold more than 50 million records, spinning a dozen into gold, including some of the most beloved songs of the '50s and '60s. His parents encouraged him to study music and by age 16 he had formed his first band, which played clubs in the Pittsburgh area. He financed his college education and graduated with a degree in musical composition from Duquesne University, which recently conferred an honorary doctorate on Bobby. After a stint in the army he returned to performing and soon appeared on Guy Lombardo's *TV Talent Scouts*. A subsequent four-week run on the show landed him a contract with Epic Records, leading to his first epic success, "Roses Are Red," and launching him to superstardom. The Hollywood Chamber of Commerce confirmed his enduring pop-icon status by bestowing its ultimate accolade: a bronze star on the Hollywood Walk of Fame. Owning his own theater has enabled Bobby to bring a lifelong dream to fruition. He grew up in Pittsburgh on the big-band sound—his father (Stan Vinton) had his own big band—and now has fulfilled a longtime goal by singing with the Glenn Miller Orchestra. ***Popular songs:*** *"Melody of Love"* (1974), *"Roses Are Red"* (1956). ***Popular albums:*** Sealed with a Kiss *(Epic)*, Blue on Blue *(Epic)*, Mr. Lonely *(Epic)*, There I've Said It Again *(Epic)*, I Love How You Love Me *(Epic)*, Melodies of Love *(ABC)*.

LAWRENCE WELK CHAMPAGNE THEATER

1984 Rte. 165, tel. 417/337–SHOW or 800/505–WELK. 2,268 seats. Admission: $18.10 adults, $9.56 children. Lennon Brothers: Apr.–mid-Dec., Tues.–Sun. 10 AM. Matinee and evening shows: Nov.–mid-Dec., Wed.–Sun. 2 and 8; Apr.–Oct., Tues.–Sun. 2 and 8.

Your favorite TV show comes to life during matinee and evening performances, which begin an hour before the curtain rises with video clips of the old TV shows. The audience can dance in the aisles or on the small dance stage. Then a handpicked crew of fondly remembered cast members—the Lennon Sisters, Jo Anne Castle—and rotating hosts including Ron English, Arthur Duncan, Myron Florin, and Tom Heatherington bring back Champagne Time with favorites such as "Bubbles in the Wine." The production is sumptuous, ranging from a 1940s stage-door canteen, a stylized re-creation of Hollywood, to one set where columns are draped with more than 1,000 yards of chiffon. The nostalgic sounds of Dixieland, polka, waltz, and old-time gospel fill the theater. Of course, the show closes with "Auf Wiedersehen," and, yes, there are bubbles galore. The attractive complex includes a restaurant and a gabled Tyrolean chalet–style motel, linked by a series of brick-colored loggias. A big neon stage-door-canteen sign welcomes you to the restaurant, which serves buffet and à la carte meals; the waiters are smartly garbed in military USO-style outfits. Piano or harp music plays softly during lunch and dinner; after the show a limited supper menu is available, and a four-piece combo plays for anyone who wants to dance the night away.

In the morning the Lennon Brothers harmonize on big-band songs and golden oldies from the 1930s, '40s, and '50s.

ANDY WILLIAMS' MOON RIVER THEATER

2500 W. Rte. 76, tel. 417/334–4500. 2,000 seats. Admission: $18 adults, $8 children. Apr., Tues.–Thurs. and Sat. 3 and 7, Fri. 7 PM; May–mid-Dec., Mon.–Thurs. and Sat. 3 and 7, Fri. 7 PM.

Andy and his 11-piece international orchestra play past and present favorites, with nostalgic video tributes to friends who performed on his TV show. As dapper and elegant as ever, Andy retains his boyish charm. His smooth, sly, slightly nasal voice still dips and swirls around the notes. He soothingly sings many of the songs he introduced to the world: Expect to hear "Days of Wine and Roses," "Love Story," "I Can't Stop Loving You," "Help Me Make it through the Night," and, of course, "Moon River." You'll float out of the theater.

Andy Williams got his start singing in the church choir with his brothers Bob, Dick, and Don back in tiny Wall Lake, Iowa, before they made a splash on a Des Moines radio station in 1938 when Andy was just eight years old. The act (now dubbed The Williams Brothers Quartet) hit the road throughout Andy's childhood, making stops in major cities, including Cincinnati and Los Angeles. In 1951 the group disbanded, and Andy pursued a solo career. A stint on Steve Allen's *Tonight Show* led to his first recording contract in 1954 with Cadence Records, the label on which he recorded standards such as "Butterfly," "Lonely Street," and "Hawaiian Wedding Song." Andy went on to garner 20 gold and platinum records, five Grammy nominations, three Emmy Awards, and a Golden Globe nomination as Most Popular Male TV Star for the much-loved *Andy Williams Show*, which ran on NBC from 1963 to '71. He started performing in Branson in 1992, paving the way for such noncountry Vegas performers as Wayne Newton, Bobby Vinton, and Tony Orlando. Andy fell in love with Branson not only because of the opportunities it offers performers but also because of the Ozarks' natural beauty. He considered the natural surroundings when building his theater. "When I saw the dramatic limestone formations along the highway, I knew I had to include them in the design," he says. The edifice duplicates the rock bluffs, waterfalls, and foliage typical of the region, and in 1992 the design won a Conservation Award from the state of Missouri for developed land use. The theme continues inside, incorporating soothing earthtones in what Andy terms an "oasis." His multimillion-dollar art collection graces the lobby walls, with Navajo rugs, sculptures by Willem de Kooning, Jacques Lipchitz, and Henry Moore, and paintings by Donald Wilson and Kenneth Noland. Inside Andy's dressing room are works by Helen Frankenthaler, Richard Diebenkorn, Jackson Pollock, Claes Oldenburg, Fernando Botero, Paul Klee, and Pablo Picasso. **Popular songs:** *"Moon River" (1962), "Days of Wine and Roses" (1963), "Call Me Irresponsible" (1964), "The Shadow of Your Smile" (1965), "Born Free" (1967), "Love Story" (1971), "Merry Christmas" (1989).* **Popular albums:** Moon River *(Columbia),* The Wonderful World of Andy Williams *(Columbia),* Love Story *(Columbia),* The Andy Williams Christmas Album *(Columbia).*

● ● ● ● ● ● ● ● ● ● ●

CELEBRITY QUOTE

Andy puts the Branson-Vegas connection in perspective: "The best you can get in Vegas is a royal flush. But here in Branson the best you can get is a full house!"

OTHER ENTERTAINMENT AFTER DARK

Some visitors are surprised that there are no regular boot-scooting palaces or karaoke bars here. But most of Branson's nightlife revolves around the shows, and with so much to do, see, and hear, it's early to bed, early to rise. This is not to say, however, that 76 Country Boulevard rolls up its sidewalks once the theaters go dark. After all, locals have their hangouts, and performers often need to wind down after their shows. The legal drinking age in Missouri is 21. Most venues close by 1 AM.

BARS AND DANCING

B.T. Bones, which holds theme nights featuring comedy showcases (usually Monday and Tuesday), hypnotists (usually Tuesday), and karaoke sing-alongs (Sunday), also presents Route 66, a country band that plays every evening from 9 until closing. *See also* Chapter 8, Dining. *2346 Shepherd of the Hills Expressway, tel. 417/335–2002. No cover or minimum.*

Confetti's is the only one true disco in town, attracting crowds of all ages, usually ranging from 21 to 50, who enjoy the live bands. It's *Saturday Night Fever* revisited, albeit on a small scale, with pulsating lights and crystal disco balls galore. *Holiday Inn, W. Rte. 76, tel. 417/334–5101. Cover: $6. Closes 1 AM and Sun., Mon.*

The **Cowboy Cafe** attracts 21- to 50-year-olds who come to the lounge for the DJ's mix of oldies and C&W. It's very casual here, even when they do the occasional karaoke night. *526 Shepherd of the Hills Expressway, tel. 417/335–4828. No cover. Closed Mon. and winter. Closes 1 AM Mon.–Sat., midnight Sun.*

Crockey's Show Biz Theater, at the durable local hangout Crockey's, attracts people who come for the dancing (the largest dance floor in the area) and live entertainment. Look for the Young Branson Stars, tomorrow's recording artists ranging in age from 13 to 19, performing the latest country hits, as well as old standards on a changing schedule several times weekly at noon or 4 PM. There's a country band Wednesday through Sunday, a talent show on Monday, and a DJ on Tuesday. Lunch and dinner are served daily. *Rtes. 65 S and 165, Hollister (2 mi south of downtown Branson), tel. 417/334–4995. No cover. Closes 1 AM.*

Dimitri's is the place for fine dining and soothing piano music, every night but Wednesday (when it's closed). *Lake Taneycomo at the end of Main St., tel. 417/334–0888. No cover. Closes midnight.*

At **Down Under,** next door to the Ozark Family Restaurant, you can dance to live rock 'n' roll in the closest thing Branson has to a roadhouse. Although not strictly a singles hangout, Down Under attracts a 21- to 45-year-old crowd with theme evenings and competitions such as the "Cutest Tush" contest. *1580 W. Rte. 76, tel. 417/334–1207. Cover: $2 weeknights, $3 weekends. Closes 1 AM.*

Rocky's is a smoky, crammed, dimly lighted joint that heats up on weekends after 11 PM, thanks to a smokin' jazz-blues combo led by tenor saxman Dock Butler and singer Brenda Stevenson. They, and other bleary-eyed musicians, jam well into the night, and there's no cover or drink minimum. *120 N. Sycamore St., tel. 417/335–4765. No cover. Closes 1 AM.*

Roy's Loft keeps the party going long after Roy Clark's show ends. Live country music (what else?) gets a crowd of all ages dancing. *3425 W. Rte. 76, tel. 417/334–0076. No cover. Closes 1 AM and Nov.–Mar.*

● ● ● ● ● ● ● ● ● ● ● ●

CELEBRITY QUOTE

"I feel sorry for all my non-drinking friends," Mickey Gilley confesses, "'cause when they wake up in the morning, it's the best they're gonna feel all day."

DINNER SHOWS

The **Hay Loft** has two shows nightly and features acts on a rotating basis. Among the performers are gospel groups and a magician. Of course kids love the magic, but the singers attract a family crowd, too, and you can enjoy this show without missing a performance at one of the bigger venues. *2005 W. Rte. 76, tel. 417/334–7676. $10.95 adults, $5.95 children, including dinner. Apr.–Nov., daily 5–6:30 and 10:30–11:30.*

The **Settle Inn** stages a whodunnit comedy/murder-mystery dinner theater with audience participation. Children enjoy the interaction as much as adults. Shows last about two hours. *Green Mountain Dr., tel. for reservations 417/335–4700 or 800/677–6900. $75 per couple, $25 children. May–Oct., Thurs.–Sat. 7:30 PM.*

MOVIES

If you're in the mood for a feature flick, you have four choices at the **Table Rock Cinema Four** (W. Rte. 76, tel. 417/334–6806), which screens the latest first-run hits.

There's also the **Ozarks Discovery IMAX Theater** (*see* Chapter 4, Other Fun Things to Do in and Around Branson), where nature and science films are projected on a six-story-tall screen. Features change every few months.

Tony Orlando,
entertainer, singer, playwright

Jordan Simon: How did you discover Branson?

Tony Orlando: About four or five years ago I
bumped into Jim Stafford, and I said, "So, how's
it going, Jim?" He said, "Tony, I'm in Branson,
Missouri." At the time I didn't know what
Branson was. He said, "Branson. You know,
where Boxcar Willie and Roy Clark are. I got a
brand-new theater there." Then, like the rest of
the world, I started to hear about Branson. I got
a call from Roy Clark, who asked me to fill in
one weekend for someone, and I said, "But I'm
not a country singer. Will they know me there?"
Then Jim and Mel encouraged me to consider it.
Jim's point was that the audiences here have
great feelings for America and traditional values
and that the yellow ribbon is a significant symbol
and that the audiences relate to a good show. So
I took the job last November and did three days.
The first thing that happened was I fell in love
with the terrain. The second thing that happened was I fell in love with the people. Big
time. I sensed this wonderful community spirit,
and I've been friends with all the performers
here for years. Ray Stevens was here. In 1961,
when I was 16, I did my first tour with Ray in
1961. And I've know Andy [Williams] since
1957. When I was 12 I was the kid in school
picked to interview stars. He came to our local
school, and I interviewed him for

WNYC radio. And Mel Tillis and Roy Clark were semi-regulars on my television show. And Jim Stafford and I go way back together. So these are all old friends. It's like, wow, I can have a social life here that I enjoy. We opened July Fourth [1993].

JS: So you really jumped right in.

TO: We did. And we came in the middle months, which are tough. We had no buses. We were dealing with just word of mouth. And the city of Branson, the city of Springfield, and Hollister and Ozark really came out for the show.

JS: The locals.

TO: Yeah, they came out big time for the show. They made this theater happen. They really did.

JS: You're very involved with the community, aren't you?

TO: I think all the artists are. One thing about show people, it's part of our responsibility to give back. I mean, you can use fame for bad, you can be self-destructive, or you can be sane and really do something constructive. And we're here for the locals, we're here for the charities. So we're blessed with fame. Fame is a responsibility that even Branson has. Branson is taking on a responsibility big time. We're also the heartland of America, where we hold traditional values high. If you wave the flag here no one will snicker at you. You can be proud of it here. You have God, family, and country in the right perspective, the old-fashioned way. You walk on a stage here and see Grandma and Grandpa, their children and their children, all in the same row watching the same show. That's very rare.

JS: It's a real family destination. Unlike, say, Vegas, where you've also played.

TO: Absolutely, it's not a gaming town. You leave here with the same amount of money in your pocket. So it doesn't have the trappings of a gaming town. You know, I don't think gambling's gonna come. I think it would spoil the area. It would be devastating. Branson has all the values that everyone who comes here wants to keep: family values and traditional values, along with some of the most beautiful terrain in America. And the guys who are putting on the shows have been around long enough to know how to do it right. You're not gonna get a novice. You walk in to see a show here, you're seeing guys who have been doing this all their lives. You're not gonna see a bad show in town.

JS: You're pretty versatile, with the acting career and now playwriting.

TO: Oh, I'm just dabbling in that. You know what it really is? When I did *Barnum* on Broadway and I did the television show, I developed great respect for the writer. Now playwriting has made me realize why writers are willing to starve and not make more money doing something else. I'm flexing muscles now I never thought I'd flex. I'm having more fun letting my creative juices flow and enjoying my life as an entertainer than I ever have. It's a blessing, it's a chance to work, in a multimillion-dollar theater, no less. I haven't had a hit record since 1977, yet we're doing 4,000 people a day——performances twice a day, six days a week. Twenty-seven buses pulled up to this theater last night. I had 1,903 people here, and I'm only here eight months. The yellow ribbon, the symbol of homecoming, renewal, and love, has surpassed anything any entertainer could ever do. The American people have made it a symbol, it's now part of American history. I'm born and raised in New York City, I never saw high school, I never went past the eighth grade. Yet I've shaken hands with the last five presidents of the United States and sung at the White House three times. All because of this yellow ribbon. It's unbelievable. I mean, here I am at the Yellow Ribbon Theater in Branson, Missouri, the heartland of America.

JS: It's the American Dream.

TO: Oh, I call it Field of Dreams, Branson. Every entertainer talks about how they've dreamed about this. You drive up this Strip, your name is on the theater—-wouldn't it blow *your* mind?

JS: What gives you the ultimate satisfaction now? Playwriting, acting, singing?

TO: All of it. I love all of it. When I started out, I saw myself doing it for the pure enjoyment of it, not for the money. And I'm just beginning to learn how to do it well. I can say when I walk off that stage, I know I did my best. It may not be your taste or his taste or hers, but I know that what I'm putting out there is professional and first-class. And good. You can't please everybody, but you can try. And that's what I try to do, I try to please everybody in that audience, so when they go home they can say, "I got more shows, more good shows, for $19, than I can get any-where in the world. And if Branson can keep those prices down, keep the product affordable, no one will ever be able to compete with this town.

JS: How do you maintain that energy level day in, day out?

TO: I'm conditioned because I was one of those guys who loved to perform. Two shows in Vegas, seven days a week, week after week. Or Broadway, eight shows a week.

JS: And it never gets old or boring?

TO: No, absolutely not. You know why? Because every audience has its own personality. It becomes like any one person, different eyes, nose, mouth, personality. It's not two thousand people. All the brainpower in that room creates this one person. Some days it's a conservative person. Some days you meet a partying person. Some days you meet a person who's a little to the left or the right. So it's never boring. No matter what you do, it can't be boring. Because people aren't boring. I will change that show according to the mood of the audience.

JS: So you ad-lib?

TO: Oh, yeah. I'll do an opening and closing song, but everything in the middle has to change, because some people don't want to hear four bal-lads in a row. Some people do. An afternoon audience is different from an evening crowd. A summer audience in Branson is different from a spring audience. Guys who've done Vegas, like me or John Davidson, couldn't have survived if we hadn't ad-libbed.

JS: You were involved in a weekly variety series, with all the attendant worries about ratings and coming up with new material. You've done live theater: *Barnum, The Boys Next Door.* You've per-formed two shows a day. Ultimately, what's the greatest challenge?

TO: The TV show was a killer because while I was rehearsing the show for the week, I also had to be there for my guests, be there for the changes in rehearsals, *and* be involved in next week's show, approving the scenes, checking in on the writers' room to see if next week's show is gonna work. Meanwhile they're starting to write the third week's show, and we only got three days to rehearse, because Thursday is blocking, Friday is the show. We shot live to tape. In other words, you saw the show, from beginning to end, like a live show. No stopping. The pressure of five new musical numbers, a guest sketch spot, the big finale sketch, and the last twenty minutes ad-libbed every week was enormous. Believe me, it was draining. It was the hardest work I've ever done, not to mention the stress of ratings. And I was only 27 years old, working with guys who'd been around. Jackie Gleason was my first guest.

JS: No wonder you appreciate Branson.

TO: Yeah, this is grueling but not as hard. Nobody gets away with not working. From the person in marketing to the chamber of commerce to the waitress to the hotel desk clerk to the person on stage. It's a hard-working town. Seven million people a year to please.

JS: With all its explosive growth, are you worried about Branson losing its small-town warmth and charm?

TO: Of course you worry about it, but I think there's a natural base that we're gonna see preserved in our lifetime. Because we have a fishing base here and a Bible Belt base that wants to keep things green. I think the performers here want to keep it that way, too. The Ozark Mountain marketing people know that the real star of the Ozarks is the Ozarks. I think we're living in a time in which people are a little more sensitive about the environment. If this was twenty years ago, I'd say no, but in the nineties we're down to counting trees. I think it'll be a big surprise how well they'll preserve this area. You'll never see skyscrapers in this town. Unfortunately, with the rest of the world, the planet—I don't know. I think we need to gain respect for our planet.

JS: It's inevitable with a phenomenon like Branson that it will attract its share of negative publicity. Is that fair? It's been said that Branson excludes people. If you're not Christian from middle America, don't bother coming. If you're black, Jewish, gay, from the East Coast, forget it.

TO: Obviously, whoever said that didn't do his homework. We have three black musicians in our show and a Jewish musical director.

JS: And you're a New York boy.

TO: Half Greek, half Puerto Rican. I don't understand that rap at all. Not when you look around. You'd be blind not to see that there's a Christian base here, but is it anti-Jewish? No. Anti-black? No. You wanna look at any place, you'll find something wrong. Yeah, we have our problems in Branson. But our positives outweigh our negatives. And anything negative can be fixed.

JS: And that's why you and your family have moved here?

TO: I'm gonna raise my children here. My two-and-a-half-year-old daughter and my twenty-three-year-old son. I'll tell you how definite it is: I know where I'm gonna be buried. I passed the cemetery here, and I said, "Oh, so that's where I'm gonna be?" And, believe me when I tell you, there was a kind of peace in that. "Oh, that's where I'll end up." That's how real it is to me. And I tell you this. If I never had a theater, never had one here, I'd still be here. If God said tomorrow, "Tony, I'm sorry, you only got fourteen people coming in to see you today and twenty more tonight," I'd say, "That's okay, I'm still living here in Branson." I've found where I want to be. Because it's beautiful. Because the people are kind. They care.

Other Fun Things to Do in and Around Branson

DOWNTOWN

Most of Branson is brand-spanking new, with construction springing up all over town, especially along the side streets that feed the Strip. But there was a Branson before the music shows came to town, and the compact four-square-block area that makes up the city's downtown offers a peek into the town's past. Give yourself an afternoon to walk along Main and Commercial streets, which are lined with historic buildings housing interesting shops. (For shopping, dining, and lodging suggestions *see* Chapter 7, Shopping; Chapter 8, Dining; and Chapter 9, Lodging.)

Branson sprouted in the early part of the century as a railroad town and tourist attraction, thanks to the enormous success of Harold Bell Wright's novel *Shepherd of the Hills*. By 1907, Main Street boasted two hotels, a bank, a newspaper office, and several other businesses. Fire swept through the center twice between 1912 and 1913, destroying most of the wood-frame buildings. The oldest remaining structure, the **Union Pacific Railroad Depot** at the foot of Main Street, dates from 1906. From here you can see the *Sammy Lane* cruising Lake Taneycomo, much as it did on its maiden voyage in 1913.

Continuing up the Main Street hill, you'll see the **Branson Bank Building,** also dating to 1906. Inside are a number of gift shops. Farther along Main Street, on your left, is the venerable **Branson Hotel** (*see* Chapter 9, Lodging), which opened its doors in 1906; this building is the hotel's second incarnation, built in 1913. Today it is one of the area's most charming bed-and-breakfasts. The Presbyterian Church atop the hill is modern (built in 1966), but the adjacent original structure dates to 1907. It houses several social organizations, including the Senior Citizens Center, Habitat for Humanity, Youth Life, and the Women's Crisis Center.

Perhaps the most important edifice on Commercial Street is the venerable **Owen Theater.** The story of Branson as America's live-music capital began in this building, when visionary—and huckster—Jim Owen opened the theater as a "movie palace," offering the occasional live act, including Western star Gene Autry and his horse, and local beauty pageants.

THEME PARKS

MUTTON HOLLOW ENTERTAINMENT PARK AND CRAFT VILLAGE

Rte. 76 and Shepherd of the Hills Expressway (western end of Strip), tel. 417/334-4947. Admission for rides and entertainment: $9.95 adults, $3.95 children under 12. Open late Mar.–Oct., daily 9–5; Nov. 10-Dec. 11, Thurs.–Sun. 9–5 for Ozark Mountain Christmas celebration.

The idyllic retreat in the novel *Shepherd of the Hills* was the inspiration for this charming re-creation of a pioneer village. Mutton Hollow is set on 45 acres amid a grove of ancient oak. The beautifully landscaped gardens are laced with silvery brooks, and the streets are lined with crafts shops, theaters, restaurants, and a county-fair area, all carefully modeled on historic photos. Because the park is on level ground, senior citizens, young children, and visitors with mobility problems should be able to access most areas.

RIDES AND ATTRACTIONS
The county-fair area is home to an ornate Ferris wheel and 1930s carousel, as well as a Tilt-a-Whirl. The Harold Bell Wright Museum, built by Wright's son, contains the original manuscript of the masterpiece, among other memorabilia.

SHOWS
Five theaters host 40 music shows per week, which range from country and bluegrass to big-band to gospel music. Special events include Square Dance weekends, farriers' (horseshoeing) contests, clogging championships, and antique-tractor pulls. Call ahead for a weekly schedule.

SHOPPING
Mutton Hollow is noted for its 30 crafts and specialty shops, where you can watch artisans at work on quilts, dolls, clothes, and other crafts. **Amanda's** is the place to shop for dolls, quilts, Christmas ornaments, afghans, and unusual items such as crocheted butter-

flies and animals crafted from pecan shells. **Sweet Annie's** is fragrant with sachets, potpourris, and essentials oils in exquisite old bottles. You'll also find meticulously made paper angels, mountain-flower baskets, and scarecrow wreaths. The **Bull Traden Co.** traffics in Mexican wool shirts, embroidered blouses, and a large assortment of earrings. You can dip your own candles at the **Wic and Wax Candle Shop** or choose from candles in all shapes, sizes, and fragrances: Look for fearsome dragons, fanciful clowns, dripping ice cream sundaes, and prickly cacti. Special items include onyx figurines and quartz crystals buried in "Treasure Candles," and aromatic eucalyptus, popcorn, cranberry, or rose candles. The **World Famous Woodshed** cobbles everything from toys to trucks to canes (walking sticks, measuring sticks, even mule clubbers). **Katie's Fancy Goods** sparkles with its baubles, bangles, and bright shiny beads: trinkets to wear or dress your Christmas tree. **Leathers Etc.** hawks not only well-crafted belts, wallets, and buckles but Confederate caps and handcarved wooden mushrooms. And the friendly folks at **Mountain Dulcimers** will entertain you with the instrument's history while they show off their wares. (For the record, cherry wood creates the clearest, sharpest tone, and walnut and oak produce a deeper, mellower sound.)

DINING

Aunt Parthene's specializes in scrumptious pies (try the sour-cream raisin or blackberry cobbler), creamy ice cream (not home-made, though), and tasty sandwiches (wash them down with fresh apple cider). Walls papered with old newspaper headlines ("Dewey Defeats Truman") and red tablecloths contribute to the convivial setting.

Try **Sammy's Kitchen,** a full-service restaurant, or open-air **Jake's Rib House,** or stop by one of the many **food tents** erected for special events such as the Cajun Festival (replete with fried okra, red beans and rice, and jambalaya) or the German Polka Festival (a two-month-long Oktoberfest, where bratwurst, dirndls, and oompah bands are the rule). Five or ten dollars should burst your seams. No alcohol is served.

SHEPHERD OF THE HILLS HOMESTEAD AND OUTDOOR THEATER

W. Rte. 76 (2 mi west of Shepherd of the Hills Expressway), tel. 417/334-4191. Homestead Park open Apr.–Labor Day, daily 9–5:30; Labor Day–Oct., daily 9–4:30. Admission: $12 adults, $7 children 4–12. Shepherd of the Hills Theater open Apr. 30–Labor Day, daily 9–8:30; Labor Day–Oct., daily 9–7:30; shows at 8 PM. Admission: $17 adult, $8 children under 13; combination ticket, $22 adults, $11 children under 13; Christmas Show (Nov. 9–Dec. 11, Wed.–Sun. 6 PM), $12 adults, $6 children. Inspiration Tower open daily 8–8. Admission: $4 adults, $2 children under 13.

At the turn of the century, a writer named Harold Bell Wright made a trip from upstate New York to the Ozarks, in hopes that the mountain air would help him recover from tuberculosis (eventually, he did). While here he was befriended by a local family, the Rosses, who permitted him to camp on their homestead while he regained his health and strength. His experiences inspired the bucolic novel *Shepherd of the Hills*, which was based on his encounters with the family and other memorable hill folk. The book became a national sensation and, using the new railroad, droves of tourists came to gawk at landmarks mentioned in the book. The Rosses were virtually driven from their home ("Uncle Matt's Cabin" in the novel) by all of the attention.

In 1911 the cabin was purchased by M.R. Driver, a physical education teacher from Wichita, Kansas, who converted it into an inn for travelers. By the early 1920s Driver lost interest in the inn, letting it fall into disrepair, but in 1926 Lizzie McDaniel bought and restored it with the help of her wealthy family, who owned the United National Bank of Springfield. At that point, McDaniel replaced Driver's furniture with some original pieces. She operated the homestead as a tourist attraction and inn until she died in 1946, at which time the Civic League of Branson assumed ownership. Dr. and Mrs. Bruce Trimble, Kentuckians who moved to the Ozarks that year, bought the surrounding land, including Inspiration Point, where Wright camped for many years. The league and the Trimbles restored the property to its original condition and turned the cabin into a museum, which displays clothing, tools, and cookware that belonged to the Rosses and Wright.

These steps toward preserving a national literary landmark proved instrumental in furthering the tourist trade in Branson. People came to see the cabin, and in 1960 (the same

"Uncle Matt's cabin," the home of the Rosses; photo courtesy Shepherd of the Hills Homestead.

year Silver Dollar City opened) the Trimbles produced an outdoor stage epic based on the beloved bestseller. The show became so popular that the Trimbles added another activity—tours of the homestead. More than 35 years later the drama is still being performed on the grounds, for more than 2,500 people per performance.

RIDES AND ATTRACTIONS

You can take a **Jeep-drawn wagon tour** of the 160-acre site and visit **"Old Matt's" cabin,** which contains many original furnishings, including "Aunt Mollie's" clothes and such Wright memorabilia as the typewriter on which he pecked out his masterwork. At the **gristmill** next door you can watch an old steam engine grinding corn.

The tour includes **Inspiration Point,** where a dilapidated 1901 church has been born again, a reminder of an important focus of Ozarks life at the turn of the century. Atop the point is 230-foot **Inspiration Tower,** built in 1989 and standing as the second-highest such structure in the state (after the Gateway Arch in St. Louis). More than 4,400 square feet of glass envelop the tower, affording sensational 360° views of the countryside from the observation deck, which is reached by elevator. Bronze plaques, many quoting the novel, tell you about the view from each side of the deck.

Inspiration Tower; photo courtesy Shepherd of the Hills Homestead.

Kids will love the **Clydesdale-drawn wagon rides** through the grounds; the **Flag Museum,** displaying American flags of many years; and the new unsupervised **"City Kids and Country Cousins" playground,** with a slide, teeter totters, and such rustic touches as tire swings. They'll also like the **Championship Frog Track,** where they can cheer on—even coach—their favorite amphibian throughout the day.

SHOWS

The *Shepherd of the Hills* performance is monumental in every way: There are 80 actors, 25 horses, 30 sheep, 3 mules, 3 buggies, 4 wagons, a 1906 DeWitt automobile, and a virtual arsenal of 12-gauge shotguns and 45-caliber pistols. All of these participants and props make a remarkable showing in an amphitheater surrounded by the lush green Ozark Mountains. Enhancing the two-hour performance are natural sound and light effects such as lightning, chirping crickets, and tree frogs, and pyrotechnics such as a burning cabin. During intermission the audience is invited onto the stage for an energetic square dance.

After *Shepherd of the Hills* shuts down for the season, *The Newborn King* drama takes the outdoor stage, also with great fanfare. The Nativity play tells the story of Jesus's birth and the visit of the Three Wise Men. (As heartwarming as the drama is, remember that it can get quite nippy at night, so dress warmly.) A trail of more than 18,000 lights decorates the grounds, transforming Inspiration Tower (*see* Rides and Attractions, *above*) into the state's largest Christmas tree. "Flying" to the observation deck is a 12-foot-high, 45-foot-long Santa, riding a sleigh pulled by reindeer.

SHOPPING

The homestead has fewer shops than Silver Dollar City, but it, too, has authentic local crafts and offers demonstrations. Try **Lizzie McDaniel's Craft Shop** for coin-cutting, leatherwork, handpainted china, jewelry, and the like. **Suzie's T-Shirts** is a great place to pick up last-minute gifts and keepsakes from Branson. There's a branch of the **Precious Moments chapel,** selling Sam Butcher's delicate figurines. If you like handmade comforters and lace items, stop at **Mandy's Quilts and Things.**

DINING

No doubt you'll get hungry after spending a few hours here, and you have two choices. **Aunt Mollie's Country Coffee Shop,** built in rough-hewn rustic style, spreads lavish all-you-can-eat buffets that include the house specialty steak sandwich and Polish sausage. It's an eat-in, serve-yourself affair. **Mrs. Wheeler's Fast Vittles** serves bulging sandwiches and tasty barbecued chicken, plus sinful desserts. Prices of entrées at both places range from $5 to $10. No alcohol is served, and reservations are not accepted.

SILVER DOLLAR CITY (SDC)

Indian Point Rd. (off W. Rte. 76, 5 mi west of Branson), tel. 800/952-6626. Admission: $23.50 adults, $14 children 4–11 per day; $36 adults, $25 children for season pass (June–Oct.). Open Apr. 19–May 19, Wed.–Sun. 9:30–6; May 20–Aug. 20, daily 9:30–7; Aug. 21–Labor Day, daily 9:30–6; Labor Day–Oct. 29, Tues.–Sun. 9:30–6; Nov. 9–Dec. 23, Thurs.–Sun. 1–10; Dec. 26–30, daily 1–10; closed Thanksgiving.

It all started with an attraction called Marble Cave, now a National Natural Landmark. Local lore has it that the Baldknobber vigilantes dispensed with their enemies by throwing them into a supposedly bottomless pit then known as the Devil's Den. In 1894 Missouri's first commercial cavern began luring visitors into its yawning black depths.

The trip down was no doubt an arduous, spooky experience for those first tourists, wandering the cathedralesque rooms by lantern, squeezing through narrow passageways, struggling up a seemingly endless ladder to reach the sunshine again.

In 1946 a couple named Hugo and Mary Herschend toured the area. Enchanted by the attraction (now known as Marvel Cave), they leased it in 1951 from Genevieve and Miriam Lynch for 99 years. In 1957 the Herschends modernized it, installing a tram to transport guests more easily and comfortably. They kept the remains of a mine shaft to remind visitors of the cave's earlier incarnation as a fertilizer factory during the 1880s. (Inordinate amounts of bat guano coated the cave floor, under which they expected to find marble—hence the cave's original name. But its foundation turned out to be ordinary limestone, and the operation shut down in 1889.) With the cave's popularity came long lines of restless people waiting to take the tram down. Realizing that these people needed to be entertained, in 1960 the Herschends designed an 1880s-style village replete with crafts and food stalls. Before long, visitors were wandering through an old blacksmith's shop, a doll shop, a general store, a print shop, and a candy store, all constructed with native materials and run by local people garbed in mountain attire and sharing their time-honored methods of pulling taffy, chiseling wooden dolls, and forging horseshoes. That was the origin of Silver Dollar City, a remarkably authentic, respectful re-creation of frontier American life. It was so realistic that when "The Beverly Hillbillies" television show needed to film a "genuine" Ozarks town for several episodes, the Hollywood Hills came to the hills of Branson—and Silver Dollar City.

Although it's grown by leaps and bounds and is now one of the state's premier attractions, Silver Dollar City has retained its warmth and remained true to its mission of keeping Ozarks arts-and-crafts traditions alive. Almost 50 shops offer wares as they might have been made in the 1880s, along with demonstrations by artisans who clearly love their work and are scrupulous about using only tools from the last century. Actors in late-19th-century dress roam the park, to the delight of visitors: A snake-oil salesman might try to sell you elixir, and the sheriff might warn you about the low-life rustlers in town. You can duck into a one-room log church (transported from nearby Wilson Creek) for services every day at 10 AM (or renew your wedding vows at 3:30). Even if you have don't want to attend a service, stop by for the fantastic view. The attention to detail is such that a turn-of-the-century Bible serves as guest book in the chapel. Several "citizens" of Silver Dollar City lounge about the 1843 McHaffie's Homestead, painstakingly reassembled log by log when it was moved from nearby Forsyth.

Silver Dollar City is built on a series of small hills, making it difficult for travelers with mobility problems, the elderly, and the very young to move around (the steepest incline is nicknamed "Cardiac Hill" by locals). Yet the very setting contributes to a natural Ozarks atmosphere. The sheer size and number of attractions can be overwhelming; plan to go early or spend two days enjoying it all. There's something for everyone here. Weekends in season (May–October) can be a madhouse. If you can, plan your trip during the week to avoid the crowds. Try to hit the popular rides (like the roller coaster and the train that circles the park) first thing in the morning, before the lines swell, or you could be in for a wait of an hour or longer at each attraction.

RIDES AND ATTRACTIONS
There are 10 rides in addition to attractions like Marvel Cave and McHaffie's Homestead. Most rides are suitable for small children, although

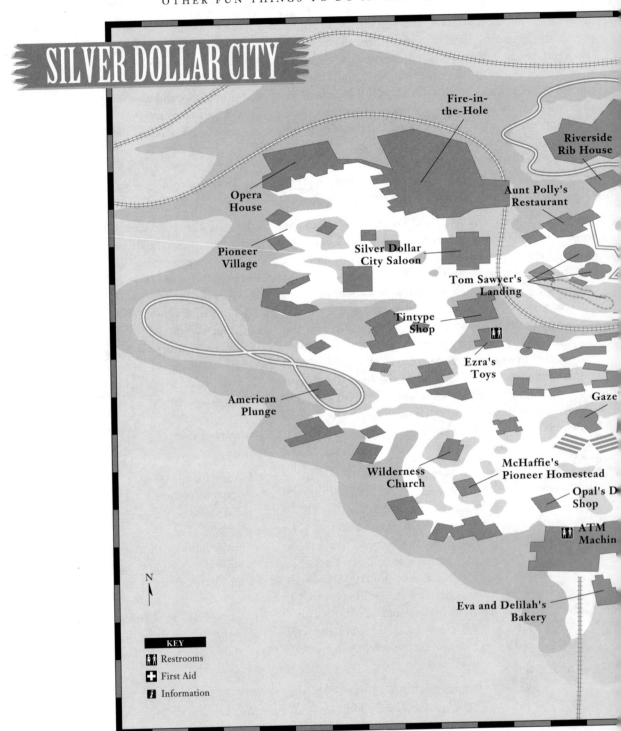

SILVER DOLLAR CITY

Fire-in-the-Hole

Riverside Rib House

Opera House

Aunt Polly's Restaurant

Pioneer Village

Silver Dollar City Saloon

Tom Sawyer's Landing

Tintype Shop

Ezra's Toys

Gaze

American Plunge

Wilderness Church

McHaffie's Pioneer Homestead

Opal's D Shop

ATM Machin

Eva and Delilah's Bakery

N

KEY

Restrooms

First Aid

Information

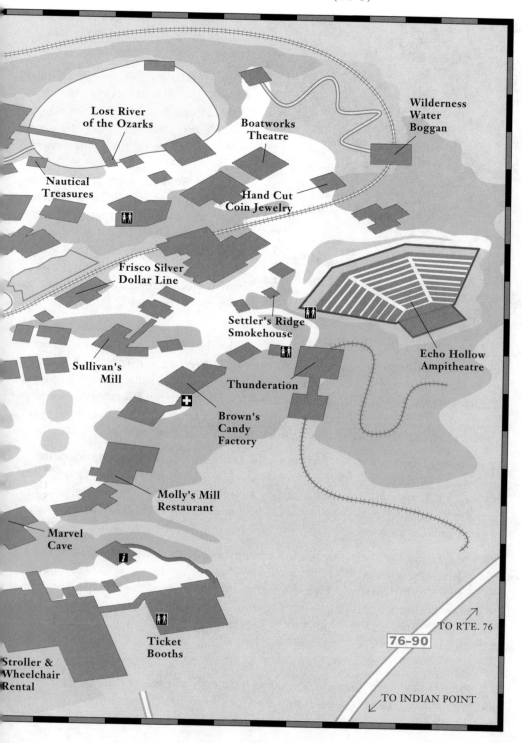

Lost River
of the Ozarks

Boatworks
Theatre

Wilderness
Water
Boggan

Nautical
Treasures

Hand Cut
Coin Jewelry

Frisco Silver
Dollar Line

Settler's Ridge
Smokehouse

Echo Hollow
Ampitheatre

Sullivan's
Mill

Thunderation

Brown's
Candy
Factory

Molly's Mill
Restaurant

Marvel
Cave

Ticket
Booths

TO RTE. 76

76-90

Stroller &
Wheelchair
Rental

TO INDIAN POINT

The Wilderness Church at Silver Dollar City; photo courtesy Silver Dollar City.

the Thunderation rollercoaster is limited to those 40" or taller, and the Fire in the Hole might scare younger kids.

The biggest attraction in Silver Dollar City is the **Marvel Cave,** which is entered through the "ceiling," actually a sinkhole that leads to the top of a tower in the vast Cathedral Room (dimensions a staggering 411 x 225 x 204 feet). The tour then winds through several rooms and passageways, highlighting different calcite and limestone formations before ending up in the Elves' Chamber (so named for its whimsical, natural sculptures). This chamber leads to the train tunnel, which takes the tour group up to the surface, reemerging in the large gift shop.

Silver Dollar City has lots of water rides, which can be fun and fast on a warm day, but if it's cold or damp outside you may consider just standing on the sides watching, unless you have a change of clothes. Among the water rides are **Lost River in the Ozarks** (a whitewater raft ride), **American Plunge** (a dugout log journey to splashdown), **Wilderness Waterboggan** (a flume ride in covered toboggan boats), and **Fire in the Hole** (a roller coaster through a "blazing" town).

If you prefer to stay dry but don't want to miss the action, ride the new **Thunderation,** a roller coaster that zooms 81 feet, to tree level. For a calmer adventure, try **Tom Sawyer's Landing,** jam-packed with kids (most of them are under 7) milling around the Ferris wheel, carousel, hot-air balloon rides, and miner's carts, replicas of original carts, that travel around a flat track.

Other features for the fun-loving but less adventurous are the **Critter Corral,** a petting farm where hungry goats and calves nibble on shoelaces, buttons, lapels—anything, if you let them; and **McHaffie's Homestead,** an authentic late-19th-century cabin (with Ivy Jean cookin' up a storm and Granmaw pickin' banjo) that brings pioneer America to life. The 1930s **Frisco Line Train Ride** weaves through the park, stopping occasionally when bandits hold it up.

SHOWS
Nine theaters host more than a dozen shows (pick up a schedule at the park entrance), most beginning at different times throughout the day so you can see several. All shows are free with regular daily admission. There are no name acts, but SDC prides itself on

hiring the best local talent. Many of the venues are open-air, so melodies and laughter waft down the streets of Silver Dollar City. The 3,700-seat **Echo Hollow Amphitheater,** the largest stage at SDC, showcases *Country America* magazine's "Top 100 Country Songs of All Time" every evening at 7; admission is free for day visitors, $13.95 for adults, $7.50 for children 4–11 attending just the evening show. All other shows are performed during the day.

Kids are mesmerized by the street show staged by actors three times daily on Main Street. Granpaw comes out to do some old-fashioned banjo pickin' at **McHaffie's Homestead**; passersby are invited to come listen. Those who like to kick up their heels should join the come-one-come-all **barn dance** at the homestead, held Saturday at 3:30. At various times throughout the day there's more fiddling at the **Gazebo,** rambunctious zydeco (a mix of French, Caribbean, and blues) at the **Boatworks Theater,** a sassy cancan with women in period dress at the **saloon,** and a choir singing angelic hymns at the **Wilderness Church.** The nostalgic musical "Listen to the River" is performed in the **opera house.** If you're looking for entertainment, just walk around and see (or hear) what strikes your fancy.

SHOPPING

There are some 50 shops in Silver Dollar City, many offering crafts demonstrations, and some artisans give impromptu lessons. The crafts tend to be fairly priced, and the quality is generally good. Among the more interesting shops are **Scrimshaw,** specializing in intricate bone and fossil carvings; **Ezra's Toys,** selling old-fashioned wooden games, toys, and puzzles; **Tintype Photos,** taken in authentic turn-of-the-century attire, from cowboys to saloon girls; **Opal's Doll Orphanage,** with old-fashioned rag dolls and collectors' items like Kewpies; **Ray Johnson's Damascus Steel Knives,** where Ray hones his creations and recites hillbilly poetry; the **Coin Cutter,** for jewelry fashioned from old money; and **Sullivan's Mill and Bakery** and **Brown's Candy Factory,** two places you'll find just by following your nose.

DINING

There are 12 restaurants and stands selling candy apples, funnel cakes, and homemade cider, among other treats. But even with all the food options, lines for seating can be long during lunch and dinner time, and reservations are not accepted. Eat early or late to avoid the crowds. Major credit cards are accepted at the larger restaurants. Hours are the same as the park's.

Try **Mollie's Mill** for sumptuous all-you-can-eat breakfast buffets, including homemade breads and muffins, then come back for lunch for scrumptious fried catfish and chicken; compare and contrast the huge juicy ribs and chicken at **Riverside Ribhouse** with the smoked meats smothered in tangy, mouth-watering barbecue sauce served up at **Settler's Ridge Smokehouse**; or stop in at **Aunt Polly's Parlor** for spicy, eye-watering, Cajun fare.

WATER, WATER EVERYWHERE

CINEMA 180 THRILL BUBBLE AND COOL-OFF WATER CHUTE

Thrill to a 15-minute, 70-millimeter action film—of anything from a roller-coaster ride to a volcanic eruption—projected onto a 30-foot-high, 180°, wraparound screen with stereophonic sound. Then for a real-life adventure, shoot down the water chute next door. You'll most certainly get wet, so bring a change of clothes (there's a dressing room at the chute). *W. Rte. 76 (across from Wal-Mart), tel. 417/334–1919. Cinema 180: admission $3.50 for both. Open Mar.–Nov., daily 10–10, shows every 60 min. on the hour. Water chute: $6 per person per hour. Open May–Sept., daily 10–10.*

RIDE THE DUCKS

Imagine riding in amphibious vehicles that transported troops and equipment over land and water during World War II. It's certainly more fun than taking a bus tour. The company's owner, Bob McDowell, has spent the last 25 years painstakingly collecting and adapting (installing seats and removing artillery) more than 30 ducks that take tourists on a 70-minute tour of a military museum. Among the items housed in the museum are unusual vehicles such as the Gamma Goat (a cargo truck) and the snow-worthy Studebaker Weasel. At the end of the tour the ducks splash down into Lake Taneycomo for a quick sightseeing cruise. (Sit in front if you want to get wet). *W. Rte. 76, tel. 417/334–5350. Admission: $9.95 adults, $4.95 children under 12. Open Apr.–Oct., daily 7:30–5:30, tours every 15 minutes on the quarter hour (weather permitting); Nov. and Feb., daily 7:30–5:30, but tours are less frequent so call ahead.*

SAMMY LANE PIRATE CRUISES

Ever wanted to play swashbuckler à la Errol Flynn? Here's your chance, as the *Sammy Lane*, a 49-person passenger boat, whisks you off on a Lake Taneycomo adventure.

You'll hear the history of the White River (impounded to become Taneycomo and Table Rock lakes) before you tangle with a fearsome band of pirates who are after the gold the *Sammy Lane* picked up from the Boston Ridge Gold Mine. The 70-minute excursion is a great way to see the lake and enjoy a little swashbuckling while remaining dry. *280 N. Lake Dr., tel. 417/334–3015. Admission: $6.95 adults, $4.50 children under 12. Open Apr.–mid-Oct., daily; 10 shows throughout day.*

SHEPHERD OF THE HILLS FISH HATCHERY

This is the largest trout-rearing facility operated by the Missouri Department of Conservation, producing up to 400,000 pounds of trout annually. Eighty percent of the rainbow and brown trout raised here are used to stock the cold waters of Lake Taneycomo. At the visitor center you can see a multimedia presentation and exhibits on trout spawning, fishing, and the Department of Conservation's role in aquatic-resource management. Also at the visitor center are trailheads for hikes (none strenuous, mostly loops less than 1 mile long) that follow the shore and the rocky bluffs above. Indigenous flora and fauna are labeled. *Rte. 165 (6 mi southwest of Branson), tel. 417/334–4865. Admission free. Open Mar.–mid-Nov., daily 9–5; mid-Nov.–Feb., weekends and by appointment 9–4:30.*

WALTZING WATERS

Depending on your mood, you'll find this water show featuring several rows of lighted fountains dancing to the thunderous crescendos of "Hello, Dolly," "Hooked on Classics," and the like either hokey or mesmerizing—maybe both. More than 40,000 gallons of water in flumes up to three stories high move to the music, forming twirling lariats, triple-tier wedding cakes, and even the Manhattan skyline; there are more than 200 buttons and nearly 42,000 possible combinations on the sophisticated control panel that guides the water's movement. John Cody and his son Shane Dalton sing rousing country hits with their backup band, using the liquid fireworks as a backdrop for their "Fountains of Fire" musical extravaganza. An engineer runs the panel during the show, but audience members can make the waters dance after the performance. Next door is the Carolina Mills Factory Outlet (*see* Chapter 7, Shopping), which is under the same ownership. *W. Rte. 76 (west end), tel. 417/334–4144. Water show: admission $4 adults, $2 children under 12; open Nov.–Mar., daily 10–6 and Apr.–Oct., daily 9 AM–11 PM; 45-min show every hour on the hour. Fountains of Fire: admission $7 adults, $3.50 children under 12; daily 10 AM and 1 PM. Reservations accepted and recommended for groups of 15 or more.*

WHITE WATER

You won't think Branson is landlocked when you're relaxing under palm trees by a blue grotto, sipping a tropical fruit punch, playing beach volleyball, or cooling off on one of 12 water rides at this park. Among the rides are the heart-pounding, triple-cascade Paradise Plunge (a speed slide), a Tropical Twister (a five-person water-boggan), and the undulating SurfQuake Wave Pool. These rides are suitable for children three years and older, but they are not equipped for people with disabilities. You can also come here simply to relax by the palms (admission remains the same). When you need a break from the action, stop at Islander Pizza, the Tradewinds Café (offering counter service for burgers, taco salads, and other light fare), or Beachcomber, a deli serving soups, salads, and sandwiches that are ideal for poolside nibbling. *3505 W. Rte. 76, tel. 417/334-7488. Admission to park: $15.50 adults, $11 children 3–11, $5.50 senior citizens 55 and older, $3 off admission when you purchase a ticket to Silver Dollar City. Open May 20–June 9, Aug. 14–27, and Sept. 2–4, daily 10–6; June 10–25, daily 10–8; June 26–Aug. 13, daily 9–8.*

MUSEUMS

BONNIEBROOK

Rose O'Neill Kewpie doll; photo courtesy Lois Holsman, Bonniebrook Historical Society.

Rose O'Neill was one of the few women at the turn of the century who were recognized in the notoriously male-chauvinistic world of publishing. Her illustrations for *Puck* and *Life* magazines delighted millions. In 1907, Rose retreated to Bonniebrook, the Ozarks home she purchased for her parents, after an emotionally draining breakup with her husband, Harry Leon Wilson (author of the classic *Ruggles of Red Gap*). "The Tangles," as she dubbed the house, was her respite, concealed within a hollow surrounded by trees, rocks, bushes, and flowering vines. From the moment she saw it, Rose wrote, "My extravagant heart was tangled in it forever." One night some impish figures appeared to her in a dream; small plump creatures with a startled look in their eyes bounded about her bedroom. A year later the Kewpies made their first appearance in illustrations for the *Ladies Home Journal*, and soon they were reproduced as the now-famous dolls.

Despite the fragile beauty's Bohemian lifestyle (would-be artists and dependents constantly descended on Bonniebrook), her neighbors adored her, as she tirelessly promoted education in the community and donated valuable artworks to local museums. In 1946, two years after her death, Rose's beloved home caught fire, but neighbors and Kewpie fans never forgot her. The Rose O'Neill fan club (today boasting more than 1,000 members worldwide) led to the formation of a Bonniebrook Historical Society, which has spent the last two decades rebuilding the home; today it is on the National Register of Historic Places, along with the grounds. Slowly but surely the society is furnishing each room in lavish period detail, and the home is now open to the public. You'll see—and be able to purchase—Kewpies in all shapes and sizes, as well as Rose's "Sweet Monsters," languorous figurines with a disturbing sensuality. *481 Rose O'Neill Rd., Walnut Shade, MO (east of Rte. 65, 9 mi north of Branson), tel. 417/561–4797. Admission: $9.50 per person; group rates available. Open Apr.–Sept., daily 7–5.*

BOXCAR WILLIE MUSEUM

See Boxcar Willie in Chapter 3, The Theaters and the Stars.

RALPH FOSTER MUSEUM AT COLLEGE OF THE OZARKS

Nicknamed "The College that Works," and "Hard Work U," this university is reknowned for its innovative program that requires students to work full time (often in their chosen fields of endeavor) in lieu of paying tuition. Students work 15 hours a week during the school year and 40 hours a week in summer to pay for room and board. Among the many on-campus attractions open to the public are Edward Mills, a replica of an old-fashioned mill where students grind whole-grain meal and flour; a weaving studio where they create rugs, shawls, and place mats on traditional looms; greenhouses with some 7,000 plants, including many hothouse varieties of orchid; and a fruitcake-and-jelly kitchen where more than 25,000 cakes are baked annually. Only the jelly is offered on sale to the general public.

The main reason to visit the college, however, is the astounding Ralph Foster Museum, the "Smithsonian of the Ozarks," named in honor of the man who founded KWTO radio station in Springfield, Missouri, and gave many country stars their first break on his "Ozark Jubilee" show. More than 750,000 items are displayed on the museum's three crowded floors. Among the most notable exhibits in this wildly eclectic treasure trove of Americana are galleries devoted to Foster's life and interests. You'll see Grammy certificates, gold records, and old fiddles; collections of rare Kewpies and ethnic dolls; the original *Beverly Hillbillies* buggy; and a large gun collection that Smith, Wesson, and Colt could spend hours happily cataloguing. One of the incidental pleasures of the Ralph Foster is that its holdings are so vast and its space so cramped that some objects are oddly juxtaposed. The taxidermy collection scattered over two floors includes the usual deer, moose, and elk, along with a replica of movie cowboy Tom Mix's horse (with his original saddle). Glittering geodes stare down shrunken heads and stuffed polar bears. Other galleries focus on decorative arts, school history, the music industry in Branson, the pioneer days, and antique agricultural equipment. You name it, it's here at this gloriously eccentric delight. *College of the Ozarks, Point Lookout, tel. 417/334–6411, ext. 3407. Admission: $4.50 adults, $3.50 senior citizens, children free. Open year-round, Mon.–Sat. 9–4.*

HAROLD BELL WRIGHT MUSEUM

See "Mutton Hollow," *above.*

RIPLEY'S BELIEVE IT OR NOT MUSEUM

"Was there an earthquake?" you may wonder, as you approach this museum, opened in 1994 and devoted to the macabre and the bizarre. The edifice is uniquely designed with an ominous crack running down the center—a tribute to seismologists who predicted a "Really Big One" for Missouri (which sits on the New Madrid Fault) in 1990. (It never happened). During construction, the crack looked so real that concerned locals called the museum's public relations director at home to commiserate. One room is tilted to reproduce a feeling of disorientation, and contractors had difficulty finishing the museum because of equilibrium problems.

The structure was built around the World's Largest Ball of Nylon String, weighing in at 7 tons. This ball was created by Texan J.C. Payne, who saved string for 10 years so he could beat an existing record. Ripley's bought it from him to feature at this museum. This infuriated the good people of Crocker City, Kansas (whose citizens save up string year-round and add it to *their* ball in the social event of the year), and Darwin, Minnesota (theirs is bailing twine, not string). One man from Kansas sniffed on *ABC World News Tonight*, "It's so squat, how can they call it a ball?" (Gravity tends to flatten a 7-ton ball at its axis). Ah well, it's all in the name of preserving "genuine American folk art," claim Ripley's executives.

Displays include an antique bedpan, chimney pot, and toilet seat collection, a limo with a heart-shaped Jacuzzi, New Guinea penis sheaths (they protected the wearer against insect bites), and necklaces fashioned from human teeth. In the country gallery you'll see the score of Jim Stafford's "Spiders and Snakes" scrawled inside an egg, and a plaque from the *Guinness Book of Records* attesting that a woman saw the Dondino show 2,700 times. Even the lavatories are unusual, with a pipe collection in the men's room and mounted butterflies in the ladies' room. *3326 W. Rte. 76, tel. 800/998–4418. Admission: $8.95 adults, $5.95 children 4–11. Open daily 9 AM–10 PM. Closed Christmas.*

OTHER ATTRACTIONS

BRANSON SCENIC RAILROAD

Relive the romance of old-fashioned rail travel aboard these elegant, air-conditioned art-deco Zephyr cars built in the late 1940s. The three to six cars are equipped with "Vista Domes" that have panoramic windows affording 360° views. There are two routes, each taking about an hour and 45 minutes round-trip. The route is determined each day, depending on Amtrak traffic. The north route passes through rich farmlands following the Roark Creek and by waterfalls and wildflowers—cascades of yellow daisies staining the hills and hollows. Many locals come out to greet the shrill whistle. The southern route features wilder scenery, as the train clings precariously to the hillside and clatters over trestles spanning yawning gorges. Soft drinks, coffee, and snacks are available on both trips. *Depot at foot of Main St., tel. 417/334–6110. Admission: $17.42 adults, $16.33 senior citizens over 54, $9.78 children 3–11. Trains run Apr.–Oct., Wed.–Mon. 8:30, 11, 2, and 4:30.*

OZARKS DISCOVERY IMAX CENTER

IMAX award-winning film technology allows audiences not only to see a movie but to feel the action, as well. How does it work? The largest film frame in motion-picture history (more than 10 times bigger than a conventional 35-millimeter frame) is projected onto a screen six stories tall (and 83 feet wide) to the accompaniment of a 22,000-watt sound system filtered through 44 speakers. The larger the image, the greater the clarity. The production crews specialize in shooting the world's most spectacular locations and capturing unique experiences. You'll feel you're hanging over the rim of the Grand Canyon, wandering amid penguins in Antarctica, sinking with the *Titanic,* or on stage in concert with the Rolling Stones. The main feature changes every few months, but the short that precedes it was created for Branson and is always run. Entitled *Neighbors,* it focuses on Ozarks people and places, as well as on Branson personalities gathered at a picnic. It makes them seem truly larger than life. IMAX is working on a new film titled *Ozarks, Legacy and Legend,* which will depict the history, culture, and geography of the Ozarks. It is scheduled to premiere on May 1, 1995. The IMAX Center also features 14 shops (*see* Chapter 7, Shopping) and a full-service restaurant, the Pioneer (*see* Chapter 8, Dining). *3069 Shepherd of the Hills Expressway (off W. Rte. 76), tel. 417/335–4832. Admission: $8 adults, $7.50 senior citizens over 59, $4.75 children 3–12; $25 single-household family. Open Jan.–Mar., daily 9:30–7:30; Apr.–Dec., daily 8:30 AM–11:30 PM, shows every hour on the hour.*

KRAZY HORSE RANCH AND RAILROAD PARK

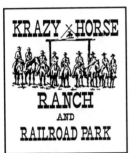

This little-known attraction is a paean to two older forms of transportation: the horse and the Iron Horse. You can mount a steed for a peaceful trail ride, climb aboard an 1880s steam train for a scenic one-hour trip through the White River Valley, and enjoy a chuck-wagon cookout/trail ride for a hearty breakfast or a steak dinner. *Shepherd of the Hills Expressway, tel. 417/334–5068. One-hour trails rides every hour on the hour, late May–late Oct., daily 9–5. Admission: $12.50 adults, $6.50 children under 6 riding double-saddle with adult. Breakfast cookout/ride twice a week (days vary; call ahead) 8–10 AM; admission $25; dinner cookout/ride twice a week 6–8 PM $30.*

STONE HILL WINERY

Once upon a time, Missouri's wine production was among the largest of any state in the nation, and its vintages regularly won medals in international competitions. But that was well before Prohibition. It took decades to get the industry started again, and Stone Hill pioneered its renaissance. The vineyard is in Hermann on the Missouri River (220 miles away), but the Branson facility blends and bottles many of the wines. You can take a free tour of the winery and learn how the grapes are grown, crushed, and fermented. The tour winds down in the tasting room, where you can sample the product, which contains mostly French-American grape hybrids such as Norton (a dry, slightly spicy red), Seyval (a smooth white with an apricot bouquet and a hint of grapefruit), Vidal (a crisp, slightly tart and herbal white), and Verdelho (a fresh, lively white with a touch of green apple). Several other blends will appeal to those who prefer sweeter wines. *Rte. 165 (south of W. Rte. 76), tel. 417/334–1897. Tours and tastings free. Open Mon.–Sat. 8:30–6, Sun. noon–6.*

TALKING ROCKS CAVERN

One of the most impressive caves in this vast underground world of caverns and sink-holes is Talking Rocks, which was discovered by local homesteader Arthur Irwin while on a hunting trip in 1883. In what is essentially one giant room, you'll see an incredible variety of formations—including translucent draperies, soda straws, and calcite curtains, all formed over eons by dripping water. Among the most spectacular sights are the 100-foot-tall Cathedral (which you can actually walk through), the towering Powell's Column, and the Angel, a formation replete with wings. The 45-minute tour is made more dramatic with the use of colored lights that highlight the formations while intense background music is played. *Rte. 13 (1 mi south of Branson West, about 8 mi from Strip), tel.*

800/600–CAVE. Admission: $7.95 adults, $4.50 children and youths 5–21. Open Apr.–Sept., daily 9:30–5; Oct.–mid-Dec. and mid-Jan.–Mar., Fri.–Tues. 9:30–5

THUNDER ROAD AMUSEMENT CENTER

This family park offers something for everyone: two miniature golf courses, bumper cars, an arcade with everything from pinball to Pac-Man, batting cages, a bungee-trampoline (10-foot poles on either side of the trampoline are attached to bungee cords that are secured around your waist, enabling you to do flips and jump even higher, thanks to increased momentum). *Rtes. 76 and 165, tel. 417/334–5905. Admission free; ride and attraction prices vary. Open daily 9 AM–midnight.*

OTHER ACTIVITIES

BOWLING

Dogwood Lanes (2126 E. Rte. 76, tel. 417/336–2695); **Hillbilly Bowl & Restaurant** (Rte. 13, Kimberling City, about 15 mi southwest of Strip, tel. 417/739–4425).

BUNGEE JUMPING

For $24.95 for the first jump and $19.95 for the second, **Outback Bungee Jumping** will give you the thrill of a lifetime and a free fall—from a 75-foot T-shaped tower—to remember. *1924 W. Rte. 76, tel. 417/336–5867. Open weekdays 4–midnight, weekends noon–midnight. Children under 18 need parent or guardian's signature.*

GO-CARTS

Kids Kountry (2505 W. Rte. 76, tel. 417/334–1618), **The Track** (1116; 1615; 2505; 3345; 3525 W. Rte. 76, tel. 417/334–1610, 417/334–1611, 417/334–1613, 417/334–1617, or 417/334–1619). Children must be 54" or taller to ride the standard-size go-carts alone and at least 6 years old to ride the bumper boats alone. Only **Kids Kountry** has a track for 4- to 6-year-olds (admission $3). Admission for all others is

$4.50 (good for all rides); children can ride with an adult for 50¢. *Open June–Sept., daily 9 AM–midnight; Apr.–May and Oct.–Nov., daily 10 AM–midnight.*

HELICOPTER RIDES

Table Rock Helicopters (W. Rte. 76, tel. 417/334–6102) offers thrilling tours of varying mileage around the Branson Lakes region, with a running narrative on the area's past and present. A 5-mile (three-minute) trip costs $14.95, a 10-mile (six-minute) trip costs $19.95, and a 15-mile (eight-minute) trip costs $24.95.

MINIATURE GOLF

There are several courses to choose from. Among the most elaborate are **Indoor Mini-Golf** (1807 Neihardt St., tel. 417/334–3919); **Pirate's Cove** (2901 Green Mountain Dr., tel. 417/336–6606), which has two outdoor ranges; and another indoor range at **76 Music Hall** (1919 W. Rte. 76, tel. 417/334–3919).

RECORDING STUDIOS

You can become a recording star (at least in a select family circle) at **Singing Sensations** (Stacey's Ozark Village, W. Rte. 76, tel. 417/335–4435), where you select and sing a song and receive a cassette of your performance. You can even have a music video shot.

ROLLER-SKATING

Skateworld Amusement Center (W. Rte. 76 at Truman Rd., tel. 417/334–1630) has a roller rink, trampoline, and—in summer—bumper boats and line dancing. Skating costs $3 per hourly session. Line dancing costs $5.95 and includes a lesson.

A PEEK INTO THE FUTURE

Be on the lookout for three exciting new developments in the Branson/Lakes area, all currently in various stages of completion.

The *Showboat Branson Belle,* a 1,000-seat paddle wheeler co-owned by Kenny Rogers and Silver Dollar City, is scheduled to ply the waters of Table Rock Lake starting in April 1995, departing from its berth at White River Landing. There will be four cruises daily: breakfast, lunch, dinner, and late dinner. Meals are sit-down, with a fixed menu.

Breakfast is ham and eggs, muffins, and fruit. Lunch is salad, chicken or beef, rice or potatoes, and dessert. Dinner is salad, vegetables, chicken or beef, beverage (no alcohol), and a sundae. A musical production with an 1890s showboat theme has been created by Marilyn Magnis and Jim Carroll, who have written for Disney and Jim Henson's Muppets. The cruise will last 90 minutes to 2 hours. Although White River Landing won't be finished until 1996, there will be a ticket booth, rest rooms, and at least one shop open by April 1995. Ultimately, the 55-acre wharfside development will feature landscaped gardens, restaurants, and shops; plan to arrive for the show a couple of hours early so you'll have time to mosey around. *Rte. 165, HCR 9, tel. 417/336–7171 or 800/227–8587. Breakfast cruise $19; 8–9:30. Lunch $23.20; 11–1. Dinner $31.75; 4:30–6:30. Late dinner: $31.75; 8–10.*

The $40 million first phase of the 360-acre **Branson Meadows** development, at the intersection of Route 248 and Shepherd of the Hills Expressway, should be up and running by summer 1995. This venture of the local Motley family will feature three theaters, condominiums, restaurants, retail shops including Factory Stores of America, a 300,000-square-foot factory outlet mall, a golf course, and 2,000 motel rooms.

The biggest news at Branson Meadows, however, is the coming of "Sportopia," a 62-acre theme park—the first of its kind—slated for completion in late 1996 or early 1997. Designed by LucasArts Attractions, an affiliate of the Oscar-winning special-effects wizards at Industrial Light and Magic, Sportopia will combine sports activities with multimedia simulation technology to create such sensations as batting in a major league stadium, driving a race car at LeMans, climbing a cliff in Yosemite, kayaking through or hang gliding over the Grand Canyon, and many more once-in-a-lifetime athletic experiences. Sportopia will be open March through December

The Ozarks Quilt

There's an old Ozarks joke that goes something like this: St. Peter is escorting a tour group of prospective entrants around heaven when they happen upon two hillbillies shackled to the Pearly Gates, looking miserable as can be. Horrified, one good soul demands to know the reason. "Did those poor boys do something wrong to be chained up like common criminals? Is this how you do things in heaven?" "No, ma'am," replies St. Peter humbly, "but it's springtime in the Ozarks, and if we don't chain 'em up, they'll leave here!"

For many residents and return visitors, the Ozarks have an almost mystical, spiritual attraction that defies explanation. The mountains are beautiful, of course, yet they lack the showy grandeur of the Rockies. In fact, the Ozarks, one of the oldest ranges on the planet, have been whittled down by erosion and seem tame by comparison. On the other hand, they are of a more human scale. They are approachable rather than awe-inspiring, making communing with nature that much easier. Everywhere you look are verdant "hollers" and a cathedral of vaulting oak, cedar, and hickory trees, interspersed with jagged outcroppings and sheer bluffs whose colors shift with the sun's progress. Each season yields its own rewards. In winter, dew freezes into a shimmering curtain of icy fog, lacquering the ancient rocks and trees. In spring, blossoming dogwood and redbud trees daub the roadside with white, pink, and carnelian. In summer, a virtual color wheel of wildflowers pokes through the carpet of pine needles and transforms the rugged hills into a gigantic rock garden. In autumn the turning leaves blaze a trail of fire through the woods.

The name "Ozarks" is thought to be derived from the French *aux arcs*, but etymologists dispute its definition. Some claim it was simply an abbreviation for "to the Arkansas Post," a fur-trading center. *Arc* also means "bow" in French; the term might refer to the sturdy bows fashioned by the region's original Osage and Choctaw residents. Still others believe it refers to the bow-wood tree, or *bois d'arc*, itself.

Many Native American tribes settled the region during the prehistoric era. The Osage nation was indisputably dominant when the first Europeans—mostly French and Spanish explorers and missionaries—arrived, during the early 17th century. Tall, athletic, and extraordinarily graceful, the Osage were superb hunters and farmers; their highly evolved society scrupulously provided for its poor and infirm members. The imprint and legacy of the Osage linger most vividly in the "thong trees" that dot the plateau—saplings intentionally bent as directional finders, usually pointing the way to freshwater springs, medicinal herbs, and caves for shelter.

The Osage and other tribes were gradually supplanted by settlers—mostly of Scots, Irish, Welsh, English, Dutch, or Scandinavian descent—moving west from the Appalachians. Thousands of acres had been set aside for reservations (most notably for the Cherokees, who were forced to migrate from their southeastern homes), but the pioneers' continual demand for land pushed the Native Americans farther west into Oklahoma and Kansas.

Despite its undeniable allure, from a strictly financial standpoint the land was never worth fighting over anyway. The ancient rock, blasted by wind and water over eons, made for poor soil, at times so thin and porous it was unfit even for grazing. The area's many fast-flowing rivers carried away what remained of the rich, loamy topsoil and its nutrients. This is a land forged by the elements, defined by the earth and water. The plateau is a vast dome patiently sculpted over time. It was once covered by a roiling inland sea, which formed the sedimentary base of the mountains; volcanic uplift gradually thrust the dome higher and higher. But although the mountains are ghosts of their former selves, the region remains incredibly rugged, etched with rivers and streams. As a local saying goes, "It ain't that the hills are high, but that the valleys are deep." Indeed, the entire Ozarks Plateau functions as one giant watershed. Water flows everywhere: from a torrent above ground in the fast-coursing rivers (even when dammed they periodically reassert themselves when heavy rain floods their banks) to a steady trickle underground in caves and sinkholes carved from the limestone.

The geological term for this topography is karst country. Karst is formed when water seeps into limestone, eroding increasingly larger basins, called sinkholes, which function like drains, coaxing still more water underground. Karstic hillocks, known as mogotes, result as the bedrock dissolves, and the subterranean streams resurface as springs. The Ozarks are literally eating away at themselves, explaining both the dramatic terrain and nutrient-poor soil.

As the surrounding waters receded and lower-lying areas were clawed by floods and glaciers, flora and fauna took refuge on the plateau, leading to a remarkably diverse ecosystem. This abundance, as well as unique geological formations, formed the background for lore and legend that bear imprints of the region's many inhabitants, members of diverse cultures and religions from Christianity to Native American to Norse and Celt. The myths of the origins of the dogwood (whose brown stain on the cruciform white blossom represents Christ's wounds on the cross) and redbud (from which Judas is said to have hanged himself) derive from Christian symbolism. Many of the legends surrounding the more unusual natural landmarks recall Native American lore.

This rich oral folkloric tradition arose not only to illustrate values that elders wished to inculcate in younger generations but also as entertainment—a welcome break from hardscrabble daily lives. The harsh existence and long distances fostered a strong sense of community (and concomitant distrust of "furriners," who might come from the next county!), as well as a tremendous yearning to socialize. Music played a vital role. In almost every household, a banjo, fiddle, or dulcimer held an honored place above the mantel. Even the music seems to take its cue from nature; anyone who has heard both the screech of a turkey buzzard and the scrape of a fiddle knows the two are oddly harmonious.

Granted, "civilization" came late to the Ozarks, thanks to the rugged terrain. But although the region is remote, it was never quite the backwater outsiders believed. Most of the area lacked a paved road system until well into the 20th century, but the many navigable rivers were harnessed for transportation, ensuring that the Ozarks wouldn't be totally isolated. The myth of the ignorant, backward hillbilly persists, however: The very wealth of folklore has often been cited as proof that Ozarkers were superstitious and uncultured, stubbornly clinging to old ways and resisting progress.

The misconception has at times been fostered by hill folk themselves. The demanding lifestyle made natives infinitely resourceful, as well as intimately knowledgeable of their surroundings, forging a strong independent streak and a wry sense of humor. They're not above playing hillbilly for profit, which is not to say they're cynical or money-grubbing—just practical. Hillbilly sells, even today. That explains the quaint misspellings on so-called primitive, hand-painted signs; more often than not, the shop owners and artisans are college educated. They'll even don ill-fitting clothes and black out their teeth, tongues firmly planted in cheeks (along with a wad of chawin' tobacky), for the fast-paced stage shows typical of the region. Broad slapstick alternates with surprisingly sharp barbs—usually reserved for people and places that are symbols of authority. When it comes to politics, Republican and Democrat alike are targets. A standard bit of unsophisticated rube humor might run like this: "I heard in Washington they were gonna put on a show about the life of Jesus, only they had to cancel it when they found out there weren't three wise men in the whole city."

At the same time, the hillbilly image has been romanticized—a peculiar 20th-century twist on Jean-Jacques Rousseau's "enlightened" concept of the noble savage. It is thought that, somehow, the simple way of life imputes a purity of spirit, as if literal impoverishment paved the way for spiritual wealth. (Harold Bell Wright's monumental best-seller, *The Shepherd of the Hills*, depicts just such a story.) The massive Christ of the Ozarks statue sits atop a hillock outside Eureka Springs, arms outstretched, as if to gather the flock from the surrounding valleys and begin the Sermon on the Mount. Throughout the century, various media portrayed the hillbilly as wiser than the city dweller. Among these contributions to popular culture are Ma and Pa Kettle (centerpieces of a series of 1940s B movies), the cartoons' L'il Abner, and TV's Beverly Hillbillies. Ozarkers embodied the family values that have become the stuff of political campaigns: a strong sense of independence, hard work without complaint, pride in one's family and heritage. And if their ways seemed oddly quaint, at least they honored their roots, unlike a contemporary society in a constant state of flux and drift. Even today, hill folk cannily play upon the city dweller's nostalgia for a better time and place—one that he or she usually never knew to begin with. No wonder the popularity of such heritage and historical theme parks as Branson's Silver Dollar City and the Ozark Folk Center in Mountain View, both dedicated to re-creating a lost time and perpetuating regional crafts, continues to soar.

John Ross and Will Powell at sawmill, 1908; photo courtesy Walker Powell, Reeds Spring, and Branson Tri-Lakes Daily News

Of course, progress is inevitable, and it's come to the Ozarks with a vengeance. You can't travel more than a few miles without running into a Burger King or Dairy Queen. Fleets of tour buses circle the area like birds of prey. Giant billboards proclaim the gospel according to Andy, Tony, Mel, Glen, and the like from Springfield clear to Eureka Springs. Happily, however, the exponential growth has given the younger generation reason to stay put and run the tourist industry. The steady influx of newcomers, fleeing the big cities in search of what is missing from their lives, brings still more talent to the region, making Branson and Eureka Springs comparatively enlightened bastions of the arts and crafts.

And through it all the siren call of nature persists. Just a few miles outside Branson, the interstate slices through a thick tangle of hardwoods and meanders past rolling green meadows, a reminder that state-of-the-art theaters, imposing man-made dams, and the inevitable traffic jams are merely pockets of civilization stitched into the surrounding wilderness. Time screeches to a halt, willing you to stop and take stock.

Excursions in Ozark Mountain Country

5

Ozark Mountain Country, a triangle enveloping Branson, includes Springfield at the northern apex, Eureka Springs at the southwest point, and Mountain View at the southeast. The area is within an hour's drive of Branson, and you can easily spend two or three days taking in all the sights.

History buffs will want to see Wilson's Creek National Battlefield, an important Civil War site, as well as Eureka Springs' exquisitely preserved Victorian National Historic District and the Ozark Folk Center in Mountain View. For those wanting to commune with nature, there's a vast network of caves accessible by underground tram and a turn-of-the-century spa for luxuriating. With all its beauty and historical significance, Ozark Mountain Country has much to offer, especially to families with diverse interests.

TOURIST OFFICES

For information, contact the **Springfield Convention and Visitors Center** (3315 E. Battlefield Rd., Springfield 65804-4048, tel. 417/881–5300 or 800/678–8766), the **Eureka Springs Chamber of Commerce** (Box 551, Eureka Springs, AR 72632, tel. 501/253–8737 or 800/643–3456), and the **Mountain View Tourist Information Center** (Box 133, Mountain View, AR 72560, tel. 501/269–8098).

GUIDED TOURS

SPRINGFIELD. Aquatic Adventures (1833 S. Holland St., tel. 417/887–2509) tour organizers will take you flyfishing, hunting, canoeing, even scuba diving on a variety of half- and full-day excursions.

The **Ozark Balloon Port** (Rte. 6, Ozark, tel. 417/485–7373) provides colorful hot-air balloon rides over the Ozarks at dawn or dusk.

EUREKA SPRINGS. The chamber of commerce runs trolley tours April–October (all-day pass $3.50, one stop $1) in color-coded cars that travel five loops through the town. The folksy drivers are a font of local lore and gossip. Tickets can be purchased from most downtown hotels and shops, the trolley depot on South Main Street, or from the chamber of commerce.

If you prefer the comfort of an air-conditioned motorcoach, **K-Tours** (Passion Play Rd.,

BRANSON AREA

TO SPRINGFIELD

13

176

65

248

176

Galena

160

13

Reeds Spring

Walnut Shade

39

Cape Fair

248

76

65

Branson West

Silver Dollar City

Forsyth

65

Lake Ta (SEE DETA

Kimberling City

76

Branso

MARK TWAIN NATIONAL FOREST

39

Shell Knob

Point Lookout

Kirbyvi

Hollister

86

Table Rock Lake (SEE DETAIL MAP)

Table Rock Lake

Eagle Rock

Viola

13

Lampe

86

Ridgedale

MISSOURI ARKANSAS

Blue Eye

65

23

Omaha

14

221

Oak Grove

21

Eureka Springs

Urbanette

103

62

Berryville

23

Green Forest

103

62

21

Alpena

65

N

206

Connor

412

HARRISO

0   10 miles

0   15 km

Osage

TO HOT SPRINGS

128

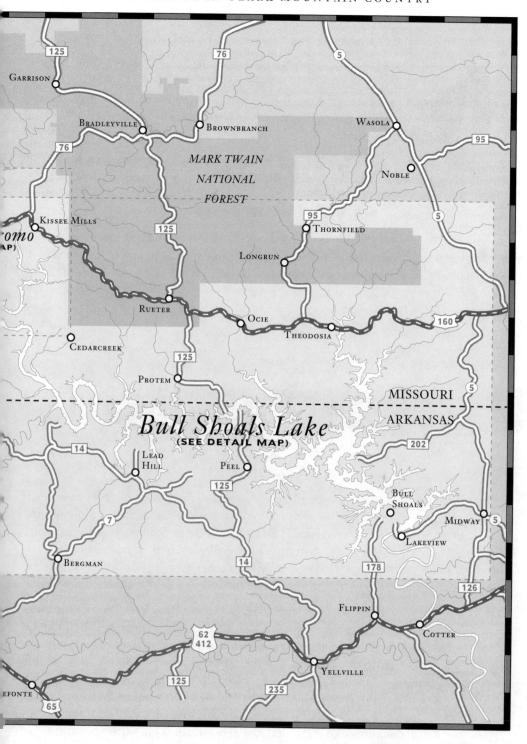

tel. 501/253–6559) offers a 2½-hour whirlwind excursion that takes in the downtown area, the Christ of the Ozarks statue, and Thorncrown Chapel.

Touring the **Eureka Springs and North Arkansas Railway** (299 N. Main St., tel. 501/253–9623; admission $8 adults, $4 children under 12; Apr.–Oct., Mon.–Sat. 10–4 on the hour) offers an opportunity to recall the town's golden era in a "Cabbage Head" locomotive—an old-fashioned train with a comfortable, restored parlor car and an extravagant engine car up front.

Another way to see Eureka Springs is in a surrey drawn by horses called Duke and Danny. They prance up and down Prospect Street, drawing an elegant white carriage behind them, courtesy of Southern Pride Carriage Tours. *Carriages depart from Crescent Hotel, 75 Prospect St., tel. 501/749–2665. Cost: $15 per couple.*

For sea salts, the *Belle of the Ozarks* chugs along the shores of nearby Beaver Lake, making stops at Beaver Dam, the White House Bluffs (spectacular limestone escarpments), and a 200-acre game-preserve island. *Starkey Marina, off Rte. 62W, tel. 501/253-6200. Admission: $10 adults, $5 children under 12. Departures May–late-Oct., daily at 11, 1, and 3; sunset cruises June–Aug., daily at 7.*

IN AND AROUND THE TOWNS

SPRINGFIELD

Springfield is the largest city on the Ozarks plateau and has a population of more than 140,000. Most of its top attractions are far-flung, making a car desirable, although the historic downtown is easily walkable. The town is home to Southwest Missouri State University, Drury College, and Southern Baptist College. To drive here from Branson, travel 40 miles north along I-65. *See also* Getting There in Chapter 1, Essential Information.

One of the most notable attractions in Springfield is the **Bass Pro Shops Outdoors World,** visited by 3.5 million sports and nature enthusiasts annually. The 150,000-square-foot property retails everything from sporting gear and outdoors attire to environmental art. It's the Great Outdoors indoors, with wildlife mounts, a four-story waterfall, trout streams coursing through fishing displays, and a 140,000-gallon aquarium teeming with game fish, including leviathan bass (among the largest in captivity, weighing more than 50 pounds) and catfish. (One of the big thrills for shoppers is watching the scuba diver feeding the fish.) The store is impressively designed, and displays are even altered to reflect the changing seasons.

Not only does Bass Pro offer the largest selection of any outfitter, but the salespeople are knowledgeable about their merchandise. The person who fits you for hiking boots is probably an enthusiastic hiker, and an avid angler will advise you about which lure to purchase. Bass Pro also offers extras and conveniences such as an archery and firing range in the hunting department, weekend seminars and lectures, even a barber shop and a McDonald's. Also on the premises, overlooking the bustling main floor, is **Hemingway's Restaurant.** Ernest Hemingway, author of *Islands in the Stream* and *The Old Man and the Sea,* was an avid fisherman, and his estate loaned the restaurant several photos of Papa battling 100-pound tarpon and carousing in his marina bars of choice. You can ogle the sharks cruising through the 29,000-gallon saltwater aquarium here while enjoying well-prepared—what else?—seafood.

While you're in the complex, you may want to wander through the **National Hunting and Fishing Museum,** in its own 10,000-square-foot facility. You can learn about North American wildlife and habitats from the lifesize dioramas. There's also an extensive exhibit of nautical technology, with antique boat motors and lobster and tuna boats. One of the shark models used in the movie *Jaws* is on display, as well as one of Hemingway's fishing boats. *1935 S. Campbell Ave. (about 1 mi south of downtown), tel. 417/887–1915. Open Mon.–Sat. 7 AM–10 PM, Sun. 9–6.*

You could easily spend a half-day at Bass Pro, but save time for Springfield's other attractions. It has a thriving city center, with a wealthy historic section called **Walnut Street National Historic District,** lined with grand old walnut, sycamore, and redbud trees that explode with color in spring and fall. The eclectic architecture documents more than a century of building styles, ranging from Queen Anne to Moorish. You can pick up walking- and driving-tour brochures at the chamber of commerce (*see* Tourist Information, *above*).

There are several museums in town worth exploring, all within a mile or so of downtown. The peaceful, uncrowded **Springfield Art Museum** presents rotating exhibits in 11 gracefully designed galleries. It's particularly strong in etchings; you can view superb examples by Rembrandt, Albrecht Dürer, Goya, Picasso, George Grosz, and Fernand Léger, among others. There's also a small but choice permanent collection, containing primarily work by regional artists. Most of the rotating exhibits feature contemporary works and themes. *1111 E. Brookside Dr., tel. 417/866–2716. Donations accepted. Open Tues. and Thurs.–Sat. 9–5, Wed. 6:30 PM–9 PM, Sun. 1–5.*

The **Museum of Ozarks History** fills the third floor of the august stone Springfield City Hall with clothes, tools, letters, and other artifacts that exhaustively trace the life of a typical Ozarks pioneer. No tours of City Hall are available. *830 Boonville St., tel.*

417/864–1976. Admission: $2.75 adults, $2.50 senior citizens, $1 children 6–12. Open Feb.–Dec., Tues.–Sat. 10:30–4:30.

The **Frisco Railroad Museum** is in the midst of a major expansion. Its new exhibit rooms (when completed in 1997) will re-create a traditional dining car, boxcar, and caboose. There are dining-car and Pullman displays, a re-creation of a turn-of-the-century ticket agent's office, and more than 2,000 memorabilia. A gift shop within the museum sells replicas of many of the pieces on display. *543 E. Commercial St., tel. 417/866–7573. Admission: $2 adults, $1 children under 12. Open Tues.–Sat. 10–5.*

Just outside city limits are other attractions that can be reached by car. For a pleasant urban respite, head south on U.S. 65 to the edge of town to reach the **Springfield Conservation Nature Center,** with 5 miles of interpretive trails winding around Springfield Lake under canopies of vaulting oak and hickory trees. Informative exhibits include replicas of Ozarks habitats from forests to wetlands. Children love the hands-on displays, the nature and conservation films screened in the auditorium, and the dark room, where they can hear nocturnal animal sounds. *4600 S. Chrisman St. (off U.S. 65), tel. 417/882–4237. Admission free. Open May–Oct., daily 8–8; Nov.–Apr., daily 8–6.*

If the nature center seems too tame, go on safari through **Buena Vista's Exotic Animal Paradise.** Take your own car over 9 miles of paved roads that meander through the 400-acre compound, where herds of zebra, llama, yak, ostrich, emu, antelope, elk, and buffalo roam (behind fences). *Exit 88 off I-44, Strafford, tel. 417/859–2159. Admission: $8.95 adults, $3.95 children 3–11, under 3 free. Open year-round 9–5.*

Another enjoyable activity is a journey through **Fantastic Caverns,** part of a vast underground system below the city. The tram tour—the only one of its kind in North America—takes you through a guided mile-long passage following an underground river. Among the rare species down here are pipistrel bats, the endangered Ozarks' blind cave fish, Ozarks' blind cave salamanders, and Ozarks' blind crayfish. Also in the cave are examples of stalactites and stalagmites, as well as other formations such as soda straws, columns, drapery, and flowstone. A film explains the cave's drainage system and how the community watershed affects the creatures' delicate existence. The cave was used as a speakeasy during the 1920s, then as the site of the secret "Rites of the Dead" ceremonies attended by 7,000 Ku Klux Klansmen. *Cavern Rd., off Rte. 13N (follow signs to Cave Rd.), tel. 417/833–2010. Admission: $12.50 adults, $6.50 children 6–12, 5 and under free. Open May–Sept., daily 8–6; Oct.–Apr., daily 8–4. Closed holidays.*

The Springfield area's turbulent history is on display at **Wilson's Creek National Battlefield,** commemorating the first major battle west of the Mississippi; a 15-minute film gives an overview of the battle's strategic importance for the Union and the Confederacy. Although Missouri was a slave state, it chose to remain in the Union, and sympathies here were fiercely divided. Agitators on either side outweighed the moderates who preached strict neutrality. The Springfield area controlled both the state's river routes and many vital supply lines into Arkansas and Texas. Several skirmishes resulted in this bloody four-day battle, with several thousand casualties. The "mighty mean-fought fight," as newspapers called it, resulted in a Confederate victory but at a cost so great that Missouri was preserved for the Union. You can pick up a driving tour that hits the important sites, including the 1852 Ray House, the only surviving structure associated with the battle. Owned by a local farm family—the battle was fought on their corn-field—it had been commandeered by Confederate troops for use as a hospital. *Rte. 13 southwest out of town, follow signs to Battlefield, MO, about 5 mi past town. Rte. ZZ, tel. 417/732–2662. Admission: $2 per person or $4 per car. Open daily 8–5. Closed holidays.*

Adjacent to (though not part of) the national battlefield is **General Sweeney's Civil War Museum.** The beautifully preserved battlefield is complemented by General Sweeney's collection, a labor of love painstakingly assembled by his great-great grandson Dr. Tom Sweeney. Exhaustively detailed and beautifully mounted, its more than 5,000 artifacts focus on the trans-Mississippi arena, vividly re-creating the brutal series of skir-mishes fought in Missouri (which saw the third-most battles

Daguerrotype from the Civil War period; photo courtesy A. Beck.

during the war, after Virginia and Tennessee), Arkansas, Kansas, and the Indian Territory (now Oklahoma). Other displays shed light on little-known aspects of the war, including the roles played by Native Americans and the daily lives of soldiers' wives and medicos. It's organized chronologi-cally, starting with John Brown and "Bleeding Kansas" (the vicious fight over whether to make the state slave or free) during the 1850s. If Tom's around and has time, he may even give an informal tour. *MO ZZ, Republic, tel. 417/732–1224. Admission: $3.50 adults, $2.50 children 5–11. Open Mar.–Oct., daily 10–5; Feb. and Nov., weekends 10–5.*

EUREKA SPRINGS

The area's original residents, the Osage Nation knew about the healing properties of the mineral-laden waters for centuries. Native lore relates that the magical springs' fame was so widespread that even the mighty Sioux had ventured to the "Land of Blue Skies and Laughing Waters" to cure the blindness and rheumatism of Mor-I-Na-Ki (Beautiful Flower), daughter of their great chief. Rumors would later attract explorer Ponce de León as he sought the legendary Fountain of Youth.

By the mid-19th century the area had become increasingly popular with hunters, among them a Dr. Alvah Jackson. His son Bill, afflicted with granulated eyelids (sties), got dirt in his eye as father and son dug out a "varmint" the dogs had cornered. Alvah advised Bill to wash his eyes out in the spring, and, miraculously, his chronic pain lessened. After several days of taking the "cure," Bill was completely healed. After the Civil War, Alvah returned to the area with his powerful, influential friend, Judge L.B. Saunders. The doctor tactfully suggested Saunders bathe a chronic sore in the water. Once again, the spring eased the condition, and the waters' healing properties were advertised far and wide. By the 1880s a huge settlement straddled the bluffs, crags, and grottoes surrounding the Old Indian Healing Spring, to which cures were now attributed for cancer, dyspepsia, ulcers, piles, asthma, catarrh, scrofula, and many other complaints. In the late 1880s and 1890s, a series of fires swept through the ramshackle wooden buildings, but the town rose from its ashes on limestone foundations to become one of the country's most fashionable Victorian spas.

After the spa craze died down during the Great Depression, Eureka Springs dozed for many years, until the counterculture generation discovered its exquisite if dilapidated Victorian homes in the 1960s. These new inhabitants transformed the town into the chic artists' colony that it is today. It's home to the most vibrant, eclectic mix of people in the Ozarks, from hard-core, Bible Belt mountain folk to New Age mystics. The Hell's Angels hold an annual convention here (a former Eureka Springs mayor was a card-carrying member); there's an irresistible charm about a quaint storybook town filled with tattooed, pony-tailed bikers. But that's fitting for Eureka Springs, which in its first heyday played host to both temperance leader Carrie Nation and goodtime gal Diamond Lil who both lived here.

The place is quirky in more ways than one. Eureka Springs is nicknamed the "crazy-quilt" town, because the original residents had no choice but to build their houses up—and down—the steep hills. Rickety wooden stairways careen drunkenly in all directions, at times leading nowhere in particular. As one incredulous Ozarker remarked, "Why, there isn't a spot on the whole hillside level enough for a house, let alone a town!" And as *Ripley's Believe It Or Not* marveled during the early part of the century, one hotel (the Basin Park) actually has "eight floors and every floor a ground floor," while St.

Elizabeth's Catholic Church is entered through the belfry. Even today the town seems to have been hacked from the surrounding wilderness: Terraced gardens nestle under bluffs or perch on boulders, and foliage pokes through cracks in weathered limestone walls.

But the town's glory remains its almost-perfectly preserved Victorian architecture. The entire downtown is listed on the National Register of Historic Places. The original gazebos shelter the springs, which are now cracked and crawling with undergrowth. Old-fashioned trolleys wheeze up and down the hills. Rough-hewn limestone edifices emblazoned with fading signs advertising 5¢ COCA COLA and BLOCKSON & CO., UNDERTAKERS alternate with whimsical, gingerbread-covered homes painted with cotton-candy colors. The Eureka Springs Historic District Commission zealously enforces zoning bylaws to ensure authenticity. Residents can't even apply a coat of paint unless they can prove it was a color commonly used during the Victorian period.

To reach Eureka Springs by car from Branson you can take the one-hour scenic route: Route 65 south onto Missouri Route 86 west, then Arkansas Route 23 south into town. The road dances in and out of oak and hickory groves and yields breathtaking views of Table Rock Lake. The longer but slightly faster route is Route 65 south to Route 62 west. Shuttle service is sometimes offered Memorial Day–Labor Day from Branson; call the Eureka Springs Chamber of Commerce (*see* Tourist Information, *above*).

Attractions in Eureka Springs range from exquisite to oddball, and most of the top sights are within walking distance of downtown. The best way to experience the town is on foot: Stop by the chamber of commerce (*see* Tourist Information, *above*) and ask for their pamphlet detailing six tours. Other renowned attractions, including the Christ of the Ozarks statue and Passion Play, are only reachable by car.

A stroll around the historic loop—Main, Center, Spring, and Prospect streets—will transport you to the golden days at the Springs. It's a Disneyesque fantasia of towers and turrets, stained glass and beveled bay windows, fish-scale shingles and gables galore. A perfect example is the resplendent **Crescent Hotel** (75 Prospect St., tel. 501/253–9766), nicknamed the "Castle in the Wilderness" when it opened in 1886. Like the town itself, the Crescent has enjoyed a strange, checkered past. During the spa town's gradual decline during the early part of the century, the grand edifice fell into disrepair. From 1908 through 1932 it remained a hotel during the mild winters only. The rest of the year it was rented out as dormitories and classrooms for the Conservatory for Young Women. A junior college subsequently struggled and failed here during the Depression era. In 1937 the building was sold to the colorful "Doctor" Norman Baker, who advertised miracle cures for cancer but neglected to inform patients that he had just completed a prison sentence in Texas for fraud. A flamboyant character, Baker wore imperial-purple silk shirts over a bulletproof vest and also did a brisk side trade in goat glands (apparently for renewed sexual vigor). His tenancy was the only time until the present that the Crescent made money. Alas, he was convicted in 1940 of mail fraud and carted off to Leavenworth Penitentiary, where he died of cancer. Among the Crescent's more notable features are exquisite wainscoting and period furnishings throughout, balconies supported by old railroad tracks, and a fourth-story observation deck overlooking a tangled hollow and the Christ of the Ozarks statue in the distance.

Across from the hotel is the tranquil, aforementioned **St. Elizabeth's Catholic Church** (Crescent Dr., tel. 501/253–9853), which is entered through its bell tower. Other homes of historic importance include temperance leader **Carrie Nation's house,** a simple affair befitting her convictions, and **Rosalie House,** possibly the most elaborate dwelling in town. The 15-room 1883 redbrick structure was built in a melange of Victorian styles; painted red, maroon, cream, and green; and hung with fanciful gingerbread curlicues and icicles. The interior design is just as intricate, with handcarved yellow-pine woodwork, gold-leaf picture moldings, and plaster ceiling frescoes. Both houses are on the chamber's walking tour.

For an overview of the town's founding, golden age, decline, and revival, visit the fine **Historical Museum** (97 S. Main St., tel. 501/253–9417; open Tues.–Sat. 9:30–4, Sun. noon–4; admission $2 adults, children free). A typical small-town tribute to itself, with little apparent design, it offers a fascinating potpourri of objects, from old light-bulb and coke-bottle collections to exhibits on the evolution of the washing machine from 1890 to the present. There are also dedications to important local women in history and to locals in the armed forces from the Spanish-American to Persian Gulf wars. A case displaying the tools of a frontier doctor is a grisly affair, including nerve pills and bloodcurdling forceps and scalpels.

If you're an avid museum-goer and haven't gotten your fill of displays and exhibits, you're in luck. Eureka Springs is nationally known for its strange assortment of museums, each cataloging someone's magnificent obsession and put together haphazardly with fine contempt for the curator's art. There's **Frog Fantasies** (151 Spring St., tel. 501/253–7227; open daily 9–6; admission $1), in the store of the same name, where you can find ballerina frogs, frog candelabra, handpainted frog china, frog boxer shorts, and the like, for amphibian fanciers. Pat and Louise Mesa claim to own more than 5,000 frogs of all descriptions. As their brochure states, "the gift of a frog, with expressions varying from sad and lonely to mischievous to exultant, is sure to please."

When you're finished toadying to Pat and Louise (who could resist schmoozing a little to discover the origin of their collection?), ring the day in at the **Hammond Museum of Bells** (2 Pine St., tel. 501/253–7411; open Apr.–Nov. 10, Mon.–Sat 9:30–5, Sun. 11:30–4). Bells in all shapes, sizes, and tones, as well as wind chimes (from melodic five-pipe Westminsters to the long Cathedral series that duplicates the sonorous sound of a church organ) are the attraction here. Needless to say, many examples are also on sale in the attached Collectabells shop.

The dulcet sounds continue at the **Miles Musical Museum** (Rte. 62W, tel. 501/253–8961; open May–Oct., daily 9–5). A cacophony of sounds—some melodious,

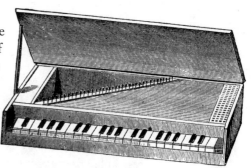

some woefully out of tune—follows you down the halls of the 12,000-square-foot exhibit space. It contains thousands of instruments from around the world, from old-fashioned to newfangled. It's all here—somewhere—from old-time cylinder music boxes to castanets, sitars and zithers to seemingly every description of piano and organ, including many fine player varieties. Miles Musical Museum also holds other unusual collections, including one of "button" pictures.

If you prefer the soothing sound of a choo-choo whistle, visit **Little Trains of the Ozarks** (Rte. 62W, tel. 501/253–5845; open Thurs.–Tues. 9–5). The 20-by-100-foot working display of model electric trains runs through real waterfalls and past a working gristmill, bridges, tunnels, and trestles galore, all placed amid 52,000 pounds of native rock.

Queen Anne and **Wings** (Rte. 62W, tel. 501/253–8825; open daily 9:30–5; admission $4 for 1 adult, $7 for two, children under 12 free) are side-by-side Victorians owned by Bob, Mary Lou, and Heather Evans. The Queen Anne mansion (which doubles as an inn) was built in 1891 in Carthage, Missouri, then disassembled and painstakingly transferred board by board and stone by stone to Eureka Springs in 1985. Forty trucks were required for the move. The exterior is notable for its more than 2,000 hand-chiseled stones. The interior oak, walnut, poplar, and cherry woodwork is extraordinary, with especially fabulous handcarved wainscoting, central balustrade, fireplace mantels, and pocket doors. But what catapults this attraction into the eccentric category is its dainty powder-blue sidekick Wings. The downstairs is decorated in a Christmas theme year-round, including an entire life-size crèche, elaborately wrapped gift boxes, delicate ornaments made of everything from paper to crystal, and an 8-foot-tall, edible, Hansel and Gretel gingerbread house. The upstairs has been transformed into a giant aviary, with more than 20 tropical birds, resplendent in their rainbow-hue plumage, including rare Gouldian finches, Goffin Cockatoos, and red lory parrots.

Quigley's Castle (Rte. 23S, tel. 501/253–8311; open Apr.–Oct., Mon.–Wed., Fri., and Sat. 8:30–5; admission $3 adults, children under 15 free) is perhaps the most intriguing structure in town. One fine June morning Mrs. Albert Quigley took advantage of her husband's departure for work and tore down the house. Albert returned after a hard day to find a chicken coop in place of his abode. Mrs. Quigley explained with her usual common sense: "I knew he'd never do anything about a new house as long as the old one was standing." She wanted to feel like she was "living in the world and not in a box." Welcome to the result: The four two-story walls are covered with rocks she carefully chose for their color and texture. To achieve her "worldly" effect, Mrs. Quigley insisted that 4 feet of earth be left bare between the floors and the walls on three sides of the house. She then planted her indoor garden—everything from subtropical flowering shrubs to Southwestern cacti. The second-story rooms are suspended, through clever placement of oak pillars. Mrs. Quigley died in 1984, but a granddaughter runs the house and tells fond stories of growing up Quigley.

You can cap your tour with a natural oddity, **Pivot Rock** (end of Pivot Rock Rd., tel. 501/253–8860; open daily 8–7; admission $2.50 adults, 50¢ children under 12). Immortalized by Bob Ripley in his "Believe It or Not" column, the rock is nature's supreme balancing act: it's 32 feet wide at the top but only 16 inches wide at its base. The surrounding park is ideal for nature hikes: Trails wind around eroded bluffs that resemble abstract sculptures and through bucolic woods that offer smashing views of Lake Leatherwood and are alive with the screech of owls and whippoorwills.

The **Passion Play** and **Christ of the Ozarks statue** (end of Passion Play Rd., tel. 501/253–9200 or 800/882–PLAY; performed late Apr.–late Oct., statue and grounds open daily; admission to grounds free, tickets for Passion Play $3–$13) are two of Eureka Springs' most enduring attractions. The Institute of Outdoor Drama in Chapel Hill, North Carolina, called the Passion Play the world's number-one outdoor drama. First performed by locals on July 15, 1968 (children have literally grown up in the production), it is the pious retelling of the events of Jesus Christ's life. It features a cast of 250 actors and live camels, doves, donkeys, horses, and sheep on a multilevel stage that re-creates the hustle and bustle of the Biblical Holy Land.

Also impressive is the gleaming white statue itself, seven stories tall (67 feet), depicting Christ with arms outstretched as if to embrace the world (65 feet from fingertip to fingertip). Sculpted by Emmet Sullivan, who assisted Gutzon Borglum on Mt. Rushmore, it appears primitive yet undeniably powerful. It is said that if the sunlight strikes it just so, the eyes appear to follow you as you stroll the observation sidewalk.

The complex was founded by Gerald Elko Smith, a 1920s radio evangelist who fell in love with the area and dreamed of creating a replica of the Holy Land. Descendants L.K. and Elna M. Smith (and now the Elna M. Smith Foundation) carry out his vision. A full-scale reproduction of Moses's Tabernacle in the Wilderness, Ten Commandments Memorial, Golgotha Hill, life-size re-creations of the Last Supper, the Nativity, and a scaled down Sea of Galilee—all composing Smith's "New Holy Land"—sit on the Passion Play grounds. The Bible Museum holds Scripture in more than 625 languages, with more than 6,000 biblical artifacts. A 10-foot section of the Berlin Wall, inscribed by an imprisoned East Berliner with the 23rd Psalm ("Though I walk through shadow of the Valley of Death, I will not be afraid") stands as a symbol of liberation from oppression. Of course, what strikes many as reverent may appall others, who might see it as nothing more than a shrine to the commercialization of religion. There are restaurants, souvenir shops, and parking lots crammed with tour buses. Still, you'll likely find a quiet moment for reflection and renewal somewhere on the grounds.

A simpler example of heart-warming faith can be found at the transcendent, privately owned **Thorncrown Chapel** (end of Thorncrown Rd., tel. 501/253–7401; open daily

8–sunset; donation requested), nestled below a canopy of trees. Designed by architect E. Fay Jones (a protégé of Frank Lloyd Wright) and completed in 1979, it is a soaring edifice constructed of glass and native woods that seems to sprout from the surrounding rocks and trees, which are reflected in the pristine glass. Pine lattice work anchors more than 20,000 pounds of glass in 425 towering panes up to 48 feet tall—reaching as high as the surrounding forest. It represents the vision of Jim Reed, who sought to "build a little glass chapel on the side of the hill to give wayfarers an opportunity to relax in an inspiring and peaceful way." Estimates for his "little" project grew and grew, but he persevered and raised the several hundred thousand dollars needed. His faith was rewarded when the American Association of Architects saluted it in 1991 as "Building of the Decade." Mr. Reed has passed on, but his family has perpetuated his glorious obsession, sharing it with visitors from around the world (more than 3 million so far). Dedicated to the glory of God and nature, it is a place of contemplation, meditation, and repose, especially dramatic at sunset, when the 24 glowing cruciform light fixtures are mirrored in the windows. As Mrs. Reed says, "We change our wallpaper four times a year."

Another place of peace and ease is the **Eureka Springs Gardens** (Rte. 2, tel. 501/253–9244; open Nov.–Mar., daily 9–5, Apr.–Oct. 9–6; admission $6.90 adults, $4.25 children 12–17, $2.13 children 5–11, under 5 free). Thirty-three acres of hardwood trees, native plants, and lovingly landscaped floral displays weave around the centerpiece Blue Spring, the largest in northwest Arkansas and long revered by Native Americans for its healing properties (you can spy the faint tracings of petroglyphs in the surrounding limestone). The designers are still landscaping the gardens, which opened in 1993. They've done their best to preserve the natural feel, opting for discreet plantings rather than flamboyant banks of flowers. Wood and concrete walkways spill down the bluffs, and gazebos and benches are strategically placed at scenic lookouts. The odd quack of mergansers or trill of whippoorwills mingles with the singsong of distant calliopes and organs. Peak color season is April through October. An added attraction is the excellent multimedia presentation on Eureka Springs' history, held several times daily in the auditorium.

Eureka Springs' many other attractions range from **Dinosaur World** (Rte. 187, 8 mi west of Eureka Springs off Rte. 62, tel. 501/253–8113) to **Abundant Memories Heritage Village** (Rte. 23, 2.5 mi north of Eureka Springs, tel. 501/253–6764; open Apr. 15–Nov. 15, daily 9–6). The former displays more than 100 replicas of prehistoric beasts, including memorable movie creations such as King Kong. It's not Jurassic Park, but then who wants to be stalked by a T-Rex anyway? Abundant Memories is another example of the historical theme park prevalent throughout the Ozarks, whose residents are fortunately zealous in preserving their heritage crafts and traditional lifestyle. This one contains more than 25 buildings brimming with period antiques, tools, and other artifacts that re-create village life at various stages from Colonial 1776 to Victorian 1900. Crafts demonstrations are given at the many fine shops by artisans ranging from potters to woodcarvers to blacksmiths.

MOUNTAIN VIEW, ARKANSAS

Mountain View, Arkansas, is a friendly, laid-back Ozarks town, with white picket fences and neatly groomed lawns: It's a slice of classic, small-town America. This unassuming hamlet is deeply devoted to keeping Ozarks crafts and traditions alive. Its renowned Ozark Folk Center not only sponsors crafts demonstrations for the public but offers workshops and apprentice programs to perpetuate authentic folk arts.

To reach Mountain View by car follow I-65 south from Branson, turn east on I-62 then south onto Arkansas Route 14 into town. The trip will take from 45 minutes to an hour.

Courthouse Square is the town common, where musicians hold frequent concerts: There's often a community jam that anyone can join, and Saturday brings locals playing fiddles, banjos, dulcimers, and mandolins. Pickin' and grinnin' continues into the wee hours; just do what the locals do, and bring your lawn chair or a blanket.

One of the best-known attractions in town is the **Ozark Folk Center,** where Ozarks crafts and traditions are demonstrated. Daily (in season) you can smell the aroma of fresh apple pie and cherry preserves being prepared or listen in on a frenzied fiddling contest. Storytellers will invite you to listen to their histories. The so-called cabin crafts are well represented by top artisans, who weave, whittle, spin, and make baskets and candles. Evening concerts are held in a limestone-and-cedar auditorium with marvelous acoustics. Only pre–World War II music and lyrics are played, and no instruments are amplified. The sweet zing of fiddles, dulcimers, and Autoharps fills the night air as locals take to the stage for a fast and furious impromptu jig. All the people working within these log cabins and simple shacks do so on a volunteer basis and are pleased to answer any questions they can. Their wares are for sale. *Folk Center Rd., off Rtes. 5/9/14, tel. 501/269–3851. Admission free. Open May–Oct., daily 10–5.*

SPORTS

SPRINGFIELD

GOLF

There are four 18-hole golf courses among Springfield's surrounding hills and hollows: 7,001-yard, par 72 **Deer Lake Golf Club** (5544 W. Chestnut Expressway, tel. 417/865–2234); 6,043-yard, par 70 **Grandview Municipal Golf Course** (1825 E.

Norton Rd., tel. 417/833–9962); 5,900-yard, par 70 **Horton Smith Golf Course** (Scenic Ave., 1 block west of Rte. 13, tel. 417/881–9200); and 5,320-yard, par 69 **Siler's Shady Acres Golf Course** (6000 S. National Ave., tel. 417/881–9060).

SKIING
The **Snow Bluff Ski and Fun Area** (Rte. 1, Brighton, tel. 417/756–2201) has only eight trails and a vertical drop of less than 200 feet, but it's a place to ski moguls and have some fun. It's open winter weekends when the temperature is cold enough for snowmaking and daily in summer, when go-carts, bumper boats, a driving range, and miniature golf course are available.

TENNIS
Several city parks, including **Cooper** (Patterson Ave. and Pythian St.), **Meador** (Fremont Ave. and Sunset St.), and **Silver Springs** (Florence and Scott Sts.), have lighted asphalt tennis courts. Call the park board office (1923 N. Weller St., tel. 417/864–1049) for information.

EUREKA SPRINGS

BOATING
White River Canoe Rental (Riverview Resort, Rte. 2, tel. 501/253–8367) rents canoes for $25 per day, including lifejackets, paddles, and shuttles to the lazy river. They will also structure guided fishing trips in the area.

FISHING
Beaver Guide Service and Lodging (Rte. 2, tel. 501/253–5048) offers guided fishing tours on Beaver Lake.

HORSEBACK RIDING
Happy Trails (*see* Chapter 6, The Outdoors) leads horseback rides through the wilderness.

SPAS
You can get the works at the **Palace Bath House** (135 Spring St., tel. 501/253–8400), a spa in the turn-of-the-century hotel of the same name. Services include a mineral whirlpool bath in an old claw-foot tub and a eucalyptus steam treatment, clay mask, and half- or full-hour massage. The price for all that pampering is even more refreshing: $38 to $56.

MOUNTAIN VIEW

HIKING AND RAFTING
Mountain View is one of the gateways to the pristine **Buffalo National River** (Box

1173, Harrison, AR 72602, tel. 501/741–5443), the first river so designated, in 1972. Soaring bluffs, jagged hills and lush foliage are reflected in its emerald depths. The river's hairpin twists and turns yield stunning views of natural bridges, waterfalls, and canyons. This is the premier spot in the Ozarks for whitewater rafting and float trips, as well as camping and hiking. There's an abundance of flora and fauna: more than 50 species of fish and 1,500 kinds of plants, plus bobcats, beaver, bear, elk, mink, and white-tailed deer.

SHOPPING

SPRINGFIELD

Bass Pro Shops Outdoor World (*see* In and Around the Towns, Springfield, *above*) is large enough to be a genuine tourist attraction itself.

There's also **PFI Western Store** (2816 S. Ingram Rd., Rte. 65 and Battlefield Rd., tel. 417/862–1614 or 800/284–2191), a 30,000-square-foot, brick-and-stone structure designed like an old-fashioned railway station. It's most impressive after dark, when two bucking broncos are illuminated on the facade. The theme continues inside, where a giant hand-painted mural of six mustangs jockeys for attention with a 16-screen video wall playing the latest country music videos. The merchandise caters to the Marlboro Man in us all, from Stetson hats to barbecue sauce, leather boots to the latest in clothing designed for celebrities such as Moe Bandy and Tanya Tucker.

There's no shortage of shopping malls in Springfield: There are more than 30 enclosed shopping areas, of which **Battlefield Mall** (Battlefield Rd. and Glenstone Ave., tel. 417/883–7777) is the largest by far. Numbering among its 150-plus stores are such national retailers as Sears, J.C. Penney, and Montgomery Ward.

Galloway Village is a series of smartly remodeled turn-of-the-century shacks housing trendy boutiques, antiques shops, and home-furnishings stores selling everything from duck decoys to Adirondack chairs, weather vanes to water pitchers. Notable shops include **Coming Up Roses** (3545 S. Lone Pine St., tel. 417/883–7673), all of whose items are scented or decorated with roses; **Countryside Cottage** (4064 S. Lone Pine St., tel. 417/882–7997), specializing in regional crafts and collectibles from around America; and **the French Door Boutique** (4112 S. Lone Pine St., tel. 417/886–0423), a virtual hope chest of lace and linens imported from France and Italy. The French Door also carries a selection of gourmet foods and Crabtree & Evelyn bath products.

The mile-long **Commercial Street Historic District** is chockablock with antiques stores and flea markets where patient sifting can unearth a treasure. It's approximately 2 miles north of the historic downtown.

EUREKA SPRINGS

Thanks to a large artist population, eccentricity abounds in Eureka Springs. There are many shops selling a variety of crafts and original artworks, and every shop is at least slightly whimsical, if not downright bizarre or macabre. Don't be surprised if you find such oddities as miniature bears sculpted out of coal dust, stuffed rattlesnakes, steer-skull lamps, or leg-iron sculpture.

Among the top-notch galleries are: **Uptown** (123 Spring St., tel. 501/253–8313), specializing in pottery and jewelry, and **Quicksilver, the Nature Gallery** (99 Spring St., tel. 501/253–7679), with one-of-a-kind objects fashioned from lacquered wood, "perfume pens" coaxed from molten glass, and turquoise and hand-woven jewelry embellished with stones and trinkets. **Spring Wind Gallery** (84 Spring St., tel. 501/253–6257) counters with miniature dragons bursting from ceramic eggs and raku sculpture. **Satori Arts** (81 Spring St., tel. 501/253–9820) is another store trafficking in exotic fantasy art.

Looking for crafts? There's the local branch of the **Arkansas Craft Guild** (33 Spring St., tel. 501/253–7072), featuring woodcarvings, handmade dolls, and ceramics. Quilts lovers will want to visit **Cotton Patch Quilts** (1 Center St., tel. 501/253–9894) and **Sharon's Quilts** (2 Center St., tel. 501/253–7889). If it can be beaten or tanned, you'll find it at the **Nelson Leather Company** (Spring St., tel. 501/253–7162). Candle mavens will wax glorious at **Eureka Springs Candles** (Rte. 1, tel. 501/253–9136).

If you're buying gifts for the kids, try **Happy Things** (55 Spring St., tel. 501/253–8011), which is all dolled up with everything from Kewpies to Cabbage Patch Kids, plus model cars and other toys. **Clothing Etc.** (1 Spring St., tel. 501/253–9582) sells wearable art and accessories, such as hand-painted or appliquéd T-shirts, scarves, and dresses. Costume jewelry aficionados should head for **Now & Then Antiques** (95 Spring St., tel. 501/253–7747) for its assortment of pieces from Victorian times to the 1950s.

MOUNTAIN VIEW

If you're in the market for crafts, the **Ozark Folk Center,** where many craftspeople work and sell their wares, is *the* place to shop. Among the artists is Joe Bruhin, who creates superlative stoneware, including striking 2-foot-high urns. His wife, Terri, is a weaver who fashions everything from stylish women's clothing to traditional lace-weave table linens.

Another such outlet is the **Arkansas Craft Guild** (2 mi north of town on Rtes. 5/9/14, tel. 501/269–3897). More than 300 artists, all of whom have met the guild's exacting standards for membership (their eligibility is reviewed every five years), offer their wares through this first-class store.

The **Ozark Artisans Mall** (Main St., tel. 501/269–4774) showcases the work of 80 local craftspeople, including woodcarvers, silversmiths and potters.

If the music inspires you, stop by **McSpadden's Dulcimer Shop** (Sylamore Rd., tel. 501/269–4313), where the workers will take a break to give you a quick lesson. Here you'll also find superb leatherwork, basketry, and dolls.

DINING AND LODGING

DINING

Both Springfield and Eureka Springs offer a range of eateries from upscale to down home, but Mountain View's selection is somewhat limited. Dress is invariably casual but neat wherever you go, and reservations (except where noted below) are rarely necessary. Prices quoted are for an average three-course meal, excluding drinks, tax, and service.

SPRINGFIELD

Carriage House Pub and Eatery. Buggies and surreys adorn the front lawn of this whimsically painted Victorian house, whose men's-clublike interior includes an eye-popping collection of steins and mugs (many for sale). This turn-of-the-century London-style pub offers an extensive selection of international beers, ales, porters, and stouts. The truly parched can opt for one of three gargantuan sizes: a yard, half-yard, and boot. The food is standard pub grub elevated to an art form: mouthwatering prime rib, toasted ravioli, and hearty soups, salads, and sandwiches. The sausage supreme, garnished with a heaping helping of delectable German potato salad, is one of the house specialties. For dessert try the excellent rocky-road mousse cake. *820 E. Walnut St., tel. 417/862–7783. D, MC, V. $10–$20.*

Clary's American Grill. This is as civilized as dining out gets in the Ozarks, with soft jazz playing in the background and a subdued clubby decor favoring tartans and mahogany. The town's movers and shakers dine here, presenting a handsome picture as they chat discreetly in booths or at the old-fashioned bar. Waiters politely murmur, "Good choice," no matter what you select. Although good, the food can't quite match the near-perfect ambience. The ambitious menu has been influenced by too many cuisines. Among the better appetizers are pepper-cheese ravioli with tomato jalapeño relish, and Chinese gold coin crab cakes (the crab meat delicately wrapped in fried wonton skins resembles gold coins) marinated with cilantro, ginger, and rice vinegar. Recommended main courses include tilapia swimming in a banana-citrus sauce with a touch of cinnamon and clove; roasted king salmon in almond-and-black-pepper crust and cabernet butter; grilled beef medallions with chipotle and browned garlic butter; and sherry-vinegar chicken served over wild-rice pancakes. Avoid the bland, low-fat entrées, unless you want to justify the sinful chocolate intemperance or lemon-buttermilk pie topped with port-marinated strawberries. The wine list is comprehensive and fairly priced, with several daily specials by the glass. *3014-A E. Sunshine St., tel. 417/886–1940. Reservations advised. AE, MC, V. $20–$30.*

Leong's Tea House. This restaurant has achieved minor fame as the place where cashew chicken was first created, during the early 1960s. Although nearly every Chinese restaurant in town claims its own "authentic" recipe or the "tastiest" variation, owner David Leong admits that his recipe isn't Cantonese at all but as American as apple pie. Noting that fried chicken was a favorite in Springfield, Leong adapted one of his chicken dishes to include breading and oyster sauce, and cashew chicken was born. Unofficial surveys claim that today Springfield's 40-plus Chinese eateries serve more than 8,000 orders daily. Other authentic Cantonese specialties include butterfly shrimp and pepper steak. The dimly lit restaurant eschews most of the usual ersatz-Oriental decorative touches, such as golden lions and paper lanterns, favoring booths in dark colors. *1036 W. Sunshine St., tel. 417/869–4444. AE, MC, V. Closed Sun. $10–$20.*

EUREKA SPRINGS

Crystal Dining Room in the Crescent Hotel. Details within this splendid dining room include baroque ceilings, six teardrop-crystal chandeliers, mahogany moldings, and crisp maroon and white napery. The chef doesn't try to match the sumptuous decor but opts for solid home-cooking. Trout prepared several ways is a house specialty, and steaks and the mountain fried chicken are menu stalwarts. For dessert, don't pass up pecan-caramel cheesecake with chocolate-cookie crust. It is sublime: not too sweet but slightly bitter, lightly charred, and oh so rich. *75 Prospect St., tel. 501/253–9766. AE, MC, V. $15–$20.*

Ermilio's. This genuine Italian restaurant housed in a charming converted Edwardian is an ideal place to dine if you're looking for a place to spend that special evening. The lovely ocher and seafoam-green interior retains the original brickwork and hardwood floors. Heavy floral curtains, hanging plants and bulbs of garlic, displays of old china, and brass pots complete the picture of a Tuscan cottage. The restaurant is named for owner-chef Paul Wilson's grandfather, a Neapolitan immigrant who would undoubtedly appreciate Paul's zesty sauces and unabashed peasant cooking. You have your pick of six pastas and nine sauces (including among others pesto, Gorgonzola, garlic and oil, primavera, Alfredo, and tomato basil). Dinner specials include perfectly grilled snapper or tangy, marinated filet mignon. Portions are ample. *26 White St., tel. 501/253–8806. MC, V. Closed Thurs., Sun. lunch. $15–$20.*

Ol Bo's. Residents have long debated about which barbecue house is the best in town. Some rival restaurants may offer equally good eats, but Ol Bo's offers an added attraction: the owner's wacky sense of humor. Don't make the mistake of reading the hilarious menu while you eat: "No one who was sober would hire me. The only thing I could do was barbecue meat that most folks seemed to like, especially free-loadin' relatives," writes Bo. Indeed, the smoky, tender meat, served with enormous sides of barbecue beans, coleslaw, corn on the cob, and chips, makes a great meal. The decor leaves a lot to be desired (you might think the sauce stains are part of the tablecoth design), but the mirrors and old photos make this a homey, cozy place after all. *Rte. 62E, tel. 501/253–5797. AE, MC, V. $10–$15.*

The Plaza. This is the choice of many locals and tourists who are celebrating a special occasion or having a big night out. The service is efficient, meals are expertly prepared, and the wine list is impressive. In fact, *Wine Spectator* annually cites the list as one of America's best. You might start your meal with escargots *vol au vent* (in puff pastry) in sauternes, sauce then segue into salmon in lemon-dill sauce or veal tenderloin with tarragon, bing cherries, and Vermont cream. In pleasant weather ask to sit on the balcony overlooking Main Street. *55 Main St., tel. 501/253–8866. AE, D, DC, MC, V. $25–$30.*

Rogue's Manor. This intimate eatery has wrested the "most sophisticated restaurant" title from the Plaza (*see above*). The exquisite, slightly fussy decor, designed by amiable co-owner Smith Treuer, includes lace curtains, dried floral arrangements, flowery wallpaper, gas lamps, and throw rugs: the feeling is that of a gentleman's digs at Oxford during the 1890s. Chef Charles Clark creates sumptuous Pacific Northwest cuisine, adding subtle Asian or sunny Provençal twists. Greek chicken is sautéed in olive oil, white wine, and garlic with onions, olives, and capers, rouged with tomatoes, and topped with feta; bonsai chicken is accentuated with ginger and red bell pepper, then tossed in a lip-smacking peanut sauce. Meat-and-potatoes types might consider the messy, delicious ribs and robust *cioppino* (a thick, sultry fisherman's stew with halibut, salmon, shrimp, and other shellfish). For brunch mavens there's an overgrown patio where you can savor specialties such as hangtown fry (oysters sautéed in white wine and curry and finished with scrambled eggs and Parmesan) or light, fluffy potato cakes that get their zest from white pepper, horseradish, and sour cream. Weekend dinners and Sunday brunch are enhanced by live acoustic music. *124 Spring St., tel. 501/253–4911. D, MC, V. $20–$30.*

MOUNTAIN VIEW

Hearthstone Bakery. This little bakery on the ground floor of the Wildflower Inn is known for its yummy muffins and pastries, as well as unusual salads and soups (try the cream of peanut butter). *Courthouse Sq., tel. 501/269–3297. No credit cards. No dinner. $5–$10.*

LODGING

The region offers a range of properties, from national hotel and motel chains to impeccably restored Victorian B&Bs. Prices quoted reflect the range of available accommodations at each property, from standard double rooms to suites, during high season (May–October). Expect air-conditioning and private bath at listed lodgings, unless otherwise noted. Phones and cable TVs are standard in hotels and motels but not in B&Bs unless otherwise noted.

SPRINGFIELD

Mansion at Elfindale. This glorious, turreted 1892 stone building is decorated in Victorian style, with floral patterns, lace curtains, and polished hardwood floors. Each sunny, spacious room is individually, tastefully adorned. Some rooms have a veranda, others a parlor; your bed might be brass, wicker, or canopied. Although the interior decor ranges from Ralph Lauren hunting-lodge to art-deco extravaganza, almost all rooms have pressed-tin ceilings, bay windows, and the original brick-and-porcelain (nonworking) fireplaces and footed tubs. All have private bath. Complimentary breakfast is served in an airy public room. *1701 S. Fort St., tel. 417/831–5400 or 800/443–0237. 13 suites. Facilities: complimentary breakfast, gift shop. AE, D, DC, MC, V. $70–$125.*

Radisson Inn. This reliable chain property offers large, comfortable rooms with faux-antique furnishings and a dark blue, jade, and burgundy color scheme. It's convenient to Battlefield Mall, Galloway Village, and Bass Pro. Children under 18 stay free in their parents' room. *3333 S. Glenstone Blvd., tel. 417/883–6550, fax 417/883–5720. 199 rooms. Facilities: restaurant, outdoor pool, airport shuttle. AE, D, DC, MC, V. $79–$85.*

Walnut Street Inn. Both the main house and the carriage house at this salmon-and-peach, 1894 Victorian bed-and-breakfast are as delightful inside as out. The shady porch with ivy-swathed Corinthian columns and a swing gives guests a place to commune after a busy day of sightseeing and shopping. Inside is the cozy sitting room, with a grand piano from 1864 that sets a sophisticated tone. Rooms in the carriage house are peaceful: Ask for the Robertson Room (named for the Springfield Symphony's founder and original conductor), with musical instruments hanging from the stucco walls, and exposed brick and rough-hewn beams; the Danzero Room, filled with steamer trunks, maps, and globes and boasting a Jacuzzi and four-poster bed; or the Maschino Room, with its skylight and handmade quilts. In the main house, standouts include the Benton Room, with numerous skylights and works by famed artist Thomas Hart Benton, and the Carver Room, with a hand-painted library wall, Jacuzzi, and fireplace. All units have a phone and private bath and are beautifully appointed with period antiques; some have TVs, fireplaces, mini-refrigerators, coffeemakers, and private patios. The sumptuous breakfasts might feature almond-cream French toast or black-walnut-and-raspberry muffins. The inn is convenient to the downtown attractions and arts scene. *900 E. Walnut St., tel.*

417/864–6346 or 800/593-6346, fax 417/864-6184. 14 units. AE, D, DC, MC, V. $80–$150.

EUREKA SPRINGS

Although the downtown has some chain hotels, Eureka Springs is famous for its ornate gingerbread houses that have been converted into charming, well-run B&Bs. Ambience and decor run the gamut from plush Victorian to posh contemporary.

Comfort Inn. A notch above its more functional brethren, this Comfort Inn replicates a grand, whitewashed southern mansion; the interior is decorated in faux-Victorian style, with reproduction cherry furnishings and pre-Raphaelite prints, all in subdued forest green and dusky rose. Ask for a Jacuzzi suite or a room that opens onto the tangled hollow in back. *Rte. 6, Box 7, Eureka Springs, AR 72632, tel. 501/253–5241 or 800/828–0109. 51 units. Facilities: restaurant, outdoor pool, gift shop. AE, D, DC, MC, V. $59–$89.*

Grand Central Hotel. One of five lovingly restored, turn-of-the-century hotels (the others are the Palace, Basin Park, Crescent, and New Orleans), the 1883 Grand Central in Eureka Springs lavishly re-creates the grandeur and graciousness of a bygone era, with original pine wainscoting and gorgeous period antiques liberally strewn throughout the public rooms and guest accommodations. All 14 units are suites, with cable TV, full kitchen, and full bath with whirlpool tub. The rooms are splendiferous, indeed, all decorated in different rich colors from magenta to jade. *37 N. Main St., Eureka Springs, AR 72632, tel. 501/253–6756 or 800/344–6050. 14 suites. Facilities: shops, free off-street parking. AE, D, MC, V. $95–$155.*

Heartstone Inn. You'll recognize this lovely, two-story, gabled Victorian inn by the white picket fence and inviting pink-and-cobalt-blue patio spilling over with Boston ferns and potted geraniums. Owners Bill and Iris Simantel are as warm and hospitable as the inn's facade, and both have brought tasteful touches to the inn. Most notable is Iris's superlative collection of antique English pottery, especially her handsome, royal blue–glazed Torquay pots and humorous Toby mugs that adorn the parlor (which doubles as her informal gallery) and sunny breakfast room. There are guest rooms in the main house and the annex, and two fully equipped cottages recall 19th-century vacation homes. All quarters feature English country antiques, including brass or four-poster beds; many have rocking chairs and intricate tracery on the walls. Each room is individually decorated. There's the Devon Wildflower Room, with a large bay window overlooking the garden and featuring framed, pressed flowers and delicate hues of teal, pink, and ecru. The English Garden Suite looks like a conservatory, replete with neoclassical garden statuary, floral wallpaper, plush forest-green carpeting, and a sparkling white trellis entwined with ivy. The inn is not recommended for children under 12. *35 Kings Hwy., Eureka Springs, AR 72632, tel. 501/253–8916 or 800/323–8534. 8 doubles, 2 suites, 1 2-bedroom cottage, 1 1-bedroom cottage. Facilities: complimentary breakfast, games room, massage therapy, free off-street parking. AE, DC, MC, V. Closed late Dec.–Jan. $80–$120.*

Rock Cottage Gardens. These quaint, flesh-tone rock cottages with shingled, smoky-blue roofs opened during the early 1930s as the first motor court in downtown Eureka Springs. The native flint and limestone used in construction is filigreed with fossils. Guests like to lounge about the tranquil sycamore bower and extended gardens. The property had fallen into sad disrepair by the time the present innkeepers, Steve Roberson and Lamont Richey, arrived, in 1992. They overhauled the cottages, retaining only the unusual exteriors. The five accommodations have stained-glass windows and vaulted ceilings and black-tile and/or gray-marble baths with jets. Furnishings are an eclectic mix of primarily English country and French provincial antiques, and color schemes and trimmings vary widely, depending on the theme of the room. Natural crystals hang in the Crystal Cottage, while the Amethyst Cottage has mauve tones, amethyst glassware, and a 75-pound piece of hand-cut Brazilian amethyst in a shadow box. All rooms have cable TV, coffeemaker, soft-drink minibar, and air-conditioning, as well as Egyptian cotton linens. Breakfast is a suitably formal affair: three gourmet courses served on crystal and bone china. *10 Eugenia St., Eureka Springs, AR 72632, tel. 501/253–8659 or 800/624–6646. 5 cottages. Facilities: complimentary breakfast, free off-street parking. D, MC, V. $95.*

MOUNTAIN VIEW

Wildflower Inn. Opened in 1907 as the Commercial Hotel, this two-story, teal-and-burgundy hostelry was saved from demolition in 1982 by innkeepers Todd and Andrea Budy. They describe the rooms as "unpretentious: not a euphemism for ugly, just not cutesy." Each air-conditioned unit is named for a wildflower and painted to match the description. Dogwood, for example, is a delicate pink, Jonquil is bright yellow, and Columbine is a soothing siena. They're furnished plainly in old-fashioned Ozarks style, most with the original handcrafted dressers and iron bedsteads, along with hand-sewn curtains and dust ruffles and modern, solid-color quilts. Some units feature what's called an Ozarks closet—embellished 2½-foot, wrought-iron rods forged into hanger units by local blacksmiths. There is no TV but usually some sort of live entertainment: People rock on the wraparound porch listening to the musicians who stop by almost every afternoon and evening. The Hearthstone Bakery (*see* Dining, *above*) provides Continental breakfast daily. *Courthouse Sq., Box 72, Mountain View, AR 72560, tel. 501/269–4383 or 800/591–4879. 4 rooms (2 with shared bath), 3 suites (1 with kitchenette). Facilities: complimentary Continental breakfast, bakery, book store. D, MC, V. Closed Jan., Feb. $41–$70.*

NIGHTLIFE

SPRINGFIELD

Because it is a college town, Springfield has an active, varied nightlife that attracts some visitors from Branson who are looking for a slightly wilder evening than they'd find in a theater on the Strip. Check local papers for listings and special events.

COMEDY
Check out the local Robin Williams and Roseanne wannabes at the **Funny Bone Comedy Nite Club** (3050 N. Kentwood Ave., tel. 417/833–2732).

MUSIC
Springfield has developed a thriving reputation in the music world for up-and-coming blues bands and underground rockers. The downtown area swings with several small, smoky clubs offering brews, burgers, and live entertainment. Among the happening spots for blues and rock are the **Antler** (319 E. Walnut St., tel. 417/862–4742), **Jamaica's** (2100 S. Pythian St., tel. 417/865–8440), and **McSalty's** (1550 E. Battlefield Rd., tel. 417/883–4324). **Midnight Rodeo** (3303 S. Campbell Ave., tel. 417/882–0309) and the **Top Tail** (631 S. Glenstone Blvd., tel. 417/869–9116) are the spots to hear country-and-western bands. For jazz and folk, stop at the **Bar Next Door** (307 South Ave., tel. 417/831–5533).

THEATERS
Touring Broadway shows, the respected Springfield Ballet, and the Springfield Symphony pack in crowds at the 2,250-seat **Juanita K. Hammons Center for the Performing Arts** (Southwest Missouri State University campus, 525 John Q. Hammons Pkwy., tel. 417/836–6776). There is also an excellent community troupe, the Little Theater, in the grand 1909 **Art Nouveau Landers Theater** (311 E. Walnut St., tel. 417/869–1334). The building is listed on the National Register of Historic Places; the elaborate Tiffany lighting fixtures are an exhibit in themselves. Among the performers who got their start here are actresses Kathleen Turner and Tess Harper. Past performances have included everything from traditional Broadway hits such as *Deathtrap* and *Guys and Dolls* to more experimental works in the intimate upstairs Studio Theater, including Stephen Sondheim's *Assassins* and John Patrick Shanley's *Savage in Limbo*.

EUREKA SPRINGS

MUSIC
Several clubs and restaurants present live acts, usually on weekends. **Rogue's Manor** (124 Spring St., tel. 501/253–4911) has live music Thursday–Saturday during dinner and

Sunday during brunch. **Fat Tuesday's** (63 Spring St., tel. 502/253–8264) is a great place to hear cool jazz and Delta blues. **Center Street** (37 Spring St., tel. 501/253–8102) has a varied entertainment menu of jazz, blues, rock, and reggae. **Sebastians'**, downstairs at the Four Runners Inn (Rte. 62, tel. 501/253–6000), offers line dancing to the music of a live country band weekend nights. The **Old Town Pub** (2 Main St., tel. 501/253–7147), a classic local hangout, keeps an open mike onstage for the courageous every evening.

VARIETY

The **Passion Play** (*see* In and Around the Towns, *above*) is the hottest ticket in town during summer.

Eureka Springs also offers family entertainment similar to the hillbilly humor of Branson's Presleys and Baldknobbers. The **Swanee River Boys Country Revue** (Rte. 62E, tel. 501/253–6011) is a dynamic mix of country music and cornball humor. Other such performances include **Ozark Mountain Hoedown** (Rte. 1, tel. 501/253–7725), the **Pine Mountain Jamboree** (Rte. 62E, tel. 501/253–9156), the **Indian Orphan Family,** featured at the Eureka Springs Music Theater (Rte. 23, tel. 501/253–5111), and the **Beyond Elvis Show** at the Aaron Patrick Theater (Rte. 62E, tel. 501/253–8832).

MOUNTAIN VIEW

MUSIC

There are informal musicales in Courthouse Square nearly every evening, weather permitting, and music shows Monday–Saturday at the Ozark Folk Center (*see* In and Around the Towns, *above*).

Legendary folk balladeer Jimmy Driftwood plays at the **Jimmy Driftwood Barn** (2 mi north of town on Rte. 5/9/14, tel. 501/269–8042), built for him by fans who are members of the Rackensack Folklore Society, a local group dedicated to preserving traditional hill music. Free Friday- and Sunday-evening concerts are performed year-round.

Fast-paced country revues with the usual dose of hillbilly antics are performed at the **Letherwoods Music Theater** (Rte. 382, tel. 501/269–2100), **White River Hoedown** (Rte. 5/9/14, tel. 501/269–4161), and **Catfish House and Mountain Music Family Dinner Theater** (Rte. 14, tel. 501/269–3820).

OTHER FUN PLACES TO GO

BERRYVILLE

Like many small Ozarks towns, Berryville seems frozen in the early 1950s. The lovely central square looks like the set of the movie *Back to the Future*, with its shade trees, benches, and Edwardian-style street lamps. For the most part, however, strolling through Berryville is a sobering experience, as several shops have been boarded up, and the charming turn-of-the-century brick buildings are sadly dilapidated. But the old-fashioned five-and-dime is still open, as are a blacksmith's shop and Fulton's drugstore (with a classic, 1930s soda fountain). Berryville is slowly coming back to life, having hopped on the historical bandwagon that helped revive Branson and Eureka Springs.

There's a living-history presentation in the **Heritage Center Museum** (1880 Courthouse Sq., tel. 501/423–6312; admission $2 adults, $1 children under 12; open daily 9–5), housed in the 1881 redbrick Carroll County Courthouse. Displays include a pioneer schoolroom, barbershop, and moonshine still. The center maintains **Pioneer Park,** two blocks west, which features a cluster of furnished, vintage log cabins that can be toured, including the original jailhouse.

The **Saunders Memorial Museum** (113–115 Harrison St., tel. 501/423–2563; admission $2 adults, $1 children under 12; open mid-Mar.–Oct., daily 9–5) was named for C. Burton Saunders, a mining and real estate magnate whose colorful career included a stint as a crack marksman in Buffalo Bill's Wild West Show. The museum's eclectic holdings include his wife's extensive wardrobe, circa 1910; a tent extravagantly embroidered with gold thread by a sheik's harem of more than 200 wives; and Native American artifacts including Sitting Bull's battle jacket and Geronimo's scalp belt. But the main attraction is Saunders's first-class collection of firearms, including Pancho Villa's elaborately embellished Colt 45 (inlaid with gold and jewels) and guns twirled by Jesse James, Billy the Kid, Belle Starr, Cole Younger, Annie Oakley, Wild Bill Hickok, Sam Houston, and Buffalo Bill. A visit to this museum will help you understand why Berryville calls itself the place "Where the Old South Meets the Old West."

HOLLISTER

Branson isn't the only town in the area capitalizing on its lakeside location. Directly across Lake Taneycomo from downtown Branson (off Rte. 65 or 65B) is Hollister, a charming hamlet light years from its bustling neighbor. At the turn of the century, general-store owner Rueben Kirkham applied for permission to open a post office in the area, and upon his appointment as postmaster in 1904 he named the settlement

Hollister, after the California birthplace of his daughter. Shortly thereafter, the arrival of the new White River Railway spurred tremendous growth, and for a time Hollister was the center of tourism in the area. Developers W.H. Johnson and Professor J.W. Blankenship built a group of Tudor-style buildings to attract visitors. The timber-and-stucco structures, constructed between 1906 and 1912, are now on the National Register of Historic Places; the original Front Street has been renamed Downing Street to give it an authentically British air.

ROCKAWAY BEACH

Sleepy Rockaway Beach was the first resort community built beside Lake Taneycomo. During its 1920s heyday, the **dance pavilion** by the dock attracted big bands from Kansas City and St. Louis. Today it houses a vast, cluttered flea market daily. The restaurants and shops along Main Street overlook an appealing waterfront park.

Shoji Tabuchi,
violinist

Jordan Simon: Tell me how you got started studying music.

Shoji Tabuchi: Well, when I was seven I began studying in Osaka under the Suzuki Method. [Later,] Mr. Roy Acuff and the Smoky Mountain Boys came to Japan, and I went to see them close up. I went out of curiosity, but I just fell in love with the music. It was because of this one song Howdy Forrester was playing, called "Listen to the Mockingbird." I never expected the violin to do that type of stuff. I just fell in love listening to it.

JS: Had you studied only classical up to that point?

ST: Oh, yes.

JS: And you decided to make a 180-degree change?

ST: I sure did. Of course, in the show I do classical. I like all kinds of music. I don't limit myself, but I love to play country.

JS: You met Mr. Acuff, and he encouraged you, right?

ST: Yes, he sure did. I came here in 1967 and 1968 and met up with Mr. Acuff in the Kansas City Auditorium. He invited me to open and said, "I'll put you on the Grand Ole Opry." I had the opportunity to play at the old Opry, Ryman Auditorium, and the new one.

That was the beginning. In 1970 I was lucky enough to hook up with David Houston, [playing in] his band from 1970 to 1975. Then I went on my own, and in 1981 I found Branson.

JS: How did you find Branson?

ST: I used to do bookings in Texas, in a place called the Grapevine Opry. The owner of the Grapevine Opry opened up a place here in Branson [called the] Starlite Theater, and I was there for four years. Before then I'd never heard of Branson, but I decided to come see what would happen. It was 1981, and there was already traffic on [Route] 76. There were all these bad theaters at that time, but I fell in love with the area. I'm a big fisherman. I love fishing. Table Rock Lake, Bull Shoals, Taneycomo are fishermen's paradise. The scenery was beautiful, and I just fell in love with the town. It's a small town, very friendly town, and I decided to take a job. I worked the Starlite Theater for four years then moved to the Country Music Theater, where I worked for another three years. Then I opened up a place that used to be an old museum, and we converted it to an auditorium. It's the Ozark Theater right now. I was there a year, then sold the lease to Mel Tillis and built this. This is our fifth year.

JS: Was it scary at first, building your own theater?

ST: Ohhh, yeah, it was scary. Oh boy, I'll tell you. We invested everything to do this. We were the first ones to do it way off [Route] 76. We went to a couple of banks that refused us because we were off the Strip. You had to be on the Strip. But I had some gut feeling.

JS: Where did the idea for the bathrooms come from?

ST: My wife knows this lady named Mona Stafford, an interior designer. She came up with the idea to do something for the ladies. I wasn't too happy about that: I thought, why spend that kind of money on bathrooms? I want people to go in there and get out as quickly as possible so they can go to the concession and gift shop. But it worked out that that was the best thing we did. We got more coverage from that!

JS: So you did the women's bathroom first?

ST: Then the men started saying, "What happened to ours?" At first I wanted to put a pond in there, you know, so I could fish. (Laughs.) But they didn't go for it. They said it was enough with the pool table.

JS: How has Branson changed in the thirteen years you've been here?

ST: There's been steady growth. Let's see . . . It really started to expand in about 1985. People from Nashville started coming, then pop artists like Andy Williams came, and that really got the momentum going. This town is built on word of mouth—you know, people come here, enjoy it, and they tell somebody else about it.

JS: Do you worry that Branson may overdevelop?

ST: Well, any town that [experiences] big growth will suffer negative results, like an increased crime rate or traffic jams. We're doing something about it by improving the roads. But this is still a small, small town, with a very friendly community.

JS: Nowhere else are performers so accessible to the audience. Do you enjoy mingling with your fans?

ST: I don't mind that at all. People come up to talk to me in restaurants, I go out to talk to the audience after the shows. It's really the only town where that happens.

JS: Do you ever worry about being so exposed?

ST: I don't worry. There are no drive-by shootings on [Route] 76.

JS: How much do you change your show every year?

ST: We do something different every year. Some songs I have to keep in, like "Orange Blossom Special." If you don't do it, somebody will complain. My wife, Dorothy, is the creative one, though, so she puts everything together. We have a group of very talented people: technicians, production crew, the best technical advisers. We get top designers from New York, and sets are built in New Jersey and shipped here. Our costume designer does "Murphy Brown" and our lighting designer did the Olympics in Barcelona. Everyone's top-notch. And our equipment is all the newest technology. We try to keep up. Everyone here does.

JS: Does Dorothy try to put one new, spectacular element in each show?

ST: Oh, there's always something.

JS: What was new this year?

ST: We cut a hole in the stage, and all the dancers came up through the floor. Last year we added laser lighting to the show. We were the first in Branson.

JS: Where do you see yourself going in the next few years?

ST: I will stay here, because I love it, and we have a house here. I'd like to be a household name. I've come this far without any hit records. Branson did it.

JS: So you feel you owe something to the town?

ST: Well, to the people who come here and the town folks, too. Because of the Branson audience,

when we do road shows we've broken two or three auditorium records—without hit records. That's something.

JS: Now that Mel Tillis is building his new recording studio, do you think Branson might become a recording center, too?

ST: I think that's a big possibility. There's a need for that here, for a great recording facility, TV facility, a soundstage . . .

JS: Do you have a desire to return to Japan, especially now that they've developed a taste for country music there?

ST: My goal is to take this whole production over there and do a grand homecoming, but that would take a major sponsor. Another thing I'd like to try out is Atlantic City or Vegas.

JS: If Vegas or Broadway or Atlantic City called and said, "Shoji, we'd like you to come, but it has to be for an open-ended run," would you do it, even if it meant leaving here for a while?

ST: Well, I don't think I'm gonna leave here. But for a certain time period, I would probably arrange that. I'd like to do that.

JS: Doing the show day in, day out, is it difficult maintaining the same enthusiasm and energy level?

ST: I have no trouble maintaining my energy level. I get psyched up on stage. Every night, every show's a challenge, different, because the people are different. Sometimes they come in a little tired, a little down, some nights they're revved up and ready to go, like there's a full moon. Every performance is different, which I like. It's nothing like playing in a nightclub, where you see the same drunk every night. I've done that. And every night, too, the musicians are in a different mood—I'm in a different mood—so it keeps things lively.

JS: Do you ever ad-lib, to keep on your toes or just for fun?

ST: Oh sure, during the Dixieland or Big Band segments we ad-lib. That's why I love to do that kind of music. It's improvisational, do your thing.

JS: Have audiences become more sophisticated since you first came here?

ST: I think so. At first people said, "Hey, that's not country." But now they love it. I have noticed that everyone has his own favorite music, but you can enjoy other music. You know, people say, "I love country music," but it can be presented in such a way that they will like other styles.

JS: Was there ever a time when people said, "Oh, you can't do that—you're Japanese"?

ST: That's why we started doing the rap music in the show. People go, "Oh no, oh gosh," but the way we do it is funny, acceptable.

The Outdoors

6

You could easily spend your entire Branson vacation indoors, in theaters, shops, and restaurants, but outdoors is where you'll find the other half of the fun. The Branson/Lakes region, comprising Lake Taneycomo, Table Rock Lake, and Bull Shoals Lake, attracted sportspeople and nature lovers long before the stars spread their glitter down Route 76. The area's popularity goes back to the turn of the century, when a music show meant an informal fiddle fest on a neighbor's front porch. Then there are the theme parks—Silver Dollar City, Shepherd of the Hills, Mutton Hollow—which take full advantage of their bucolic setting and offer rides, food, and entertainment. (*See* Chapter 4, Other Fun Things to Do in and Around Branson.)

OUTDOORS

These mega-lakes, formed by a series of dams impounding the White and James rivers, offer water sports from canoeing to jet skiing, as well as some of the finest bass and trout fishing in the country. The lakes are meticulously maintained by the U.S. Army Corps of Engineers, and the splendor of the surrounding multicolored bluffs and virgin forest has been well preserved.

BOATING AND OTHER WATER SPORTS

The lakes have been called "the last frontier" for boaters, in part because of their past reputation for lax regulations and rowdy partying. But they are strictly supervised by the Missouri State Water Patrol. While, technically, there are no speed limits, the Patrol recommends that boaters use common sense and gauge the surroundings, operating at speeds suitable for the traffic and prevailing weather conditions. Officials have no compunction about stopping and issuing warnings to any boater that seems out of control. In addition, they advise that all boaters be aware of their safety equipment, keeping PFDs and life jackets readily accessible. Weak swimmers should wear life preservers, jackets, vests or other flotation devices at all times. State law mandates that exhaust noise should not exceed 86 decibels. All rental boats' engines are muffled to conform to regulations. If you're near the dams them-

960
HALL
PHOTO
CO.

TOM YOCUM - OWNER
CAMP YOCUM - GALENA

Tom Yocum with his catch at Camp Yocum, circa 1912; Hall Photo, courtesy of Rosa House, Branson.

selves and hear the warning horn signalling the opening of the dam, leave the area immediately. You have one to five minutes before the water level rises. Boaters downstream should prepare to adjust for new currents.

Table Rock offers the most activities, including scuba diving and sailing. Wave runners, Jet Skis, and water skis are all available for rent at several marinas. Some Bull Shoals marinas also rent jets and water skis, but they're less in demand, as most people prefer to enjoy the tranquil setting. Taneycomo is limited to pontoons, bass boats, and fishing boats.

Swimming is also popular. While there are several beaches and coves, especially on Table Rock and Bull Shoals, these should not be confused for classic Caribbean crescents. They are made of predominantly small gravel, not sand, and while buoy markers demarcate a safe swimming zone, there are no lifeguards.

For information on access points, launches, and marinas, *see* "Boating," under each lake heading, *below.*

FISHING

All anglers must purchase either a three-day ($8), 14-day ($15), annual nonresident ($25), or annual resident ($8) fishing permit, available at any bait shop. Trout fishermen must also buy a Missouri Trout Stamp, available at bait shops for $6. The Branson/Lakes Area Chamber of Commerce (tel. 417/334–4136) operates a 24-Hour Fishing Hotline (tel. 417/334–6537) for up-to-the-minute information about weather temperatures, lake levels, best bait, and so forth.

✳ LAKE TANEYCOMO

Lake Taneycomo, 22 miles long, looks and feels less like a lake than like a lazy river snaking its way past downtown Branson. The warm-water lake was formed by the Powersite Dam in 1913, and at the time it teemed with bass and crappie. But when Table Rock Dam was constructed, in 1959, it drew water to generate electricity for powering the area from the chilly depths of 110 feet; the resulting runoff into Taneycomo sent its temperatures plummeting to the low 50s. The frigid waters were no longer an ideal habitat for bass, or, for that matter, swimmers and waterskiers. Taneycomo became a haven for trout (more than 800,000 are stocked annually by the Shepherd of the Hills Trout Hatchery), especially browns and rainbows, who thrive here. Try these lake-record trout catches on for size: a

15-pound, 6-ounce rainbow caught in August 1971, and a bulging, 23-pound, 4-ounce brown beaut, caught in February 1991. It's no wonder that almost year-round patient anglers perch on sandbars and rocks in the middle of the lake or along the water's edge, enveloped by a ghostly morning mist.

BOATING

LAUNCHES AND MARINAS. Public access points are the downtown **Branson Public Dock** (North Beach Park, Lake St., tel. 417/335–3085), the **Rockaway Beach Park and Dock** (Beach St., tel. 417/561–4280), and the **Empire District Boat Ramp and Dock** (Rte. Y, Forsyth, near Powersite Dam, tel. 417/546–2741).

The following marinas offer boat rentals, pontoons, and bait and tackle: **Capps Boat Dock** (Rockaway Beach, tel. 417/561–5222), **Fish Camp Company** (Rockaway Beach, tel. 417/561–4213), **J.B.'s Boat Dock** (Rockaway Beach, tel. 417/561–4115), and **Main Street Marina** (Lake Front, Branson, tel. 417/334–2263). Pontoon rentals run $70–$90 per day, fishing boats $30–$40 per day.

FISHING

Many of the casual, rustic resorts along the upper part of the lake cater to fly fishermen, who cluster near Table Rock Dam. This is the place for the best bites, but stay alert and listen for the warning horn that signals the opening of the dam. As soon as you hear the horn, run to the bank immediately to get out of the way of the rushing water.

There's also fine fishing along the bank, just below the hatchery, where a modern, elevated walkway follows the perimeter of the lake.

About a mile downstream from Table Rock Dam, where the lake widens and imposing bluffs jut into the water, it's nearly impossible for anglers to wade along the edge. Boat fishing predominates from here all the way to downtown Branson. In the jagged inlets and shallow, crystalline waters of Upper Taneycomo hundreds of thousands of fish school and dart about. These coves, especially around Point Lookout, are a favorite place for them to congregate: Many mammoth record-breakers have been caught here in the shadow of the majestic oaks lining the water.

Lower Taneycomo, the section downstream from Branson and accessible from the towns of Forsyth and

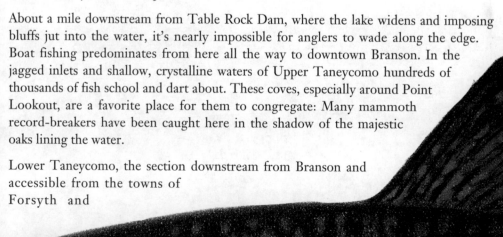

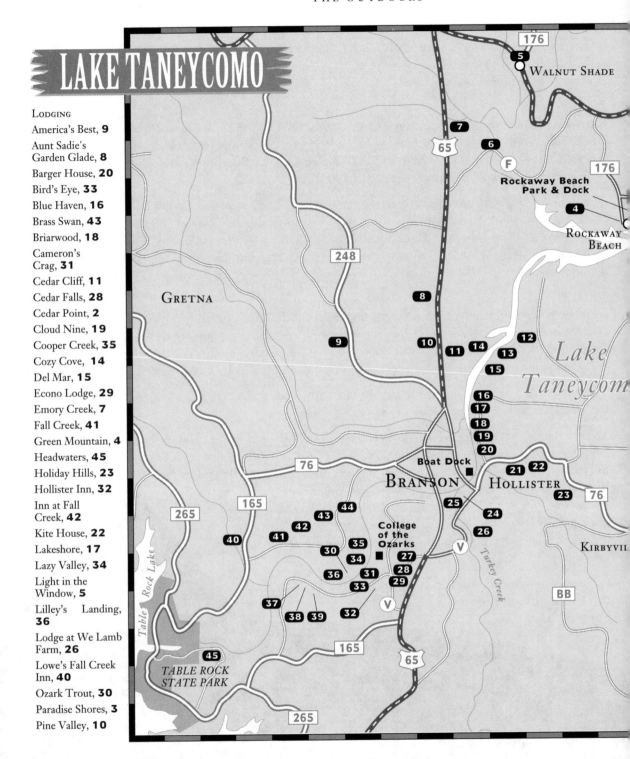

LAKE TANEYCOMO

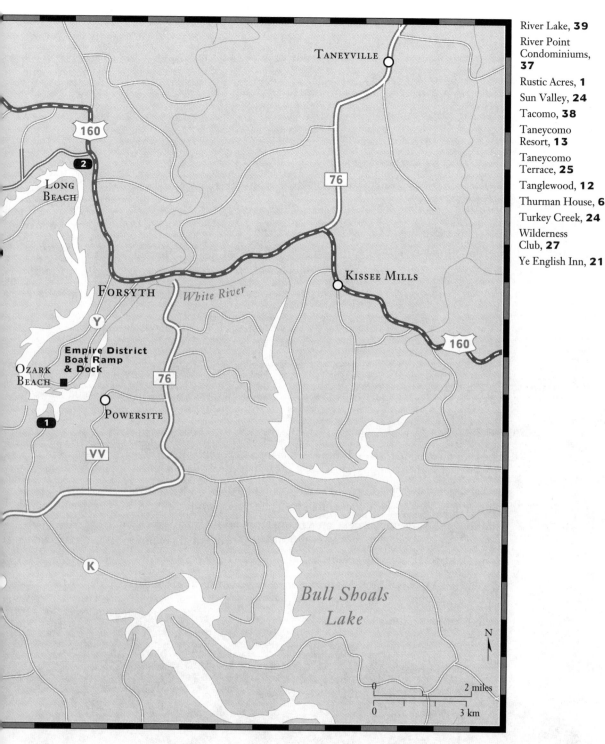

River Lake, **39**

River Point
Condominiums,
37

Rustic Acres, **1**

Sun Valley, **24**

Tacomo, **38**

Taneycomo
Resort, **13**

Taneycomo
Terrace, **25**

Tanglewood, **12**

Thurman House, **6**

Turkey Creek, **24**

Wilderness
Club, **27**

Ye English Inn, **21**

TANEYVILLE

160

2

LONG
BEACH

76

KISSEE MILLS

FORSYTH

White River

160

Y

Empire District
Boat Ramp
& Dock

OZARK
BEACH

76

1

POWERSITE

VV

K

*Bull Shoals
Lake*

N

0   2 miles

0   3 km

Rockaway Beach, has a more rural feel than Upper Taneycomo. Fewer homes and resorts dot the lakeshore, and each spring and autumn flocks of Canada geese form graceful *V*s in the sky. The water tends to be deeper and as much as 10°F warmer here, allowing a few hardy bass and catfish to swim among the trout. The many coves and creeks reward patient anglers, especially around Bull Shoals Dam, where the current washes in tiny shrimp, a favorite meal for waiting trout.

HELPFUL HINTS

Trout adore salmon eggs and corn kernels, as well as those old standbys the fly and the earthworm. Some anglers swear rainbow trout will also gravitate to spinner bait, crank bait, stick bait, and gitzits, and that brown trout gobble up minnows and any artificial lure that resembles them. In winter, midday fishing yields the biggest, best results. Spring is peak time for rainbows, and fall brings browns out in droves. In summer, night fishing is popular because the current is swifter, keeping the fish toward the surface of the water. Shy browns are best sought early or late in the day, no matter what the season, as they generally feed under low light.

✳ TABLE ROCK LAKE

Table Rock Lake is one of the premier recreational lakes in the Midwest. The lake has long been renowned as a top-notch bass-fishing locale but is also popular for sailing, waterskiing, even scuba diving.

The lake was formed when Table Rock Dam was completed in 1958; there are 745 miles of rugged shoreline. Along the water's edge, tiny caves pockmark towering bluffs colored buff and beige by the golden light, and majestic bald eagles soar overhead. Spring coaxes delicate blossoms from dogwood and redbud trees, while summer sees an explosion of wildflowers. Autumn triggers a dazzling fireworks display of turning oak and maple leaves. The ever-growing number of resorts and residential communities can't detract from Table Rock's serene beauty.

Around the **Dewey Short Visitors Center** are beautiful grounds (with panoramic views of the impressive dam), perfect for picnicking. An

interpretive nature trail snakes through the woods and along the lake. Tours of the dam and powerhouse are available on weekends; check at the tour desk for times, which vary. Four rooms of exhibits are devoted to each season in the Ozarks, and a combination of sound effects, artworks, photos, and artifacts evokes the wildlife and documents the struggles of pioneers to adapt to the environment. Films depicting the history of the early settlers, the construction of the dam, and the flora and fauna of the region are screened in a comfortable, 175-seat auditorium. *Rtes. 165 and 265, tel. 417/334–4101. Center open May–Oct., daily 9–6. Admission free.*

BOATING

LAUNCHES AND MARINAS. Among the leading marinas are **Campbell Point Boat Dock/Freeman Marine** (HCR 3, Shell Knob, tel. 417/858–6331), **Cape Fair Boat Dock** (Rte. 76-82, Cape Fair, tel. 417/538–4163), **Cricket Creek Marina** (Rte. 14W, Omaha, tel. 501/426–3474), **Gage's Long Creek Marina** (Rte. 86, Ridgedale, tel. 417/335–4860), **Indian Point Boat Dock** (Indian Point, Branson, tel. 417/338–2891), **Port of Kimberling Marina** (Indian Point Rd., Kimberling City, tel. 417/739–2315), and **Table Rock State Park Marina** (Rte. 165, tel. 417/334–3069). All offer boat and pontoon rentals, as well as bait and tackle, and eating facilities. State Park, Gage's, Indian Point, and Port of Kimberling Marinas also rent canoes, rowboats, paddleboats, wave runners, and water skis. Rental is by the hour, usually with a flat fee for the first hour or two hours and a discount for each ensuing hour. Ski boats and pontoons, with 115-horse outboard engines, generally start at $30–$40 the first hour, $20 thereafter. Bass boats average $40 for the first two hours, $10 each additional hour. Sixteen-foot fishing boats, generally with a 15-horse outboard motor, run about $25 for the first two hours, $5 thereafter. Figure $8–$10 for the first hour, $1–$2 thereafter for canoes, rowboats, and paddleboats. Wave runners and Jet Skis are $45–$50 per hour, $150 for four hours. Water skis and tubes are $6 for the first hour, $1 thereafter.

If you plan to swim or boat, note that there's a user's fee of $3 per vehicle (or $25 for an annual pass) at the following access-point parks: Aunts Creek, Baxter, Big M, Campbell Point, Cape Fair, Cow Creek, Cricket Creek, Eagle Rock, Indian Point, Joe Bald, Long Creek, Mill Creek, Moonshine Beach, Old Route 86, Viney Creek, and Viola. For more information on the above facilities and access points, contact the

TABLE ROCK

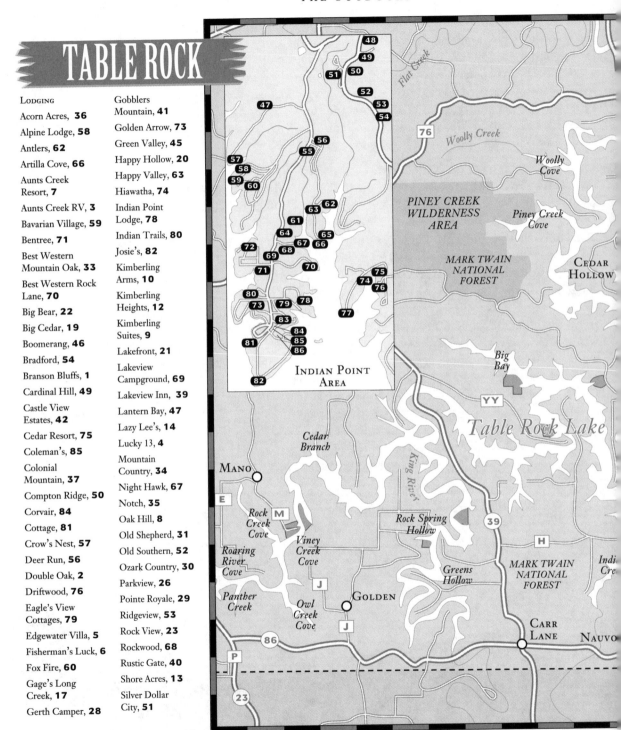

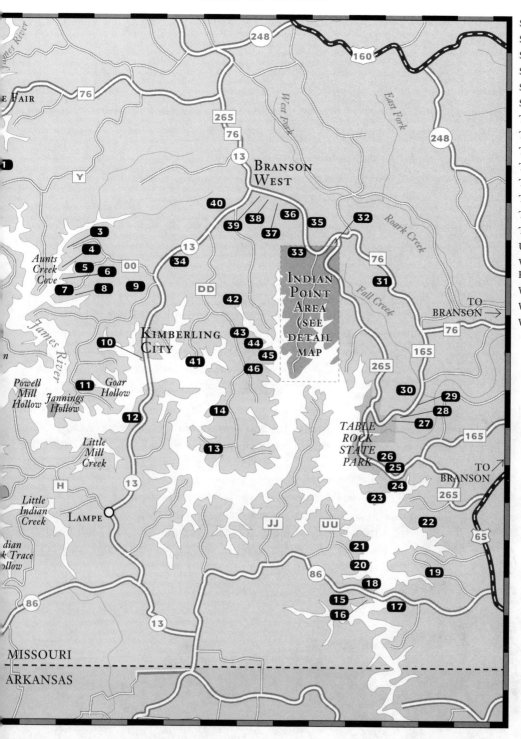

Table Rock Lake/Kimberling City Chamber of Commerce (Box 495, Kimberling City 65686, tel. 417/739–2564).

HELPFUL HINTS

Here are a few tips for landing the fish of your choice. Bass are most bountiful in spring. In April, whites run their annual mad dash to creeks and feeders, then return to the lake in May. Fall is another prime time for bass of all species. Largemouth and Kentucky bass favor the shallows, and smallmouth retreat to the depths. Summer nights are a good time to fish for largemouth and crappie. Catfish feed at night in the shallows. For most varieties of fish, you'll see a lot of action after several mild days in winter. Bass jump at minnows and earthworms, and catfish scan the muck for shrimp (but a piece of liver will do).

FISHING

On the lake, sportfishing reigns supreme. Just about any freshwater fish that enjoys a warm habitat, with waters in the 70s, calls Table Rock home. All kinds of bass, crappie, sunfish, gar, walleye, catfish, and bluegill inhabit its waters. Record fish include a 7-pound, 8-ounce spotted bass (caught in April 1966) and a 22-pound, 1-ounce long-nose gar (caught in August 1979): Table Rock grows 'em big, fast, and plentiful.

Among the best fishing spots on this lake are Long Creek, a favorite of Mel Tillis's; the James River Arm; and the Indian Point access. Waders should head for Moonshine Beach (near the intersection of Routes 165 and 265), where spotted bass congregate. The James River Arm stands in the shadow of the incomparably lovely Virgin's Bluff. Native American lore relates that a beauteous chief's daughter named Moon Song pledged herself to a handsome Spanish soldier. When her father refused the match and drove the soldier away, Moon Song pined for months and, rather than marry her father's choice, plummeted 325 feet to her death from the bluff. To this day, it is said, her ghost lingers amid the mysterious shoals and eddies beneath the jagged rock. Night anglers and nearby homeowners claim to hear her gentle sobbing.

SAILING

Sailing Charters of the Americas (Table Rock State Park Marina, tel. 417/779–4102 or 417/337–8399), an American Sailing Association certified training facility, can help you test the winds. They offer everything from 13-foot day sailers (which rent for $60–$95 for four or eight hours) to 25-foot Live-Aboard and 37-foot O'Day sailboats ($115–$245 per charter day of 21 hours), which sleep four to six people. They also offer a fun Discover Sailing cruise: two hours with a U.S. Coast Guard captain for $79.95, the set price for one to four people.

SCUBA DIVING

Divers can descend to 100 feet to check out the sunken Kimberling City Bridge, as well as rainbow-hued rock formations and giant boulders that litter the bottom like abstract sculptures. **John the Diver** (Table Rock State Park Marina, tel. 417/334–3069) is a full-service SSI-certified scuba shop. Rentals are $45 for everything, including wetsuit and single tank dive. They offer a guided lake tour for $30 per diver. Full certification runs $220 per person, including equipment.

A. L. & ...s
Silk Body

**TROUT
FLY**

ON
T.D.E. Sproat Hook
Dressed to Gut.
No. 1610.

Hook No......8....

BEAVER

BRAND

NAME;

Cowdung

The
ALLCOCK, LAIGHT
& WESTWOOD CO.,
Limited,
Manufacturers,
TORONTO.

✳ BULL SHOALS LAKE

Bull Shoals—most of which is located in the Arkansas Ozarks—was created by the Bull Shoals Dam, which was completed in 1952. Its development was bitterly controversial, as it disrupted the lives of many area residents. Local farmers resented losing their rich, loamy bottomland, environmental purists decried the impoundment of one of the wildest stretches of the White River, and four entire towns—Lead Hill, Arkansas, and Pontiac, Forsyth, and Theodosia, Missouri—had to be relocated to higher ground.

The sweet irony, however, is that the lake, scalloped by tiny coves and ringed with sheer limestone bluffs, is astonishingly lovely. With the exception of the dam itself (there's enough concrete in it to build a 6-foot-high, 1-foot-thick wall the length of the West Coast, from Canada to Mexico), Bull Shoals doesn't seem man-made. Deer and wild turkeys nibble on the lush foliage on the banks, otters and minks sun themselves on the rocks, flocks of cranes and solitary blue herons darken the sky on daily patrols throughout the year. To preserve this natural feel development by the shore is carefully protected in most places by a buffer zone owned by the U.S. Army Corps of Engineers; the small but comfortable resorts are constructed with native materials that blend with the surroundings.

BOATING

LAUNCHES AND MARINAS. Access points at Bull Shoals Lake are Beaver Creek, Buck Creek, Bull Shoals, Bull Shoals State Park, Dam Site, Route K, Route 125, Kissee

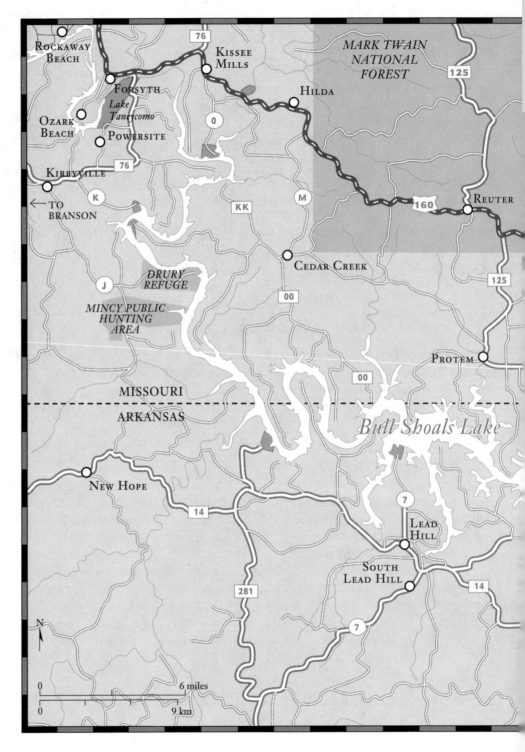

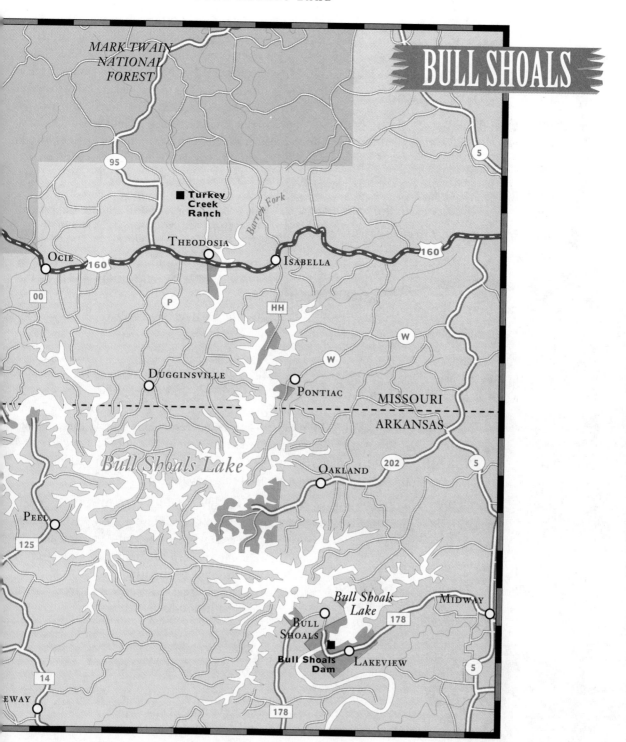

BULL SHOALS

MARK TWAIN NATIONAL FOREST

95

■ Turkey Creek Ranch

Barren Fork

THEODOSIA

OCIE 160 ISABELLA 160

5

00

P

HH

W

DUGGINSVILLE

W

PONTIAC

MISSOURI

ARKANSAS

Bull Shoals Lake

OAKLAND 202

5

PEE

125

Bull Shoals Lake

MIDWAY

BULL SHOALS 178

Bull Shoals Dam ■ LAKEVIEW

5

14

EWAY

178

Mills, Lakeview, Lead Hill, Oakland, Ozark Isle, Point Return, Pontiac, River Run, Shadow Rock State Park, Spring Creek, Theodosia, Tucker Hollow, and Woodard. The Beaver Creek, Buck Creek, Dam Site, Route K, Route 125, and River Run parks charge a user's fee of $3 per vehicle per day to swim or launch a boat. For more information about their facilities, including launch sites, boat rentals, campgrounds, picnic sites, snack bars, showers, or swimming beaches, contact the Mountain Home Resident Office (Box 369, Mountain Home, AR 72653, tel. 501/425–2700), the Bull Shoals Lake Boat Dock (Box 748, Bull Shoals, AR 72619, tel. 501/445–4424), the Bull Shoals/White River Chamber of Commerce (Box 354, Bull Shoals, AR 72619, tel. 501/445–4443), or the Mountain Home Chamber of Commerce (Box 488, Mountain Home, AR 72653, tel. 501/425–5111).

OZARKS WISDOM

Follow these old saws, and you may improve your luck. Hill folk claim that an east wind blows ill for anglers. Never step over a fishing pole or line if you want to catch any more fish that day. To guarantee good luck on your next fishing trip, hang one fish of a big catch from a tree near your favorite fishing hole.

FISHING

Anglers have made the pilgrimage to Bull Shoals since the early 1950s to battle bass of all stripes—largemouth, smallmouth, spotted, striped, and the scrappy white—along with catfish, crappies, and walleyes. The size of the catch is almost legendary; specimens here usually exceed those of Table Rock in size, and several game-fishing tournaments are held here annually. Among the state records are 5 pounds, 5 ounces for a white bass (caught April 1980); 13 pounds, 14 ounces for a leviathan largemouth (caught April 1961); and a whopping 51 pounds for a striped brute (caught July 1989).

The headwaters of Bull Shoals (accessible from Route Y off Route 160) are swifter and cooler on this side of the dam, and trout are plentiful. This is also a great place to catch walleye in late winter, before they spawn. Once they obey the call of nature in early spring, they shimmy toward the mouth of Swan Creek, which is also the spot to find the liveliest white bass. The Beaver Creek area, off Route FF, teems with smallmouth and largemouth.

OTHER FISHING HOLES

Anglers will also delight in the many streams that course through the area. Flat Creek, a wild, scenic stretch with fierce rapids, towering bluffs, and caves that hold eagles' aeries, comes highly recommended by master fisherman Shoji Tabuchi. Bull and Crane creeks are other local favorites, prized for trout and smallmouth, respectively, as well as for the parade of wildlife on their banks.

SPORTS

CYCLING AND ROLLERBLADING

There are suitable trails in **North Beach City Park** (Lake St., Branson, tel. 417/335–3085). While short, they're relatively flat and consistently paved, with some lovely peaceful vistas of Lake Taneycomo.

GOLF

There are five excellent golf courses in the Branson area, but the only championship contender is the par-70, 6,200-yard course at **Pointe Royale Golf Club,** where water comes into play on several holes. Such stars as Charley Pride often hit the tees Wednesday morning. *Pointe Royale, Rte. 165, Branson, tel. 417/334–4477. Open daily dawn–dusk. Reservations accepted. Greens fee (18 holes, including cart rental): $60 nonguests, $40 guests at the condominium complex.*

Thick stands of trees line the holes at the tricky, par-70, 5,786-yard **Holiday Hills Resort & Golf Club.** *E. Rte. 76, Branson, tel. 417/334–4443. Open Nov.–Mar., daily 9–5; Apr.–Oct., daily 7–6. Reservations accepted, at least 1 wk in advance. Greens fee (18 holes), $16; cart rental, $14.*

The challenging, heavily wooded, par-36, 2,948-yard **Oakmont Community Golf Course** plays longer than you would think. *Rte. 86, Ridgedale, tel. 417/334–1572. Open daily dawn–dusk. Reservations accepted. Greens fee (18 holes), $12; cart rental, $13.50.*

The par-35, 2,369-yard **Kimberling Hills Country Club** course demands precision thanks to short, fairly narrow fairways. There is a two-tiered green on hole five. *1 Lakeshore Dr., Kimberling City, tel. 417/739–4370. Open daily dawn–dusk. Reservations accepted. Greens fee (18 holes), $16; cart rental, $16.*

Tiny greens, rolling hills, and clusters of trees make the par-35, 2,552-yard **Lake Taneycomo Golf Course** a rewarding experience for duffers. *Rte. 160, Forsyth, tel. 417/546–5454. Open Nov.–Mar., daily 9–4; Apr.–Oct., daily 9–6. Reservations not accepted. Greens fee (18 holes), $15; cart rental, $18.*

HIKING

Don't plan to do any arduous wilderness trekking in the Ozarks: the gentle mounds and hollows are better suited to brisk walks. These ancient hills are a place for quiet reflection and communion with nature. Within a few minutes' drive of Branson you can escape the hustle and bustle, the traffic jams, and the endless drone of construction and discover the land that Harold Bell Wright called "the book of God."

The **Mark Twain National Forest** (Ava Ranger District, Business Rte. 5S, Box 188, Ava 65608, tel. 417/683–4428) is 1.5 million acres, with more than 63,000 acres congressionally designated as wilderness. The land is a habitat for more than 300 species of wildlife and has exceptional dogwood and smoke trees. There are several unmarked trailheads in Mark Twain National Forest that lead into the **Piney Creek Wilderness** (32 mi west of Branson on W. Rte. 76) and the **Hercules Glades Wilderness** (east of Branson on Rte. 76 to Rte. 12T, then south 7 mi).

A gentle, 3-mile trail winds through **Table Rock Lake State Park** (Rte. 165, 7 mi southwest of Branson, tel. 417/334–4704), beginning at Indian Point.

The comparatively rugged trails winding through the **Busiek Wildlife Area** (15 mi north of Branson, entrance off Rte. 65, no phone) are popular with mountain bikers, as well as hikers.

The trails in **Henning Conservation Area** (W. Rte. 76, east of Shepherd of the Hills Homestead, tel. 417/334–3324) are rich in indigenous flora; the Missouri Department of Conservation runs free, guided nature hikes May through October, Tuesday, Thursday, and Saturday at 9. Each week a different aspect of the region is highlighted, from wildflowers and birds to cultural history. Shepherd of the Hills is a favorite starting point.

If you don't want to venture off alone, contact **Scenic Trails Vacations** (Box 785A, Ava 65608, tel. 800/322–5048), which organizes day walks and biking/hiking trips throughout the region.

HORSEBACK RIDING

Krazy Horse Ranch (Shepherd of the Hills Expressway, tel. 417/334–5068) offers hour-long trail rides, $12.50 per person.

Red Bud Riding Stables (Rock House Rd., off Rte. 62E, Eureka Springs, AR, tel. 501/253–6556) and **Happy Trails** (S. Rte. 23, 2 mi west of Eureka Springs, AR, tel. 501/253–7146) lead rides through secluded hollows and along back roads, $12 per person for just under an hour.

You can relax in a surrey pulled by gigantic Belgian draft horses at **Wilderness Livery** (Pine Mountain Village, Eureka Springs, AR, tel. 501/253–8594).

TENNIS

There are two tennis courts at **North Beach Park** (Lake St., downtown Branson, tel. 417/335–3085) and one at **Shadow Rock Park** (Rtes. 160 and 76E, Forsyth, tel. 417/546–2741). The courts are free, open sunrise to sunset, and available on a first-come, first-served basis.

Mel Tillis,
singer, songwriter

Jordan Simon: You've been coming to Branson for some time, haven't you?

Mel Tillis: I've worked here for 20 years, since I was with the Baldknobbers.

JS: The Mabes?

MT: Uh huh, the Mabe Brothers. I've worked all around the area and all over Missouri, Kansas City, St. Louis, but I began to see Branson come up more and more on my itinerary. One day I said, "You got

me 50 dates in Branson this year?" My manager said, "Yeah, and it looks like you got more than that for next year," so I said, "Hell, I might as well lease me a place," so that's what I did. I leased the Ozark Theater, and I was there for two years, and then I built a new theater. And I had me a partner over there, and he bought me out. And I thought, "Do I wanna quit, or do I wanna continue with the Branson boom?" And I thought, "No, I wanna continue on," so we built this new one here. I think I was the first one to move off the Strip, and it worked. So I don't think you need to be on the Strip—you get so crowded up there…

…There's a story I tell about a lady who was behind me in her car, and she kept honking at me. And I stuck my head out the window, and I said, "Lady, would you please quit honking your horn at me? I can't do nothing about all this." She said, "I got to get out of the traffic, sir, I'm gonna have a baby." I said, "Lady, you ought not to have gotten in traffic in that condition." And she said, "I didn't."

JS: So, you've been coming here for 20 years. How has Branson changed?

MT: Oh my gosh, theaters, golf courses, all manner of entertainment . . . You know, there's just everything here. It's a place for everybody: for the children, for the moms and dads, the grandmamas and the grandpapas. And it's good, clean entertainment, too, and I think that's what we need in America these days.

JS: Is there concern about how quickly Branson is developing and how that will affect its small-town charm, the scenery, the recreational opportunities?

MT: Well, you can't stop that. And nine times out of ten, the community isn't prepared for it. There's a lot of discussion like "They're tearing this up, they're gonna destroy that," but that's in the name of progress. But I think Branson's a wonderful place. It is now and I think it's gonna be even more wonderful in the future. For instance, in my theater we're building a TV-and-recording studio. We're gonna have two stages, and we'll be able to do any kind of production, even interiors for movies.

JS: Aren't you worried about the financial risks? In terms of the recording industry, Branson has a long way to go before it can challenge Nashville.

MT: You see, I don't think I'm challenging Nashville at all. I'm providing a service for the entertainers who are here. They won't have to go to Nashville because they can stay here and record in a state-of-the-art studio. It'll be as good as anything in Nashville or L.A. or anywhere. And they can even do their videos here.

JS: That's wonderful and exciting. Now, this is a twenty-three-million-dollar investment, is that right?

MT: So far.

JS: How long do you expect it will take to recoup your investment?

MT: We hope to have paid it off in 10 years.

JS: Ninety-nine percent of the people who come to Branson are decent folks coming here to have a good time. But do you ever worry about being so exposed, so open to the world here?

MT: Oh no. A lot of entertainers have body-

guards, but I don't see the need for that. I don't think you need 'em around here. I can pretty well take care of myself—if I don't have to outrun a bullet.

JS: In terms of performing, who were some of your early influences?

MT: Red Foley. I loved his style. And we have almost the same kind of timbre. I think his [voice] was a little bit lower than mine, but it had a lot of the same qualities. I just recorded a gospel album, and most of the songs in it were inspired by him.

JS: What do you attribute your longevity to?

MT: Hell, I work. I said, "Hell, it's a changing of the guard, I got to get out of here and find me a new way to market myself." I got out of Nashville and found me a market in Branson.

JS: So Branson has revitalized your career.

MT: And I prepared for this. A lot of them haven't prepared, they're lazy. That ain't me.

JS: Is it ever difficult maintaining the same level of energy and enthusiasm, day in and day out?

MT: I have my days . . . Usually matinees are the toughest . . . The audience is a little laid-back, you know. You come out at full throttle, and they're not as active as they are at the 8:00 PM show. But that's anywhere, not only here but in Vegas, too.

JS: With the resurgence of country music, have you found yourself winning a new generation of fans?

MT: A new generation? No. I'm keeping my old fans, though. They're the ones who come to see us. But I think they know of me out there, and every generation has their own input. I had mine. When I first arrived in Nashville, I was a threat, and so was Waylon Jennings, Willie

Nelson, Roger Miller, Hank Cochran. We were all a threat to Roy Acuff, Carl Schmidt, Webb Pierce, and Lefty Frizzell. We were a new regime coming in. And now these guys are coming. I don't think there'll be a lot of careers like I've had—one that has lasted and lasted and lasted. It seems like they change: One year it'll be Billy Ray Cyrus, and the next year there'll be somebody else. And somebody else.

JS: You've been acting quite a bit over the last several years. Do you get more satisfaction from singing or acting?

MT: Acting's okay, but I'd rather do a live performance, where you're judged instantly and you know if they like you or not.

JS: In the current crop of singers coming up, are there any you particularly like?

MT: Oh yeah. I like George Strait. I like Alan Jackson. I like Vince Gill. I like Ricky Skaggs. I like Dwight Yoakam because he's different. Randy Travis is different. I like Sammy Kershaw, he's a little different.

JS: Any women?

MT: Oh, I like my daughter, Pam, of course. Reba. Tanya Tucker. I can't remember all the names, but there are a lot of good female singers out there.

JS: How do you feel about the diversity of talent coming in?

MT: Oh, I like it. It gives people a choice, because, you know, all of us sort of grew up together. I mean, Andy Williams, my God, I've known Andy for 37 years. And I've known Vinton for over 30 years. Jim Stafford, I've known him for years. And I was in the Air Force with Boxcar Willie. I've known him 40 years. And that Jap. I've known him forever. That's what I call him, he don't mind. I taught him stuttering—hell, he says I taught him English. So we all know each other.

JS: You guys all go fishing together?

MT: Oh yeah. That's what it's like here.

Shopping

7

With more than 6 million people visiting Branson each year, it's no wonder the city has become a shopping bonanza, where you can find everything from appliances to appliqué and zippers to zithers. Stores and souvenir stands are sprouting everywhere, in historic buildings downtown, in sprawl-marts along Route 76, even in the theaters, with annual revenues in the millions of dollars. But in spite of the competition—or because of it—the merchants are as friendly as can be, making shopping as comfortable and easy as rocking on a porch swing, chatting with a neighbor. What makes shopping in Branson even more fun is that it's one of the best ways to stargaze. After all, stars have to wear clothes, pick up groceries, and hit the hardware store like everyone else; Walmart corners the market on sightings.

Shops come in several varieties. Every attic in the region seems to have emptied its contents into a bevy of antiques stores and flea markets. Crafts shops offer all sorts of traditional Ozarks goods, from dolls to quilts to wood carvings (still known as whittlin' in these parts). Malls burst with chic boutiques and brand-name factory outlets. There are souvenir shops with the usual Branson-branded T-shirts, spoons, and other keepsakes. The stars have their own gift shops, too, usually in theater lobbies, where you can buy the latest CDs and memorabilia or share a star's favorite hobby (Shoji Tabuchi fishing rods and Glen Campbell golf clubs, for example).

Unless otherwise noted, shops along West Route 76 are concentrated on or just off the Strip. Business hours vary, although most stores are open 9 to 6. Many stores remain open on Sundays to accommodate visitors, but many smaller specialty shops close during

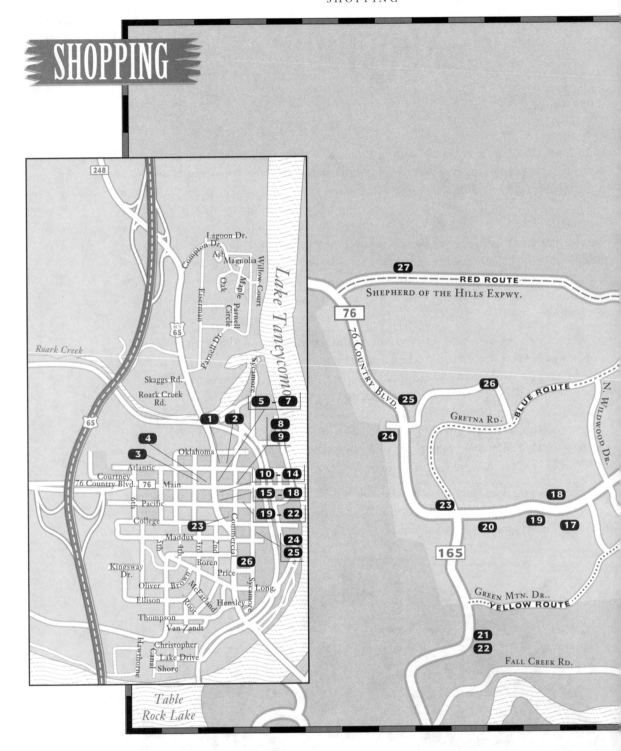

SHOPPING

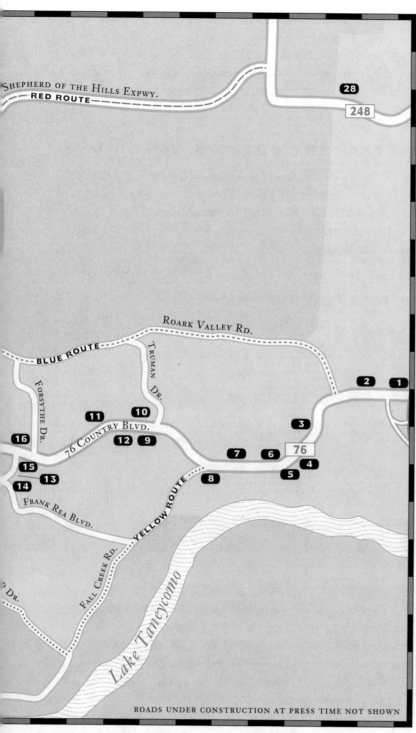

DOWNTOWN INSET

Allure, **9**

Arkansas Diamond, **6**

Australian Commercial Enterprises, **5**

Bits and Pieces Flea Market, **1**

Branson Depot, **8**

Branson Mercantile, **20**

Burlington Annex, **23**

Cadwell's Flea Market, **22**

Dick's Oldtime Five & Ten-Cent Store, **14**

Doll House, **26**

Finders Keepers Flea Market, **2**

Flea Bag Flea Market, **21**

The Fudge Shop, **17**

Grapevine Antiques, **11**

Li'l Shoppe of Leather, **12**

Main Street Jewelry, **7**

MarLea's Boutique, **10**

Mountain Man Nut and Fruit, **24**

Mountain Music Shop, **4**

Old Village Traders, **15**

One Destination, **3**

Orphanage Dolls and Pretty's, **19**

Patricia's House, **13**

Scott's Lakeside Studios and Gallery, **16**

Whole Foods General Store, **25**

Yeary's Music Stand, **18**

AROUND THE STRIP

Apple Tree Mall, **9**

Arkansas Diamond, **19**

Bob Evans' Country Store and Restaurant, **1**

Branson Heights Shopping Center, **3**

Branson Mall, **14**

Calico Cow, **4**

Carolina Mills Factory Outlet, **25**

Engler Block, **7**

Factory Merchants of Branson, **26**

Falls Parkway Center, **22**

The Gingham Goose, **8**

Grand Village, **17**

K-Mart, **28**

The Little Red Wagon, **10**

Midwest Art, **23**

Orvis Back Country Outfitters, **21**

Outback Outfitters, **12**

Ozarkland, **2**

Ozarks Discovery IMAX Center, **27**

Play Ball, **6**

Secret Garden, **13**

76 Mall Complex, **11**

Silver Spur, **20**

Stacey's Ozark Village, **18**

Tanger Factory Outlet Center, **16**

Twin Pines Antiques, **5**

Vacation Station, **24**

Wal-Mart, **15**

the winter or keep irregular hours. Celebrity shops in the theaters remain open during the evening performances. Sales tax in Branson is 7¼%. Souvenirs range from $2, generic Branson T-shirts, spoons, and other memorabilia; to tapes and CDs for $10–$15; and escalate into the hundreds for personalized gift items (like the aforementioned Tabuchi line of fishing rods or Campbell golf clubs).

MALLS, FACTORY OUTLETS, EMPORIUMS

Malls in Branson are shrines to the gods and goddesses of the shopping world. With rare exceptions, you won't find movie theaters, shake shops, video arcades, or anything to distract you from the mission at hand—shopping. In this chapter, shops within a complex note the complex name. Please refer to the following listing for addresses and telephone numbers of the primary emporiums:

Branson Heights Shopping Center, W. Rte. 76, opposite Wright Ave., no phone

Branson Mall, 2050 W. Rte. 76, tel. 417/334–5412

Engler Block, 1335 W. Rte. 76, tel. 417/335–2200

Factory Merchants of Branson, 1000 Pat Nash Blvd., off W. Rte. 76, tel. 417/335–6686

Grand Village, 2800 W. Rte. 76, tel. 417/336–7000

Ozarks Discovery IMAX Center, 3255 Shepherd of the Hills Expressway, tel. 417/335–4832

76 Mall Complex, 1919 W. Rte. 76, tel. 417/334–3919

Stacey's Ozark Village, 2855 W. Rte. 76, no phone

Tanger Factory Outlet Center, 300 Rte. 76, Tanger Blvd., tel. 417/337–9327

If your time is limited, visit the two big musts, Grand Village and the Factory Merchants of Branson.

Grand Village is a handsome, still-growing collection of upscale shops and eateries within gabled and turreted, brick-and-whitewashed buildings resembling the gracious Old Market area of Charleston, South Carolina. Among the tempting shops housed in the beautiful complex are **Earth Wonders** (tel. 417/336–7224), for environmental gifts and books, and **Backstage** (tel. 417/336–7211), for star memorabilia and souvenirs. You'll adore the delightfully odd offerings at **Reigning Cats and Dogs** (tel. 417/336–7247), a gift shop for pet owners in the market for Fido place mats, poodle pillows, and, well, cat's-eye earrings or kitty-shape brooches; or **Just for Laughs** (tel. 417/336–7212), which celebrates the world of sitcoms with items ranging from

Maryann's Gilligan's Island Cookbook to Jerry Seinfeld T-shirts. As you meander around the store you can screen classic episodes of "The Honeymooners," "I Love Lucy," and other favorites on the store's monitor. Surely you'll find the refrigerator magnet of your dreams at the **Great Stick-Up** (tel. 417/336–7256) and the rubber stamp you've been looking for at the **Artful Stamp** (tel. 417/336–7255). **Bear Hollow** (tel. 417/336–7257) carries the bear necessities for teddy bearaholics.

Factory Merchants of Branson assembles more than 90 leading manufacturers under one long red roof. Designers include Geoffrey Beene, Izod, London Fog, Evan-Picone, Bugle Boy, and Cape Isle Knitters. Among the selection of well-heeled footwear are shoes by Banister, Florsheim, Bass, and Hush Puppies. You'll find housewares by Corning Revere, Farberware, Oneida, Pfaltzgraff, and Fieldcrest Cannon, as well as discounted merchandise at such stores as Toys Unlimited, Prestige Fragrance, Totes/Sunglass World, and the Book Warehouse. To lug away your purchases, stop by American Tourister, the Leather Factory, or Bruce Alan Bags.

ANTIQUES AND COLLECTIBLES

Branson offers little for dyed-in-the-wool antiquers. In fact, in this town, antiques stores, flea markets, and thrift shops are for the most part synonymous. Chances are you won't stumble over a Louis XIV settee in mint condition, but you may find odds and ends that will finish off a treasured Hummel or Wedgwood collection or bring your end table to life.

Nostalgia nuts will have a field day combing Branson's shops. Remember the days of gas-station giveaways and dishes in detergent boxes? Do you recall the old saw, "One man's junk is another man's jewels"? Is your thing Depression-era glassware or '50s kitsch? Victrolas or Victoriana? Pink flamingoes or duck decoys? Bakelite or Baccarat? It's all here, rarely in any order but ready to be bought.

The greatest concentration of flea markets is in downtown Branson. **Aunt Tique's and Uncle Junk's** (W. Rte. 76 at Rte. 13, Branson West, approximately 6 mi west of Strip, tel. 417/272–8844), so vast it's almost daunting, is the largest in the area, with more than 80 booths selling curios and crafts. **Grapevine Antiques** (110 W. Main St., tel. 417/334–2288) has furniture, both the real McCoys and artful reproductions. The fragrance of potpourri is almost overpowering when you step into **Patricia's House** (101 W. Main St., tel. 417/335–8001), a Victorian dream, decorated with dried flowers and fruit baskets. It's the place to go for delicate porcelain dolls and frilly lace dresses, as well as home furnishings such as brass fixtures, 19th-century hutches, secretaries, and armoires. Other downtown vendors include **Bits and Pieces Flea Market** (204 N. Business Rte. 65, tel. 417/334–4564), **Cadwell's Flea Market** (114 Main St., tel.

417/334–5051), **Finders Keepers Flea Market** (204 N. Commercial St., tel. 417/334–3248), and **Flea Bag Flea Market** (106 E. Main, St., tel. 417/334–5242).

Other antiques shops and flea markets dot West Route 76, among them: **the Little Red Wagon** (1821 W. Rte. 76, tel. 417/334–2627), with a good selection of intricate brass fixtures; **Stacey's Flea Market** (Stacey's Ozark Village, tel. 417/335–4305), where you might luck into beaded vests and purses on consignment from the stars; and **Twin Pines Antiques** (1120 W. Rte. 76, tel. 417/334–5830), which might tickle your fancy with a 1850s Seth Thomas clock or an exquisite stemware set.

Collecting trading cards and celebrity autographs is a big pastime in Branson. Whether you're looking for rookie cards of the Doc and the Mick or basketballs autographed by Michael Jordan, try **Branson Depot** (123 E. Main St., downtown, tel. 417/335–4330) and **Play Ball** (1207 W. Rte. 76, tel. 417/335–4253). **Remember When** (Grand Village, tel. 417/336–7240) is a nostalgia buff's dream, displaying 1940s window cards, 1950s jukeboxes, Coca-Cola war bonds and vending machines, autographed baseballs, and Michael Garman's all-Americana sculpture.

BOOKS

For the most extensive selection of books and maps on the Ozarks as well as the latest best-sellers, try **T. Charleston and Sons** (Grand Village, tel. 417/336–7233). **Ozark Mountaineer Bookshop** (Engler Block, tel. 417/335–4195) is another source for books on regional history and folklore. **One Destination** (210 W. Main St., downtown, tel. 417/336–3493) carries paperbacks and guides to the area. **Book Warehouse** (Factory Merchants of Branson, tel. 417/334–6820) discounts the latest best-sellers.

CLOTHES

Branson shoppers searching for that special something to wear will find a dizzying selection, from the latest in haute couture, at designer factory outlets (*see* Malls, *above*) to vintage clothes at shops and flea markets (*see* Antiques, *above*) to cowboy and cowgirl duds (*see* Western Wear, *below*).

FOR WOMEN
Lakeside Traders (Grand Village, tel. 417/336–7248) and **Countrysides** (Grand Village, tel. 417/336–7220) carry women's casual apparel. **Somerset Hill** (Grand Village, tel. 417/336–7227) sells flowery fashions à la Laura Ashley. **Secret Garden** (2041 W. Rte. 76, tel. 417/334–2041) weaves a spell with its charming Victorian-style garments. If you want to ace the stars and find something they might wear, head for **MarLea's Boutique** (114 W. Main St., downtown, tel. 417/335–8393), for clothes dressed in baubles, bangles, and sequins—the glitzier the better.

FOR KIDS

Miss Maggie's (Grand Village, tel. 417/336–7252) offers dressy clothes for girls. **Gingerbread Kids** (Ozarks IMAX Discovery Center, 3562 Shepherd of the Hills Expressway, off the Strip, tel. 417/335–4832) carries fanciful children's clothing, such as red, white, and blue sequined jackets.

FOR THE FAMILY

Putting on the Glitz (Grand Village, tel. 417/336–7251) does just that to several lines of evening wear. At **Outback Outfitters** (1914 W. Rte. 76, tel. 417/334–7003) you can find clothing and other merchandise from Australia, including colorful Coogi sweaters, as well as toy koalas, Vegemite (the salty spread loved by Australians), emu-skin wallets, Crocodile Dundee hats, and opal jewelry. You'll have a ball trying things on at **Wearable Art** (1821 W. Rte. 76, Strip, tel. 417/336–3243), which carries hand-painted and -decorated shirts, jeans, and accessories for the entire family. For bargain family duds, you can't do better than **Branson Mercantile** (120 S. Commercial St., downtown, tel. 417/334–3634).

WESTERN WEAR

From country-and-western to cowboy to Native American, Branson has the shops that have it all. **Li'l Shoppe of Leather** (109 N. Commercial St., downtown, tel. 417/336–5210) specializes in fringed dresses, hats, and vests. **Silver Spur** (3210 W. Rte. 76, tel. 417/334–5026), **Vacation Station** (W. Rte. 76, tel. 417/335–4640), **Purey Country Western Wear** (Stacey's Ozark Village, no phone), and **Classic Cowboy Outfitters** (Stacey's Ozark Village, no phone) cater to the Marlboro Man—and Woman—in us all. **Tumbleweeds** (Grand Village, tel. 417/336–7225), for cowgirls, and **Tumbleweeds Gear** (Grand Village, tel. 417/336–7226), with duds for dudes, sit side by side and offer upscale ranch raiment fit for Lauren model lookalikes and the like.

CRAFTS

Locals take pride in their heritage and are dedicated to preserving Ozarks traditions. Quilting, tatting, wood whittling, glassblowing, and pottery making are time-honored skills handed down through generations. And in Branson the art of commerce has become a unique form of entertainment, as craftspeople fashion their wares right in front of you. The shops at Silver Dollar City, Shepherd of the Hills Homestead, and Mutton Hollow Craft and Entertainment Village (*see* Chapter 4, Other Fun Things to Do in and Around Branson) feature artisans at work, demonstrating, explaining, even teaching their crafts to curious onlookers. The shops listed below carry many of these and other local artists' creations, in addition to the inevitable mass-produced items. But you can usually tell the difference—especially with the artisan right there!

The granddaddy of crafts markets is the **Engler Block** (tel. 417/335–2200), a renovated 40,000-square-foot warehouse carrying "the Art of the Ozarks" in more than 25 specialty shops. It's a good evocation of bygone days, with artists demonstrating their skills, a front porch adorning the re-creation of a turn-of-the-century-style general store selling crafts, fabrics, and other goods, and a gazebo for sitting and chatting.

Apple Tree Mall is another emporium, where more than 400 merchants exhibit their wares. The scent of potpourri and fresh-baked pies greets you at the entrance to this grand establishment, which tantalizes with an almost daunting selection of goods for sale. Row after row, booths are jam-packed with colorful displays of preserves, baskets, and flowers, as well as laminated celebrity clocks, clothing patterns and afghans.

CHRISTMAS GOODS
Kringles (tel. 417/336–7246) and the **Village Emporium** (tel. 417/336–7213), both in Grand Village, carry distinctive ornaments and decorations year-round. **Engler's Antiques and Christmas Shop** (Engler Block, tel. 417/334–1223), **Christmas and More Shop** (122 S. 2nd St., downtown, tel. 417/334–1039), and the **Gingham Goose** (1534 W. Rte. 76, Strip, tel. 417/334–7870) are excellent sources of Christmas collectibles and country crafts of all kinds.

DOLLS
Befitting the home of Rose O'Neill, the beloved creator of the Kewpies, Branson is a doll-lover's mecca. (The Ozarks have a long, fascinating tradition of doll making, which has been exhaustively documented and cataloged at the Ralph Foster Museum; *see* Chapter 4, Other Fun Things to Do in and Around Branson.) Doll merchants here take their vocation seriously, carrying everything from primitive stick figures whittled from kindling and dressed in rags to elaborate porcelain figurines. Some antiques stores and flea markets have extensive collections of dolls and related paraphernalia, as do many of the crafts shops listed under other entries in this chapter.

Downtown Branson is the richest source for dolls. The cotton candy–pink **Doll House** (704 S. Commercial St., tel. 417/334–3233) carries an impressive selection of hand-sewn and -carved dolls, dollhouses, and furniture and has a doll doctor on call. **Orphanage Dolls and Pretty's** (102 W. Main St., tel. 417/334–2990) is the choice for contemporary icons from Batman to Barbie.

FOOD
Bob Evans' Country Store & Restaurant (801 W. Main St., junction U.S. 65 and W. Rte. 76, tel. 417/336–2023) sells Ozarks specialties from the kitchen from molasses to preserves, as well as locally designed napery, place mats, and the like. The sweetly pungent aroma of fruit butter, hand-stirred in copper kettles, permeates **Bekemeier's** (Ozarks Discovery IMAX Center, 3562 Shepherd of the Hills Expressway, off the Strip,

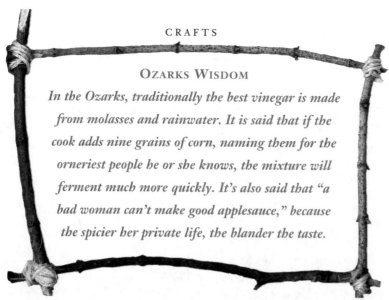

tel. 417/335–4663), where you'll also find apple, peach, strawberry, blackberry, apricot, plum, and cherry preserves. As you walk around downtown you'll surely get a whiff of chocolate from the **Fudge Shop** (106 S. 2nd St., tel. 417/334–5270), where you can watch candy-makers concoct nut rolls, chocolate logs (1 foot for 99¢), taffy, brittle—even lollipops in the shape of your favorite celebrities. (One version is shaped like Dolly Parton's breasts.) Other places to sate your sweet tooth are: the **Gourmet Fudgery** (Engler Block, no phone), **Fudgely's** (Grand Village, tel. 417/336–7254), and **Country Cookies** (Grand Village, tel. 417/336–7249).

It's difficult to count calories in Branson, with all the irresistible offerings, but for more healthful options try **Mountain Man Nut & Fruit Co.** (208 E. College Ave., downtown, tel. 417/336–6200; Stacey's Ozark Village, no phone) and the **Whole Foods General Store** (217 N. Business Rte. 65, downtown, tel. 417/335–8300), which also features essential oils and aromatherapy, as well as cruelty-free cosmetics.

GALLERIES

The definition of fine art in Branson is neither Picasso nor Rembrandt but rather expert, commercial art-school renderings of landscapes, still lifes, portraits—typically pretty if bland Ozarks scenes. For example, **Huff Gallery** (Engler Block, tel. 417/335–4458) specializes in regional oil paintings and crafts, such as hand-sewn dolls, and will personalize Ozarks scenes, adding a name or address in acrylic to a selection of prints. **Hawthorn Galleries** (Engler Block, tel. 417/335–2170) is a diverse gallery where works in various media from around America are showcased, including top-quality Western art. **Reflections** (Grand Village, tel. 417/336–7234) carries fine art, primarily landscapes, still lifes, and hunting scenes. **Midwest Art** (Hwys. 76 and 165, the Strip, tel. 417/336–3377) features an eclectic assortment of arts and crafts, including velvet paintings. The **Pottery Shop** (Engler Block, tel. 417/335–8466) sells porcelain and stoneware glazed in every color of the rainbow. **Scott's Lakeside Studios and Gallery** (118 S. 2nd St., downtown, tel. 417/335–5990) presents a lovely selection of glazed ceramics, raku, hand-tuned wind chimes, and jewelry, all created by leading regional artisans. **Wind River Gallery** (Rte. 13N, Kimberling City about 12 mi west of Branson off W. Rte. 76, tel. 417/739–5655) and **Geronimo's Den** (Stacey's Ozark Village, tel. 417/335–4440) feature Native American arts and crafts, including kachinas, dream catchers, pottery, and jewelry.

GLASS

M & K Stained Glass Collectibles (Stacey's Ozark Village, no phone), **Glass Magic** (Engler Block, tel. 417/335–8236), and the **Burlington Annex** (201 S. Commercial St., downtown, tel. 417/335–4789) make and sell stained-glass panels, windows, lamps, and fixtures. The **Helwig Art Glass Studio and Gallery** (Engler Block, tel. 417/335–2290) is a purveyor of fine handblown glass, and **Roy Clark's Celebrity Glass Shop and Crystal** (in Roy Clark Celebrity Theater, 3425 W. Rte. 76, tel. 417/335–8462) and **Traditions** (Grand Palace, tel. 417/336–7235) distribute famous brands, including Lladro, Waterford, and Swarovski.

HOME FURNISHINGS

In the market for exquisitely handcrafted country furniture and accents (they'll ship)? Try **Mountain Rockers** (Engler Block, tel. 417/335–2288) and **Bob Timberlake Collections** (Grand Village, tel. 417/336–7216). Looking for more homespun furnishings, patterns, and decor, including wallpaper and upholstery? Stop by **Calico Cupboard** (Stacey's Ozark Village, tel. 417/334–2158). **Old Village Traders** (120 S. 2nd St., downtown, tel. 417/336–2002) stocks country collectibles for the home, including baskets, dried flowers, and wood carvings. **Abbey Rose** (Grand Village, tel. 417/336–7229) displays tasteful accents and accessories such as blown-glass ashtrays, porcelain candy dishes and chintz draperies. **Victorian Garden** (Stacey's Ozark Village, no phone) sells the usual kitchenware in addition to antiques and bric-a-brac. **Sage Creations** (Engler Block, tel. 417/335–2131) is the place for scroll saws and blades.

> ### OZARKS WISDOM
> *Some hill folk believe that if you give cutlery as a present, you're bound to quarrel with the recipient, unless you receive a token in return. To give or receive a button is always lucky and ensures that the friendship will endure.*

JEWELRY

The artisans at **Ozark Mountain Gem and Clock Shop** (Engler Block, tel. 417/546–3640) sculpt polished stone into pendants, rings, and bracelets, as well as fashion fanciful, intricate clocks made from various materials from wood to stone; **White River Metalworks** (tel. 417/335–2074) creates custom jewelry from a wide spectrum of metals; **Zachary's Ozark Mountain Silver Co.** (tel. 417/335–4356) specializes in

Southwestern-theme baubles made of silver and turquoise; **Davidson Jewelry** (111 S. Commercial, tel. 417/334–3353) is Branson's oldest jewelry store; and **Norm's Cut Coin and Jewelry** (tel. 417/335–6655) fashions hand-sculpted jewelry from pounds, pesos, Susan B. Anthony dollars—you name it. **Katherine's** (Grand Village, tel. 417/336–7228) features designer creations in precious and semi-precious metals and stones. **Australian Commercial Enterprises** (113 Main St., downtown, tel. 417/335–3910) sells Aussie-themed merchandise, including black-opal jewelry. **Main Street Jewelry and Gifts** (109A W. Main St., downtown, tel. 417/335–4390), **Bitz of Glitz** (76 Mall, W. Rte. 76, tel. 417/335–8331) and **Arkansas Diamond** (3010 W. Rte. 76, tel. 417/335–3935; 116 W. Main St., downtown, tel. 417/334–7262) feature bejeweled Branson remembrances set in Black Hills gold.

LEATHER GOODS

Hillbilly Moccasins (106B Main St., downtown, tel. 417/335–8921) custom makes supple boots and moccasins. **Sunrise Leatherworks** (Engler Block, tel. 417/335–2025) and **Leatherworks Unlimited** (3106 W. Rte. 76, tel. 417/334–0775) carry soft, supple leather goods, from wallets to jackets.

MUSICAL INSTRUMENTS

Mountain Music Shop (N. Business Rte. 65, downtown, tel. 417/334–0515) offers an ensemble of fiddles, banjos, dulcimers, even a Stradivarius—plus a free quick lesson to get you pickin' if you decide to buy. **Yeary's Music Stand** (128 S. Business Rte. 65, downtown, tel. 417/335–5457) is a novelty shop that sells instruments as well as musical-theme bolos, earrings, boxer shorts, and wine glasses. They offer piano telephones, chocolate guitars, musical-note lollipops, and such lost-in-the-'50s merchandise as fuzzy dice and neon Elvis paintings. **Double Eagle Dulcimers** (Engler Block, no phone) is noted for its fine craftsmanship.

ONLY IN BRANSON

Dick's Oldtime Five & Ten-Cent Store (103 W. Main St., downtown, tel. 417/334–2410) is not to be missed. Opened in 1929, it is part of a vanishing breed. Memorabilia from its more than 60 years in business hangs from the ceiling, and in the crammed aisles you'll find Branson shot glasses, hand-painted china figurines, Ozarks cookbooks, Aunt Mollie's jams and jellies, Aunt Jemima statuettes, postcards, porcelain cherubs—just about everything imaginable.

QUILTS, PATTERNS, AND LACE

Quilts and Quilts Country Store (Branson Heights Shopping Center, tel. 417/334–3243) cozies up to shoppers with the largest selection of quilts in the Ozarks; it also sells patterns and accessories and gives (petit) pointers to those getting started. **Heirloom Lace** (Engler Block, tel. 417/334–7048) is the choice for Belgian lace and Intarsia. For ready-made clothing and linens head for the **Carolina Mills Factory Outlet** (3621 W. Rte. 76, tel. 417/334–2291).

WOOD CARVINGS

In the Engler Block, **Englers Woodcarvers** (tel. 417/335–2278) sells tools, supplies, and Nativity figures, and **Englers Emporium** (tel. 417/335–2200) creates fanciful trolls and gnomes only a mother could love. There is a large selection of wood items, even old weather vanes and carousel horses, at **Calico Cow** (Stanley Rd. and W. Rte. 76, the Strip, tel. 417/335–8941). If you're crazy about cuckoo clocks, visit **Wilderness Road Clockworks** (Hwys. 248 and 13, Reeds Spring 10 mi northwest of Branson, follow Rte. 76 to Rte. 13N, tel. 417/272–3256), which sells time pieces from Germany's Black Forest, as well as intricate music boxes, crèches, and miniature Christmas villages from around the world.

RECORDINGS

The best place to buy celebrity recordings is at the theaters. You don't have to see the show to shop in the lobby. There are surprisingly few record stores in town, but you'll find a good (if limited) selection at the **Ernest Tubb Record Shop** (Branson Mall, tel. 417/336–5605), **Backstage** (Grand Village, tel. 417/336–7211), and **Laketronics–Radio Shack** (Claybough Plaza, Branson West, approximately 6 mi west of Strip, tel. 417/272–3700).

SOUVENIRS

Almost every store sells souvenir T-shirts, key chains, buttons, and the like. For a great selection of low-price T-shirts, try **Branson Style** (Stacey's Ozark Village, no phone) and **New World Outlet** (1940 W. Rte. 76, tel. 417/334–5844). The main **Ozarkland** outlet (907 W. Rte. 76, tel. 417/334–3903) sells T-shirts as well as local products such as jams, sorghum, honey, and molasses.

SPORTING GOODS

Not surprisingly, the Ozarks have many camping and sporting-goods retailers, led by the world-famous **Bass Pro Shops Outdoor World** (*see* Springfield in Chapter 5, Excursions in Ozark Mountain Country). **Orvis Back Country Outfitters** (3265 Falls Pkwy., Suite U, approx. ½ mile south of 76 off 165, tel. 417/335–5401) stocks camping and fishing supplies and provides guides for fly-fishing and backpacking. **Ozark Outdoors** (Hwys. 76 and 13, Branson West, approximately 6 mi west of Strip, tel. 417/272–3422) is another fine source for outdoor clothing and supplies. **Right Angle Custom Rods** (Engler Block, tel. 417/335–4655) stocks quality fishing accessories from rods and reels to fishing vests. **Gibson's Golfworks** (Ozarks Discovery IMAX Center, no phone) has everything to meet a duffer's needs.

Yakov Smirnoff,
comedian

Jordan Simon: Did you perform comedy in Russia, and in what kind of venue did you get started?

Yakov Smirnoff: I've been performing since I was 15, and I was a very successful comedian in Russia. I traveled with a variety show that I hosted, performing between dancing bears and ballerinas. Then I worked cruise ships in the Black Sea, which brought me a little more [money].

JS: What kind of comedy did you do then?

YS: Oh, it was a kind of vaudeville: old jokes that were safe and clean, without political satire—no jokes about sex or religion. The Department of Jokes would censor material once a year, and comedians had to stick with it until the next year, when we'd give a new repertoire to be censored.

JS: It sounds like the death of creativity.

YS: Yeah. But, I can't complain.

JS: Are there places in the former Soviet Union that are like Branson?

YS: A lot of venues do remind me of Branson in some ways. They all have theater-style seating, with about 2,000 seats, and they don't sell liquor.

JS: I've noticed that in Branson all the celebrities get involved in the community.

YS: I'll tell you, from Russia to L.A., New York to L.A., I'd been too busy with the bigger picture to get involved in anything like this. And here, people get involved because they want to, and I think it's terrific. There's a sense of community—people helping each other help other people, which is refreshing. Some people might feel it's old-fashioned America. Well, I had never lived with June Cleaver, and I wanted to experience it. And that's why I'm here.

JS: When you were performing in the Soviet Union, did you have access to American comedians? Which ones influenced you?

YS: We had seen the Three Stooges, but that was more for propaganda [purposes than for entertainment]. They would show those guys hitting each other in the face with shovels, as if to say, "This is why we need so many missiles." But the only performer I really admired was Charlie Chaplin, because there was no language barrier. He made us laugh the same way he made you laugh; he made us cry the same way he made you cry. That taught me that language doesn't have much to do with comedy. Comedy is international: If your timing is there, if your facial expressions are there, you can probably do comedy in any language, and that inspired me.

JS: What was your introduction to Branson? How did you find out about it?

YS: I was doing FarmAid with Willie Nelson, and he was the one who said, "You know, I think your humor would go over really well [in Branson], since it's very family-oriented, patriotic." He was the one who encouraged me and my wife to come here . . . And Jim Stafford said, "I think you'd be great here." In my experience, this is unusual for people in show business. I mean, nobody says, "Hey, I want you to take a piece of my pie." They try to keep you away, but that didn't happen here. We were totally embraced by this town. And that helped me to see the natural beauty here, too, and I just fell in love with it. Before, when we were in Los

Angeles and had a two-and-a-half-million-dollar home, we had to get gates, alarms, security patrol. We had guns in the house—two little kids and guns! Then we came here, and I don't have to worry about guns. I don't have to worry about crime, and I can perform and be my own boss. No network tells me what to do, the audience is my network. If the audience comes, we're doing something right.

JS: When did you move to Branson?

YS: May 23rd [1993] was my first show here.

JS: Has Branson changed in the year you've been here?

YS: Oh, yeah, tremendously, but in a good way. Bigger acts are coming in. There's more attention from the international press.

JS: With all the explosive growth, is there concern that there will be overdevelopment?

YS: Yes, there is. But I want to enjoy it while we're here, and if it lasts forever, great; if it doesn't, I still want to be a part of it. When you announce to the whole world that this is a boomtown, everybody will come.

JS: A popularity boom can also attract negative publicity.

YS: People enjoy life here and find peace with it, and that's criticized. But that's what attracted me to Branson. Some people choose a different way of life, and God bless them. That's why it's America, that's why it's freedom, that's why people can live wherever they want. They don't have to come here, either. We're inviting everybody, but if it's not your cup of tea, don't come.

JS: Some say Branson excludes some people—that if you're black, gay, Jewish, from the East Coast, don't come.

YS: I'm from Russia; I've been embraced.

Japanese guy plays fiddle; he's been embraced. Charley Pride is doing well. Lawrence Welk, he's dead and people accept him. You know what I'm saying.

JS: How do you see your comedy evolving over the next few years? Do you see yourself moving away from the immigrant persona?

YS: I'll tell you, this has been a dilemma for a while, since the Soviet Union started falling apart. I'm not necessarily the best judge of what the audience wants; they tell me what they want, and I give them variety. My show goes from coming to America being totally naive, to marrying an American woman, to dealing with marriage, dealing with children . . . I give them a spectrum, and the response of the audience is what guides where I'm going. There was a time when I got totally away from the Russian-immigrant thing. The audience response was "Wait a minute, we came to see that guy. We don't mind you developing your other side, but don't take away the guy we fell in love with 10 years ago." So I chose to give them a little bit of everything, to take them on a ride through my life. I give them a chance to see me and get to know me . . . then the question-and-answer part of my show is open to them. They might want to talk about my parents, they might want to talk about my children . . .

JS: Is it difficult to do the act twice daily, to maintain the same level of energy and enthusiasm?

YS: Well, I love performing, so to me it's not difficult. I'm sure you get tired traveling sometimes, but you have to be somewhere, so you show up. Sometimes you get a little tired, but you still do your interview. That's what professionals are all about. I think this town demands that intensity.

Dining

8

Although Branson is a small town, it has an impressive range of restaurants with gastronomic spreads from buffet-style breakfasts with bacon and eggs to international smorgasbords featuring Mexican, Italian, Greek, and Chinese fare. This is meat-and-potatoes territory, though, and comfort food—heavy, glutinous, and drowned in thick brown gravy—dominates menus at most family restaurants. The calorie- and cholesterol-conscious needn't despair, however. Fish is popular, especially bass and trout caught fresh in nearby lakes, and restaurants are beginning to serve heart-healthy fare, offering salads and grilled and broiled dishes as alternatives to deep-fried standbys. High-end restaurants often substitute lighter dressings that use natural juices, fresh herbs, and less butter for the usual rich, cream sauces.

Country cooking is still the draw for restaurants such as Bob Evans and Branson Cafe, and an occasional "haute hillbilly" special like dandelion jelly to dress biscuits, shoofly pie (made with molasses), or persimmon bread might sneak into a daily menu. But there are no restaurants in Branson that offer traditional Ozarks cooking, a true melting pot combining Native American, Scotch, Irish, and Welsh influences. Eula Mae Stratton's *Ozarks Cookery*, on sale throughout the Branson area, is a rich source of history and recipes for everything from Cherokee fried bread to baked apples stuffed with homemade sausage.

All-you-can-eat buffets are an institution here, and because competition for the tourist dollar is fierce, restaurants outdo each other by trying to proffer the most choices and fixins'. In some establishments 10-foot-long tables are piled high with eggs, hash browns, biscuits and gravy, sausage, bacon, and ham at breakfast. Lunchtime brings out the salad bars, cold cuts, roast chicken, and deep-fried shrimp. At dinner expect the heavy hitters: roast beef, prime rib, pastas, and peel-and-eat shrimp by the bucket. The prices are right,

DINING

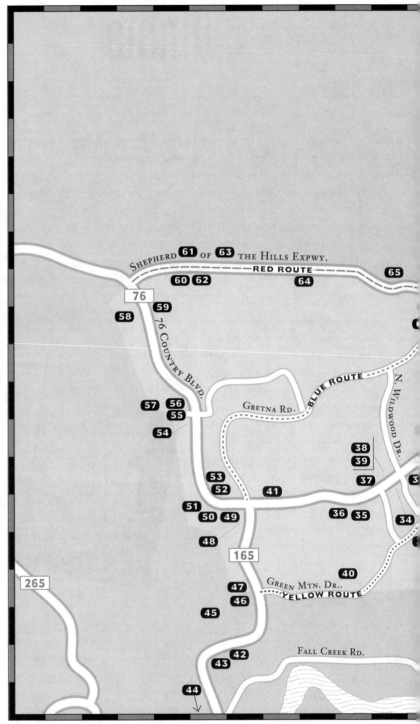

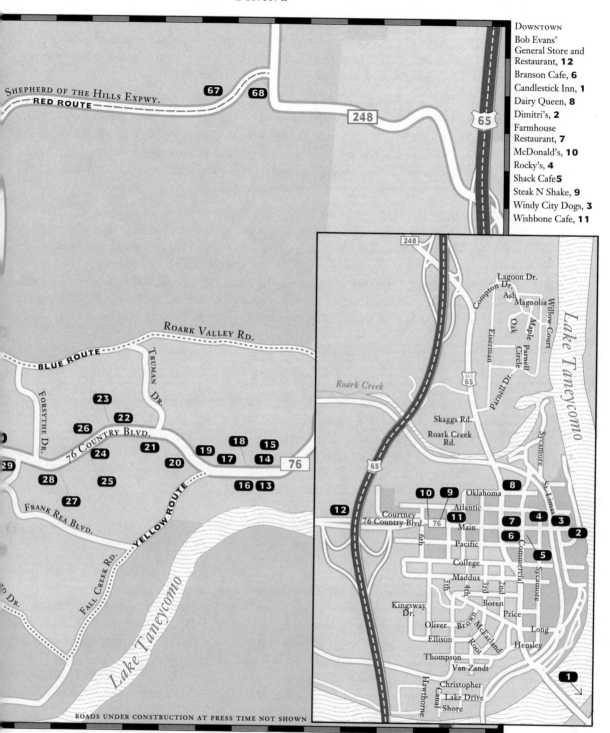

DOWNTOWN
Bob Evans' General Store and Restaurant, **12**
Branson Cafe, **6**
Candlestick Inn, **1**
Dairy Queen, **8**
Dimitri's, **2**
Farmhouse Restaurant, **7**
McDonald's, **10**
Rocky's, **4**
Shack Cafe **5**
Steak N Shake, **9**
Windy City Dogs, **3**
Wishbone Cafe, **11**

ROADS UNDER CONSTRUCTION AT PRESS TIME NOT SHOWN

too: usually $2.99–$3.99 for breakfast, $4.99–$6.99 for lunch, $6.99–$9.99 for dinner. Early-bird specials and kiddie menus (with hot dogs, hamburgers, fried chicken, and spaghetti and meatballs) help keep costs down, as well, and many restaurants run discount coupons in the local newspaper and free souvenir guides.

Generally dress is casual, but if you're going to a fancier restaurant you probably won't want to wear shorts or a T-shirt. Most sit-down eateries accept credit cards. Many restaurants don't have a liquor license. A few remain open for after-theater meals. Many restaurants accept reservations only for groups, if at all (consult the dining chart below for the restaurant of your choice). However, reservations are accepted at upscale establishments and are highly recommended if you're trying to make a show.

This chapter is divided into two parts: a list with more than 70 facilities organized by cuisine then alphabetized by name, and a Restaurant Sampler, which contains full reviews of some of the more popular eateries to give you an idea of your options in Branson. Use the list as your primary source, and when you find a property that seems interesting, turn to the map and look for the restaurant's name and corresponding number on the legend. We recommend the restaurants we have listed, but our choices are intended solely as guidelines and do not include all of the possible options.

BARBECUE

Uncle Joe's Bar-B-Que. "You'll wanna lick your fingers right down to your toes," brags the menu about the messy, delicious, hickory-smoked ribs and chicken served in dinosaur-size portions at tables dressed in red-and-white checked tablecloths. Uncle Joe's is the place to get a quick bite before going across the street to Andy Williams's Moon River Theater. *2819 W. Rte. 76, tel. 417/334–4548. Children's menu, beer and wine, senior-citizen discount, no-smoking section. D, DC, MC, V. $2–$23.*

CONTINENTAL

Buckingham's. What's most memorable about this restaurant is its African motif, with native masks, faux leopard- and zebra-skin seat covers, and a huge mural of wildlife gamboling on a savannah, painted by four artists from Springfield. The food is not nearly so exotic but is still excellent: Maryland crab cakes with aioli, chicken Amaretto, fricassee of mushrooms, and escargots or shrimp kebab with a tangy coffee-barbecue sauce are among the house specialties. Buckingham's is in the Palace Inn, convenient to the Grand Palace, and is a popular dining-out spot for stars such as Tony Orlando, Andy Williams, and Jim Stafford. *2820 W. Rte. 76, tel. 417/337–7777. No lunch Mon.–Sat. Children's menu, liquor, no smoking, reservations accepted. AE, D, DC, MC, V. $13.95–$23.*

Candlestick Inn. Perched atop Mt. Branson, 250 feet above the downtown area, is this romantic restaurant with high, beamed ceilings and expansive views of Lake Taneycomo and the city lights. Elegant tables sparkle with bone china, candles, sterling service, and crisp white napery. The menu lists mostly Continental fare, such as steak au poivre, beef tournedos (in a burgundy-mushroom sauce), and veal Oscar (with crabmeat, asparagus spears, and béarnaise sauce). Although it's not on the menu, you can request the house specialty, batter-fried lobster. If you're in Branson during Ozark Mountain Christmas, try to dine here one evening: the Candlestick Inn is one of the best seats in the house for watching the Festival of Lights around the lake. *Candlestick Rd. off E. Rte. 76, tel. 417/334–3633. No lunch. Children's menu, liquor, no smoking, reservations accepted. AE, D, DC, MC, V. $14.50–$37.*

Dimitri's. Celebrity-gazing is a popular pastime at this floating restaurant on Lake Taneycomo. Each of the two interconnecting dining rooms—one serving Greek fare, the other Continental—has its own menu and its own fabulous view of the lake through floor-to-ceiling picture windows. In the stylish gourmet section, stained-glass ceilings, a grand piano (with resident pianist tickling the keys nightly), fine china, crystal, candles, crisp white napery, and waiters in tuxedos set the tone. Here you can choose from Continental specialties such as trout almandine, duck à l'orange, and steak Diane, which is flambéed at your table. Or save the pyrotechnics for desserts such as cherries jubilee or bananas flambé. Dimitrios himself may prepare the excellent Caesar salad table-side. You may hear raucous cheers from the adjacent, more casual family room, a favorite of bus groups for its savory Greek specialties served quickly. Among the most popular dishes are the reasonably priced *spanakopita* (spinach pie in flaky phyllo), *saganaki* (flamed feta cheese), *dolmades* (stuffed grape leaves), chicken kebabs, and gyros (broiled lamb sandwiches). *500 E. Main St., tel, 417/334–0888. No lunch. Liquor, no-smoking section, reservations accepted. AE, D, DC, MC, V. $12.99–$29.95.*

Paradise Grill. If you're in the mood for fun food you'll probably enjoy this jazzy restaurant. It seems to take its cue from Shoji Tabuchi's fabulously ornate theater next door, with a brilliant explosion of fluorescent colors on its walls and unusual bric-a-brac, including clown pants and coffee mugs, hanging from the ceiling. The slyly sophisticated menu lists items such as gourmet pizza, Squawking Nachos (smoked chicken, caciotta goat cheese, and two salsas), Wild Things (wild mushrooms, leeks, and brie on focaccia), Rockhill lamb chops (coated with mustard and bread crumbs, sautéed, and served with white beans, sun-dried tomatoes, prosciutto, spinach, and arugula), and roast salmon (with tomatoes, artichoke hearts, Kalamata olives, and baby red potatoes, swimming in balsamic vinegar. Salads, from a classic Cobb to the Shanghai chicken (stir-fried veggies, spinach, chicken strips, and crispy rice noodles) are among the other standouts. *3250 Shepherd of the Hills Expressway, tel. 417/337–7444. Children's menu, liquor, senior-citizen discount, no-smoking section, reservations accepted. AE, D, DC, MC, V. $3.50–$19.*

Upstairs at Jim's. This cozy aerie above the Jim Stafford Theater looks like a fairy-tale set, with murals of trees and animals on the walls and painted cobblestone paths on the floors. Every chair in the restaurant is part of the owner's private collection, and she's painted some with whimsical scenes and patterns. The menu is concise, with a few homemade offerings each day, usually including a chicken and a meat dish, as well as bountiful salads. Among the favorite extras are a refreshing, herbal iced tea of the day; chilled strawberry soup; and delectable homemade muffins. *3440 W. Rte. 76, tel. 417/335–8080. Children's menu, no smoking, reservations accepted. AE, D, MC, V. $6–$17.*

COUNTRY

Bob Evans General Store and Restaurant. For a glimpse of what Branson was like in the early 1900s, visit Bob Evans, where local musicians pick and fiddle on the porch and artists display Ozarks crafts and offer demonstrations. Inside is a gift shop selling homemade jellies and sauces derived from old Ozarks recipes; and a huge but homey restaurant serving country cooking such as potato soup, honey-glazed ham, and chicken-fried steak. Breakfasts are excellent, thanks to the on-site bakery, which turns out scrumptious muffins and biscuits, including cinnamon-raisin, the house specialty biscuit. The yesteryear theme extends into the capacious dining room, where hundreds of old photos adorn the walls. *801 W. Main St., tel. 417/336–2023. Children's menu, senior-citizen discount, no smoking. AE, MC, V. $3–$8.*

Branson Cafe. This downtown institution, opened in the 1920s, is the oldest dining establishment in Taney County and the place to visit for heaping helpings of flapjacks, chicken-fried steak, channel catfish, and Frito pie, among other specialties. The homemade corn bread is some of the best in a town where competition is fierce. The fried chicken and fruit cobbler are so good you'd swear the recipes had been passed down and perfected through generations. They were. The dining room is cozy, with historic photos and bric-a-brac including rusting kitchen utensils and old farm tools, and 1950s carnelian Naugahyde seats and faux-wood Formica tables. *120 W. Main St., tel. 417/334–3021. Children's menu, senior-citizen discount, reservations accepted. AE, D, DC, MC, V. $1.50–$8.95.*

The Shack Cafe. Opened as a takeout food shack in 1904, this café has evolved into a respectable restaurant that charmingly recalls the turn of the century with such fixtures as faux gas-lamp chandeliers and whirring ceiling fans. This is a popular spot for locals and a good place to eavesdrop on gossip and politics. Owner Arena Creekmore encourages people to "set a spell" while she serves stick-to-the-ribs meals such as melt-in-your-mouth pot roast or chicken livers with a generous side of homemade mashed potatoes. Don't be surprised if Arena stops by to chat: She considers her customers family and will probably want to catch up on what's new. *108 S. Commercial St., tel. 417/334–3490. $3–$8.*

FAMILY-STYLE

The Frontier. This simple, home-spun restaurant decorated with saddles and horse blankets serves steaming, flaky chicken pot pie; enormous chicken fajita salad; and pot roast like somebody's grandma could make. You could fill up on the delectable fresh cornbread alone, but save room for a piece of one of the home-baked pies, rated by many locals as the best in town. Daily specials might include a memorably tart, zingy, strawberry-rhubarb; sinful, silken, peanut-butter chocolate; or yummy jumbleberry (bursting with fresh boysenberries, strawberries, and blueberries). *3562 Shepherd of the Hills Expresssway, tel. 417/336–6718. Children's menu, no-smoking section, reservations accepted for 20 or more. AE, D, MC, V. $6–$10.95.*

McGuffey's. There are five locations in Branson, but the first was built and owned by Andy Williams, whose theater is next door. All McGuffey's feature Andy's Moon River pasta (with broiled tuna, asparagus tips, and olive oil), in addition to traditional favorites such as broiled chicken and deep-fried shrimp. Except for the bright, brassy neon-and-chrome McGuffey's Diner, all locations have an attractive, dark, clubby decor and use voluminous menus designed to look like old-fashioned school primers called McGuffey's Readers. These restaurants are popular with families, so call ahead for reservations. *2600 W. Rte. 76, tel. 417/336–3600. Children's menu, liquor, senior-citizen discount, no-smoking section. AE, D, MC, V. $5.99–$13.99.*

Peppercorn's. The grand, green-and-white gabled building is a replica of a gracious Victorian mansion. However, the vast interior resembles a gussied up coffee shop, with large booths and tables ideal for family reunions. Meals of huge proportions are served either prix fixe, buffet-style, including a salad bar, or from an à la carte menu with favorites such as trout almandine, prime rib, and lobster tail. Peppercorn's is conveniently located near the Andy Willams, Bobby Vinton, and the Grand Palace theaters. *2421 W. Rte. 76, tel. 417/335–6699. Children's menu, no-smoking section, reservations accepted for 20 or more. D, MC, V. $3.99–$14.99.*

Radio Cafe. This large, bright eatery is predictably crammed with 1940s and '50s memorabilia, including old radios and autographed photos of the stars, many of whom got their start during the Big Band and Ozark Jubilee era. Radio Cafe is famous for its weekday "Pass the Biscuits Breakfast Buffet," from which KRZK radio broadcasts live music at 11 AM and presents guest stars who have included John Davidson and Ferlin Husky. The menu runs toward standard Branson fare, from fried chicken to chicken-fried steak. *3524-B Keeter St., tel. 417/335–8534. Children's menu, no smoking, reservations accepted. $5.50–$9.50.*

Sadie's Sideboard. A mannequin of Sadie at the sewing machine greets you at the door of this down-home eatery with rustic woodsy decor. You might forget that you're right on the Strip, steps away from the Grand Palace (until a tour group looms into view). The all-you-can-eat buffets feature more than 20 items such as broiled chicken, pot roast, and peel-and-eat shrimp. But the à la carte menu is diverse, too, with homemade soups, steaks, fresh trout, and catfish prepared in a variety of ways. *2840 W. Rte. 76, tel. 417/334–3619. Children's menu, no smoking, reservations accepted for 20 or more. AE, MC, V. $3.95–$11.95.*

Sugar Hill. This winsome charmer, with a Southern-mansion facade, magenta awnings, arched windows, and copper-and-aqua trim, triples as a restaurant, cannery, and bakery. All of the sunny, bright rooms have pastel napery, wrought-iron garden chairs and lots of hanging plants, giving it the appealing air of a greenhouse. The restaurant menu is simple, offering a choice of burgers, pot roast, chicken piccata, pasta specials (you're in luck if primavera is featured), and crisp salads. Items available for sale at the on-site cannery include peach preserves, pickles, and hot peppers, and the bakery offers scrumptious homemade breads, muffins, and cakes. *405 S. Rte. 165, tel. 417/335–3608. Children's menu, no-smoking section, reaservations accepted. D, MC, V. $4.95–$14.95.*

Uptown Cafe. Good, old-fashioned diner food is served in this striking, art deco–style building, painted dark blue with silver trim. The menu gives you plenty of options, from quick bites to hearty, filling meals such as the reliable brisket smothered in gravy, and crispy, tender fried chicken. While you eat, enjoy the 1930s and '40s music piped into the dining room. Uptown Cafe is a good place to eat before heading to the Osmond Theater or the Ozark Jubilee, just a block or so down the road. *285 S. Rte. 165, tel. 417/336–3535. Children's menu, no-smoking section, reservations accepted. D, MC, V. $3.50–$12.50.*

FAST FOOD

Windy City Dogs. You can eat in or take out and have a picnic by Lake Taneycomo, just a block away. Locals love Windy City for its hot dogs and made-to-order burritos that can be spiced or jazzed up with jalapeños or any of the other toppings and stuffings available from the menu, including onions, chili, cheese, bacon, and beans. The food is cheap, fresh, and fast, and sitting at the counter offers some of the best free entertainment in town, if you like people-watching. *315 E. Main St., tel. 417/335–3748. $1.65–$5.*

ITALIAN

Rocky's. This downtown eatery is popular with locals, who come for its Mamma Mia Italian fare—hearty portions with lots of garlic and attitude. (In Italian, *Mamma Mia* suggests good, home-style food in huge portions.) Superb pastas include cannelloni, linguine with clam sauce, and spaghetti carbonara, and many of the main dishes, such as chicken piccata and veal marsala, are expert renditions of classics. Rocky's has a publike ambience, with faux Tiffany glass, exposed stone walls, stucco ceilings, wooden beams, and a jungle of hanging plants. The adjacent lounge is open until midnight (1 AM weekends) and serves light fare such as nachos and burgers, along with some great talk. On weekends in season (late May—October) jazz musicians jam until the wee hours. *120 N. Sycamore, tel. 417/335–4765. Children's menu, liquor, no-smoking section, reservations accepted. AE, D, DC, MC, V. $3.95–$12.95.*

MEXICAN (TEX/MEX)

Gilley's Texas Cafe. Mickey likes his food as hot as his honky-tonk music and offers the same to his guests, so ask for meals on the mild side if your stomach isn't strong enough to handle the jalapeños. For starters, launch into nachos, piled high with toppings such as olives, cheese, beef, or chicken; chili; or Gilley's Bullets (jalapeno peppers deep fried and stuffed with cooling cream cheese). The list of entrees goes on for pages, but some favorites are beef or chicken fajitas, enchiladas, big beef burgers, barbecue chicken, and ribs. Meals are fun in this bright, friendly restaurant, where enormous papier-mâché, red and green chili peppers hang from the rafters and soothing southwestern tones prevail. Margaritas are the drink of the house, and if you're lucky, you might get to share the cantina (bar) with Mickey after his show. *3457 W. Rte. 76, tel. 417/335–2755. Children's menu, liquor, no-smoking section, reservations accepted for 15 or more. AE, D, DC, MC, V. $1.95–$17.95.*

Manny's Authentic Mexican Food. The "authentic" in the title should be taken seriously in this dimly lit, brick and adobe restaurant with the best chimichangas, tamales, *chicken caldo* (a robust stew), guacamole, and green-chili burritos in town. Manny's wife, Carmen—a native of Mexico—presides over the kitchen, cooking honest Mexican fare at fair prices. Enjoy your meal either in the dimly lit, brick-and-adobe interior, or on the colorful outdoor patio—a great place to watch traffic on the Strip while drinking a Tecate or Corona beer. The margaritas have a kick and will surely put you in a good mood for a show at the nearby Ozark, Five Star, or Country Tonite theater. *3515 W. Rte. 76, tel. 417/334–2815. Children's menu, liquor, no-smoking section, reservations accepted. D, MC, V. $3.95–$8.95.*

Taquito's. The most authentic items at this flamboyant Mexican-style restaurant are the sombreros and serapes hanging on the walls. The fire engine–red '68 Plymouth Tijuana Taxi partially embedded in the deck enhances the usually festive mood: Most nights Taquito's is as hopping and lively as a Mexican jumping bean. The food is good, if mild, with the usual fare, such as fajitas, enchiladas, and sopapillas. Taquito's is a smart choice if you're going to Shoji's or Shenandoah South. *239 Shepherd of the Hills Expressway, tel.*

417/336–5668. Children's menu, liqour, no-smoking section, reservations accepted for 10 or more. AE, D, DC, MC, V. $6.95–$12.95.

SEAFOOD

Champagne's. The fish at this down-home spot in the Blue Bayou Motel is so fresh you'd swear it could jump off your plate. You can savor the luscious trout, bass, and catfish deep-fried or simply sautéed; more adventurous palates will enjoy them blackened Cajun-style. Mouth-watering jambalaya, tasty crawfish étouffée, and fiery gumbo are among the other classic bayou choices on the menu. The restaurant's coffee-shop ambience is enlivened by knotty-pine walls and a mural depicting Cajun country. Head here Friday and Saturday nights for an 8-foot-long buffet that includes succulent shrimp and all-you-can-eat crawfish. Live zydeco music and dancing add to the high-spirited scene. *3400B W. Rte. 76, tel. 417/334–6370. Children's menu, liquor, senior-citizen discount, no-smoking section, reservations accepted. AE, D, DC, MC, V. $8–$30.*

STEAK HOUSES

Bonanza. This bustling steak house with minimal decor and comfortable booths is one of the busiest restaurants in the Bonanza chain. And why not? It serves good-quality, juicy steaks accompanied by salad from a salad bar, with more than 25 items. *1807 Neihardt St., tel. 417/335–2434. Children's menu, senior-citizen discount, no-smoking section, reservations accepted for 15 or more. D, MC, V. $2.99–$9.49.*

B.T. Bones Steakhouse. The menu won't "steer" you wrong, especially if you order one of the many cuts of thick, juicy steak (all Iowa choice, cut fresh daily in house). B.T. Bones emulates the old days of the Texas roadhouse, when ranchers/restaurateurs butchered and prepared steaks in their own backyards and served them up front. It's convenient to the Shoji and Shenandoah South theaters, but there's entertainment here, as well: Monday and Tuesday evenings are comedy and magic; Wednesday through Saturday nights live bands play foot-stomping country standards; Sunday is a raucous, riotous Karaoke Night. *2346 Shepherd of the Hills Expressway, tel. 417/335–2002. Children's menu, liquor, no-smoking section 4 PM–9 PM, reservations accepted. AE, D, DC, MC, V. $3.75–$17.50.*

Lone Star Steakhouse. This cavernous barn, decorated with neon beer signs, steer skulls, moose-head trophies, and Western murals, is a classic, beer-guzzling, sawdust-on-the-floor, sports-on-the-TV saloon. Along with your beer the waitress will bring a bucket of peanuts. Just throw the shells on the floor: they add to the ambience. The menu includes obvious but tasty fare with cute names—Bubba burgers (smothered in sassy barbecue sauce, bacon, and cheddar), Texas tumbleweeds (whole fried onions), and an assortment of mesquite-grilled foods, including ribs, chicken, and steaks. Lone Star is just down the block from the Grand Palace and Andy Williams theaters. *201 Wildwood Dr., tel. 417/336–5030. Children's menu, liquor, no-smoking section. AE, D, MC, V. $2.25–$17.95.*

Outback Steak and Oyster Bar. Crocodile Dundee would feel at home at this delightfully funky restaurant, with rough-hewn walls, corrugated-tin ceilings, and rusting signs and license plates (many from Australia). Mementos on the wall range from croco-dile skins to antique mirrors collected by owners Steve and Linda Wood on their many trips Down Under. The friendly waiters and waitresses wear khaki shorts and rival Aussies for "mateyness." You will find alligator tail on the menu (yes, it tastes like chicken, albeit a little tougher and smokier) but there are also thick steaks, lamb chops, and luscious oysters, served in a variety of ways. Try oysters Kilpatrick (deep-fried and baked with bacon and mozzarella). *1914 W. Rte. 76, tel. 417/334–6306. Children's menu, liquor, senior-citizen discount, no-smoking section, reservations accepted. $10–$20.*

OTHER RESTAURANTS IN THE AREA

COCKTAIL LOUNGES

Crockey's Restaurant
Rtes. 65S and 165
417/334–4995
Continental

Roy's Loft
3425 W. Rte. 76
417/334–0076
Continental

Wayne's Gravel Bar Restaurant
1335 W. Rte. 76
417/334–5482
Continental

Wooden Nickel
Rte. 6, Box 4690,
Reeds Spring

417/338–2737
Continental

Ye English Inn/Banjo's Pub
24 Downing St.,
Hollister
417/334–4142
Nouvelle French

FAMILY DINING

Apple Mill Restaurant
3009 W. Rte. 76
417/334–6090
American

Applebee's Neighborhood Bar & Grill
2702 S. Williams

Ave., Springfield
417/889–4501
Country Style

Baldknobber's Country Restaurant
W. Rte. 76
417/334–7202
Country Style

Captain D's of Branson
1946 W. Rte. 76
417/335–5841
Seafood

Christopher's Gourmet Restaurant
24 Downing St.,
Hollister
417/334–4142
French

C.L's Ozark Family Restaurant
1580 W. Rte. 76
417/334–1206
American

Country Kitchen Restaurant
3225 W. Rte. 76
417/334–2766
Country Style

Cowboy Cafe
526 Shepherd of the Hills Expressway
417/335–4828
Barbecue

Cracker Barrel Old Country Store
3765 W. Rte. 76
417/335–3003
Country Style

Crockey's Restaurant
Rtes. 65S and 165
417/334–4995
Continental

Dinner Bell Restaurant
200 Jess Jo Pkwy.
417/336–3540
American

Dixie Stampede
1527 W. Rte. 76
417/337–9400
Country Style

Farmhouse Restaurant
119 W. Main St.
417/334–9701
Country Style

Golden Corral
3551 Shepherd of the Hills Expressway
417/336–6297
Steakhouse

Home Cannery Restaurant
W. Rte. 76
417/334–6965
American

Iron Skillet Restaurant
3304 Gold Rd., Kingdom City
314/642–8684
American

Kentucky Fried Chicken
1206 W. Rte. 76
417/334–5700
Fast Food

Mazzio's Pizza
1167 W. Rte. 76
417/334–4054
Pizza

McGuffey's Highway 76 Cafe
120 Wildwood Dr.
417/336–4156
Continental

McGuffey's Steakhouse
3265 Falls Pkwy.
417/337–5389
Steakhouse

Mesquite Charlie's
901 Gretna Rd.
417/334–0498
Steakhouse

Olive Garden
3790 W. Rte. 76.
417/337–5811
Italian

Ozark Mountain Buffet
3099 Shepherd of the Hills Expressway
417/335–5811
Country Style

Pizza Hut
1405 W. Rte. 76
417/334–6919
Italian

The Plantation
3460 W. Rte. 76
417/334–7800
Continental

Presley's Jukebox Cafe
2920 W. Rte. 76
417/334–3006
Café

Rails Seafood Buffet
433 Animal Safari Rd.
417/336–3401
Seafood

Ruby Tuesday
3316 W. Rte. 76
417/335–5450
American

Shoney's Inc.
1950 W. Rte. 76
417/335–6855
Diner

Showboat *Branson Belle*
HCR 9, Box 1469
417/336–7400
Continental

Spaghettata
2805 Green Mountain Dr.
417/336–3376
Italian

St. Louis Bread Company
3265 Falls Pkwy.
417/336–4550
Delicatessen

Stage Door Canteen
1984 Rte. 65
417/336–3575
Continental

Steak N Shake
503 W. Main St.
417/336–5303
American

Buck Trent Breakfast Theatre
118 Hampshire Dr.
417/335–5428
Breakfast and Show

Trotter's B-B-Q and more
3559 Shepherd of the Hills Expressway
417/336–3415
Barbecue

Western Sizzlin Steak House
1343 W. Rte. 76
417/334–4845
Steakhouse

Wishbones Cafe
405 W. Main St.
417/334–2703
Continental

FAST FOOD AND SNACKS

Baskin-Robbins Ice Cream
1901 W. Rte. 76
417/334–0255

Cakes-N-Cream
2805 W. Rte. 76
417/334–4929

Dairy Queen
302 N. 2nd St.
417/334–2366

Fritz Burger Stop
5753 Rte. 165
417/336–5324

Hardee's of Branson
1809 W. Rte. 76
417/334–1121

McDonald's
515 W. Main St.
417/334–1490

McDonald's #3
179 Meadow Ave.
417/337–7744

McDonald's West
2214 W. Rte. 76
417/335–2505

Subway Sandwiches and Salads
228 Hobart Dr., Forsyth
417/334–7827

Taco Bell
2000 W. Rte. 76
417/335–2576

Wendy's #11
510 W. Rte. 76
417/334–1414

Wendy's of Missouri, Inc.
3504 W. Rte. 76
417/334–1941

Bobby Vinton,
singer

Jordan Simon: What was your introduction to Branson?

Bobby Vinton: Last year I came in for a couple of days. About two weeks before we got here I asked my agent, "So where are we going?" He said, "Branson." I said, "Isn't that country? Why am I going to a country music town? Let's cancel." So he said, "Nah, you gotta go, you're sold out." [I got] six standing ovations. They went crazy. I said, "Wait a minute, this is an entertainment town. These people just want to be entertained." And then I walked around and saw that these people looked like the people who've been coming to my shows for all these years. They said, "Hey, don't you remember me, I saw you in Buffalo. We saw you here, we saw you there." So I figured this was the place for me. The Ozark Theater [approached] me and said, "This is what we do here. . . you just play [your music] and for a percentage we'll be partners. But I decided to build my own theater and make my son, Chris, the manager. My daughters and my mother sing in the show.

JS: It must be fun getting your whole family involved in the act.

BV: We've made it a family affair. It goes over well.

JS: Is it difficult doing two shows a day and maintaining the same level of energy and enthusiasm?

BV: I'm okay once the lights hit the band. You see, the audiences are always new and fresh, they bring their own energy. I get energy from them. All that energy you see on stage is from them.

JS: Do you continually refine your act?

BV: Hey, I may just change that whole bandstand around. I guarantee when you come back it'll be different.

JS: What are the things you have to keep in your show?

BV: Our show is our hits. When you see the other shows, a lot of them do other people's songs, but we've got a broad appeal. Glenn Miller has enough songs to fill two shows. I've got enough material to fill a show. We've gotta do "Roses Are Red" and "Mr. Lonely." The challenge for next year will be to think of new ways to present them.

JS: You've worked in every aspect of the entertainment industry. What's most challenging?

BV: Television. One bad light or one bad angle and you look awful. You're at the mercy of millions of people. On stage you can make a joke out of a mistake, but on television you're up against a hundred other channels. You're under constant pressure to be real good all the time. I did my show for three years, and I had to quit. It wasn't canceled—it was top-ten—but I sang every song I knew, I cracked every joke I knew, I smiled every smile I had—I didn't know what else I could do. It would have shown that I was faking it. Movies. I did a movie with John Wayne, it was boring. We woke up at six in the morning and sat around all day doing nothing. I did one scene. I could see where it would be exciting if I were a John Wayne or a real star in the movies, and you

had control over the project, but in my case I never really paid my dues as an actor. But I paid my dues as a live performer, and that's what I do well. But I can't do that as an actor. Everybody has their forte. Mine, fortunately, fits Branson. It fits my formula, it is perfect for me. I don't think many attractions would appeal to this audience. In my case, I have always been Bobby Vinton, the wholesome, squeaky clean, mid-America kid. All my friends in New York and L.A. used to tease: Mr. Middle America, Mr. Wholesome. But, hey, now it's in! Keep on calling me what you used to call me!

JS: Do you still see yourself doing this a few years from now?

BV: Yeah, at least for a couple of years, but I bore easy. Anyone who's creative needs challenge. I'll push this to the limit, then try something else. I may do the mogul thing—build a motel, a shopping center, and still own the theater and book acts. Maybe I'll do Saturday nights. There are always new formulas to keep things fresh. Maybe I'll have someone do the matinees, and I'll do the evening shows, but I can't see doing two shows for the next 20 years.

JS: Is there something your fans might not know about you? A hobby or a way you prepare to go on stage?

BV: Well, I watch the football games during breaks when I'm not on stage. After I introduce Doris I come back here and catch up on the scores. . . . I'm on the phone, talking, making deals. It's not like I'm sitting around doing scales. (He sings ah ah ah ah ah ah ah.)

JS: That's what Mel Tillis claims he does. He lets loose in the cavernous passage under the theater. Speaking of his theater, you know he's putting in a recording studio and soundstage?

BV: He's going all out, and that's good because this town needs a good recording studio. He's smart, because there'll be so many television shows coming here, doing specials and pilots. Branson will be an important TV area.

JS: It seems that Branson is diversifying. It isn't just country, it isn't just music anymore.

BV: Yeah, it's game shows, theme parks—family entertainment. And probably the reason for its success is that in the bigger cities, the media and TV are trying to compete by making things sexier, less moral. In trying to attract an audience, the media is getting too close to the edge for a lot of people. I don't even want to watch videos anymore. They turn me off. I can't believe this is the entertainment America wants. Branson makes a statement that we want a certain type of entertainment.

JS: Obviously, with such explosive growth, there's concern about overdevelopment. Will Branson be stretched too thin?

BV: Well, I know it's gonna hurt somebody. The competition's gonna be rough, and you've got to be better than the guy next door. Only two teams can go to the Super Bowl, and the rest have to stay home and watch it. Branson is heading to the play-offs.

JS: One of the things I've noticed is the versatility of the performers.

BV: Well, that's what Branson is about. I don't

think just anyone with a top-10 hit could last nine months here. The seasoned performers are here because they're all good. There's not a bad performer in Branson. They've all been in the business at least 25 years. Nobody lasts that long unless [he's] got something the public likes and is really on the ball. Once you come to Branson you get better and better every day. The show I did today was great, but I got a lot of changes to make it even better.

JS: Any phenomenon like Branson attracts its share of negative publicity. Some recent articles suggest that Branson excludes people. If you're not patriotic, if you're not into God and country, you'll feel uncomfortable here. Is that fair?

BV: It's hard to say. Branson is not the mountain, it's not the Borscht Belt, it's not 3 AM swingers in Vegas. It is what it is: Branson, Missouri, with wholesome family entertainment. . . Anytime you're successful, whether you're a president or a millionaire, they're gonna find faults and be jealous. And there are people out there who are jealous of Branson, and I don't blame them. Nashville's jealous. Vegas is starting to get hurt. Atlantic City's starting to suffer. Whenever you take money away from there and put it here, those people there are gonna say, what can we do about this?

JS: Vegas is making a big push for the family market.

BV: Yeah, Vegas is family—now I'm laughing. A family show and nobody has any clothes on!

Lodging

9

The Branson Lakes region offers a range of accommodations, including bed-and-breakfasts, campgrounds, condominiums, hotels, houseboats, motels, and resorts. Whatever your desire—from a three-story luxury log cabin, a fully outfitted houseboat, or a Victorian B&B to an inexpensive, utilitarian motel—you'll find it in Branson. The cost of accommodations here also covers the spectrum, but most properties are moderately priced, usually between $59 and $129 for a standard double room. Bear in mind, however, that prices listed below are the published rack rates for peak season (May–September), and may drop as much as 50% at other times of the year. Also, some small motels offer lower weekly rates or special deals (advertised on their billboards) when they're not fully booked. And, of course, tour groups receive substantial bulk discounts. For information about reservations, tour groups, and discounts *see* Chapter 1, Essential Information.

This chapter is divided into two parts: a chart, listing about 275 accommodations organized by type (B&B, resort, and so on) then alphabetized by name, and a Hotel Sampler, which contains full reviews of selected properties to give you an idea of your options in Branson. Lodgings in the sampler are among the most popular in the area for their location, amenities, and comparative value. In the chart you'll find all of the necessary information, including address, telephone number, number of rooms, rates, special policies, and facilities, for *all* accommodations mentioned in this chapter—even those found in the Hotel Sampler. Use the chart as your primary source, and when you find a property you like, turn to the map and look for the accommodation name and corresponding number on the legend. Lodgings in Branson proper and on the Strip appear on the lodging map in this chapter; for locations of accommodations outside of these areas, please see the maps in Chapter 6, The Outdoors.

YOUR CHOICES

Bed-and-breakfasts are generally either historic properties or elegant, meticulously kept homes, perfect for those seeking a homey, personal touch. Some may not have private bathrooms or amenities such as in-room phones and TVs; others may have such luxuries as whirlpool baths and private terraces. Many are furnished with antiques or family heirlooms and may not be the best choice for families with small children. Breakfasts range from a simple Continental buffet spread to a three-course gourmet extravaganza. Remember that most B&Bs are the owners' home, and, although your

LODGING

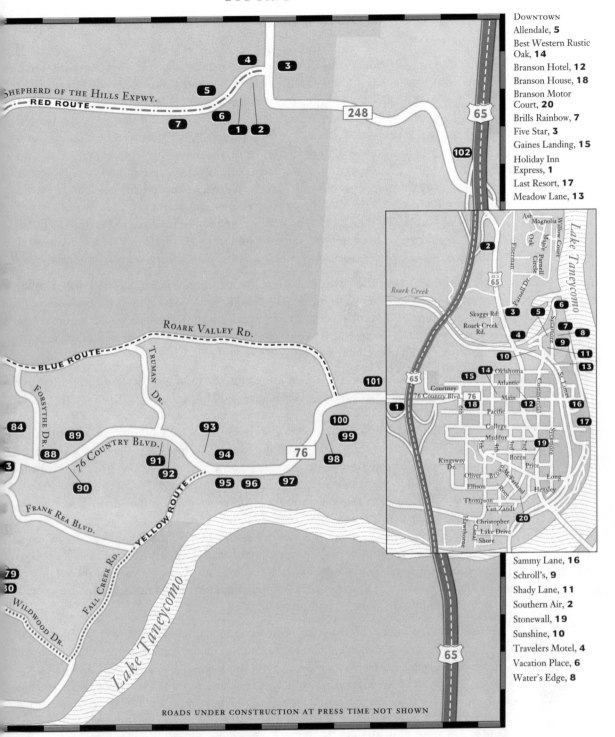

ROADS UNDER CONSTRUCTION AT PRESS TIME NOT SHOWN

hosts should be gracious and accommodating, they need their privacy, too, and can't always be at your beck and call.

Most **campgrounds,** the least expensive option, are in bucolic, out-of-the-way spots that take full advantage of the Ozarks' natural beauty. At almost all facilities, full-service tent sites and sites with RV hookups, electricity, and running water are available; at some locations you can even rent camping equipment such as tents and sleeping bags. On the other hand, a few properties may simply have primitive tent sites with no comforts, and most likely you'll have to supply your own equipment. Inquire before you go, so you don't find yourself unprepared in the woods. Although there are more than 6,000 sites available in the Branson area, it is one of the top drive destinations in the United States; many of those vehicles are RVs. Campgrounds in Branson are privately owned, except for those at Table Rock State Park and on the Taneycomo lakefront. There is no official KOA reservation center in Branson; for general information call the **Missouri Campground Owners Association** (tel. 314/564–7993). Reservations are essential.

Condominiums can offer excellent value for families, friends, and any other small groups traveling together. Condos range from efficiency studios to luxurious four-bedroom town houses, and most have a fully equipped kitchen and TV and stereo. Since condos are privately owned the decor usually varies from unit to unit: If you're unhappy with the unit you've been assigned, ask to see the other available rentals.

Most of Branson's **motels** and **hotels** are on the Strip or main thoroughfares, within easy walking distance of theaters, restaurants, and shops. In general, they offer clean, comfortable accommodations; standard amenities include cable or satellite TV, air-conditioning, and private bath. Extras may include free local calls and an in-room coffeemaker or complimentary coffee and donuts in the morning. Properties closer to downtown on the Strip are usually cheaper because they are farther from most of the action and in many cases older and more run-down than lodgings closer to the theaters. If you're a light sleeper, request a room that faces away from the street. Some hotels offer suites with connecting rooms and/or kitchenettes, a good budget option. Many low-to-moderately priced national chains are represented in the Branson area, including Holiday Inn, Budget Inn, Best Western, Comfort Inn, Howard Johnson, and Days Inn. Most such lodgings have a standardized, sterile look but also offer a standard level of service and comfort. Some of the higher-end chains have extras such as exercise rooms, shops, restaurants, or discos.

Houseboats are a unique form of Branson accommodation. They can remain moored at a marina on Table Rock Lake, or you can cruise to your heart's content. Think of them as floating apartments (or Winnebagos), with full kitchen and bath, even air-conditioning. Avoid houseboating if you're prone to seasickness: the pitch and roll of the waves on a windy night, even if your boat is moored, can be a problem if you have a sensitive stomach. If you're not an experienced boater, the marina crews will give you instructions and a quick "checkout cruise." You are responsible for gas and provisions, which are available at most marinas. Marinas are located approximately every 10 miles along the 750-mile shoreline.

Most **resorts** in Branson are on the lakes and are scenic, get-away-from-it-all options. Their styles range from no-frills with motel-type rooms to cozy, romantic, fully equipped cabins to all-inclusive, luxurious deluxe condominiums. The larger properties are villages in themselves, often replete with tennis courts, riding stables, marinas, gyms, restaurants, shops, and on-site entertainment. Many of these offer packages that translate into excellent values, especially for families. Even the smaller properties enjoy lake rights and usually have at least a launch (but no boat rentals) and small grocery store.

Following the chart is the Hotel Sampler. Its reviews describe some of Branson's distinctive choices but are not a comprehensive list: as you will see from the chart, there are many fine accommodations in Branson, and our sampler is intended simply to give you an idea of what is available at each type of establishment. After reading the review check the corresponding listing in the chart for complete service information about the specific property. Hotels in the sampler are located on the corresponding map.

BED-AND-BREAKFASTS

Branson Hotel. Built in 1907, this is the oldest hotel in Branson. The property has retained some fine details from yesteryear, including walnut, wrought-iron, four-poster, and sleigh beds, and old-fashioned shell sinks. Each room is individually decorated with a mix of antiques and period reproductions but also has modern conveniences such as cable TVs and full baths. Each room follows a specific theme: You might opt for the Duck Room, with a hunting motif in jade and burgundy, or the Wicker Room, which is dressed in lavender with intricate trim. A huge picture window dominates the sunny breakfast nook, where guests gather in the morning over coffee and a full breakfast that might include homemade muffins, pecan waffles, or French toast and fresh fruit. In the evening, complimentary sherry is served in the parlor. The spacious veranda, furnished with Adirondack-style rocking chairs, overlooks Main Street and the flurry of activity in downtown Branson. Most guest rooms, however, face away from Main Street and are sheltered from the noise.

Inn at Fall Creek. This idyllic property feels like it's in the middle of the countryside yet is only a few minutes' drive from the Strip. Americana predominates, especially in the enormous country kitchen, which is furnished with a Shaker table, copper kettles, and hand-stitched samplers. The walls are adorned with quilts, many pieced together by the grandmother of J.C. McCracken, the owner. Some of the hangings were made by members of the local quilting club and are for sale. The farmhouse antiques were patiently culled from barn sales and include an old-fashioned cedar closet used in Auntie's Attic room. Attached to the main house are the Chantilly Lace Suite, including a kitchenette and Jacuzzi, and the new Branson Broadway Suite, with canopy bed, fireplace, and kitchenette. Deer sometimes nibble the flowers lining the sun deck, which runs the length of the building and overlooks a hollow with a creek and a small waterfall.

CAMPGROUNDS

Aunts Creek Resort. Conveniently situated on a secluded arm of Table Rock Lake amid splendid gardens and woodlands, this campground—one of the most complete in the area—is only 15 minutes' drive from Silver Dollar City and 25 minutes from the Strip. Facilities include camping and fishing equipment rentals and supplies, fishing guide services, a grocery store, a laundromat, comfort stations with showers, a kennel (dogs not permitted at sites), grills, a fish-cleaning house, boat rental (and free launch), gas and oil fill-up station, and an outdoor pool (no lifeguard on duty). The campground offers electric and water hookups and shaded, level campsites. Tent and RV sites are in separate areas.

Chastains South Branson RV Park. Strategically positioned equidistant from Silver Dollar City, the Strip, and Table Rock Dam, Chastains is a popular campground with families that want to see and do everything in the area. Here, they're in the heart of the action, just 5–10 minutes by car in all directions. There are RV sites with electric and water hookups, tent sites, and rustic cabins with kitchenettes. Regardless of which unit you stay in, you'll have access to gas pumps, laundry facilities, showers, a grocery store, grills, a gift shop, an outdoor pool, a game room, and a playground.

Compton Ridge Campground. There is a total of 233 campsites here, spread across 85 wooded acres, but the main campground is just a mile from Silver Dollar City and Shepherd of the Hills. The facilities are complete, with full hookups, comfort stations with showers, a pool, laundry facilities, a grocery store, grills, hiking trails, and a free shuttle to selected local attractions. Campers have guest privileges at the affiliated adjacent Compton Ridge Lodge, which offers an indoor heated pool and children's pool, car rental, a game room, tennis court, and a convention center.

Silver Dollar City Campground. A mini–theme park unto itself, this property has its own outdoor and kiddie pools, three playgrounds, and an entertainment center with a pool table, video games, lounge with TV and VCR. Needless to say, this is a popular spot for families. Tent sites, RV sites with electric and water hookups, and a wilderness camping site with a one-room log cabin—all are within minutes of Silver Dollar City (regular free shuttle service provided) and only 10 minutes from the Strip. Facilities include a grocery store, grills, laundry facilities, an outdoor pool, and comfort stations with showers.

HOTELS AND MOTELS

Best Western Knights Inn. This centrally located, recently refurbished property is within walking distance of several theaters, including the Osmonds', Roy Clark's, John Davidson's and Jim Stafford's. The motel complex consists of three buildings, each offering the same style of room. Light sleepers should opt for the newest building in back because it's most quiet. The attractive, subdued decor features burgundy carpets, old-fashioned hardwood headboards, and dark floral spreads.

Blue Bayou Motor Inn. If you're on a tight budget, consider staying in this simple motor inn across from the Roy Clark Theater. Standard rooms are clean and have floral spreads and teal carpeting; jazzier units feature waterbeds or a Jacuzzi. Befitting its name, the Blue Bayou has an authentic Cajun restaurant, **Champagne's,** famed for its Friday- and Saturday-night seafood buffets and live zydeco music.

Branson Towers Inn. The handsome exterior introduces a southern-plantation motif that enriches the gracious lobby, with its ornate woodwork, imposing double staircase, marble floors, grand piano, and crackling fire. Rooms are slightly spartan but fresh, with wine-color carpets, salmon walls, and floral spreads and curtains. The one-bedroom suites with kitchenette and fireplace are more plush. In addition to its many facilities, Branson Towers offers a spa and masseuse services. The Shenandoah South Theater is across the street.

Comfort Inn. This ultramodern, comfortable property was built in 1992 and is impeccably maintained. Rooms are spacious by chain-hotel standards, furnished in pleasing mountain colors such as maroon, sienna, and jade. Among the facilities are an indoor pool, sauna, whirlpool, and sun deck. The Comfort Inn is within The Thousand Hills development and is a two-minute walk from Andy Williams's Theater and the Grand Palace.

Days Inn of Branson. This is the second-largest property in Branson (the Holiday Inn Crowne Plaza is the largest) and is predictably popular with tour groups because of its size and good rates. Located on a side street, just off the Strip, the Days Inn offers convenience without the noise of hotels on the main thoroughfare. Several theaters, including Five Star and the venues of Cristy Lane, Mickey Gilley, John Davidson, Jim Stafford, and Roy Clark, are within easy walking distance, as is the Factory Merchants of Branson.

Rooms are somewhat boxy but neat and are decorated with jade and peach carpets and curtains and floral bedspreads. Among the facilities are an outdoor pool, three outdoor hot tubs, and a playground.

Dutch Kountry Inn. Children particularly enjoy this property, thanks to its fairy tale–theme mini-amusement center, where kids can explore a windmill and clamber through a model of Mother Hubbard's shoe. The fun touches make sense, as the owner runs many of the go-cart and bumper boat concessions in town. (When you make reservations, ask for savings coupons for these attractions and also for breakfast buffets at Peppercorn's restaurant, next door.) Guest rooms are decorated in soothing earth tones; family units include sleeping lofts, and honeymoon suites have a whirlpool tub. Dutch Kountry is close to the Baldknobbers, Bobby Vinton, Andy Williams, and Grand Palace theaters.

Edgewood Motel. The Edgewood and its adjacent sister motel, the Shadowbrook, are set amid 25 acres of gardens and shade trees. There's plenty of beautifully landscaped space where guests can stroll, often in the company of deer and albino squirrels. Rooms, decorated in mountain colors such as maroon, jade, and dark blue, are huge, if a little spare. The **Home Cannery** restaurant, a favorite with locals for its bountiful breakfasts, deli lunches, and dinner buffets, is on the property. Facilities include two heated outdoor pools and a gift shop. Only the 76 Music Hall is within easy walking distance, but the motel is ideally situated between downtown and the main part of the Strip.

Fairfield Inn. This dependable, moderately priced hotel owned by the Marriott Corporation has average-size rooms dressed in wine and dusky rose, with jungle-print spreads. Facilities include an indoor pool and hot tub and a game room. The Tony Orlando, Pump Boys and Dinettes, and Osmonds theaters are nearby.

Friendship Inn. This reasonably priced property, built in 1993, is two blocks from the Strip, across from the Pump Boys and Dinettes theater. The appealing decor includes forest-green carpets and unusual abstract spreads. There's an outdoor pool and hot tub, and tennis courts are scheduled to be completed in 1995.

Great Western Inn. This is one of the typical big bargains on the Strip: Although the Great Western doesn't officially publish rates, there's a billboard advertising rooms for $14 and up. For that low price, you get surprisingly pleasant accommodations with a pastel color scheme. Furnishings are clean, if a little frayed at the edges, and the inn offers all of the amenities you'd expect from higher-end properties. The biggest bonus is the central location, near the Osmonds, Presleys, Ozark Jubilee, Roy Clark, Mickey Gilley, Jim Stafford, and John Davidson theaters.

Hall of Fame Motor Inn. The good-size rooms are fresh and cheerful, with powder-blue walls and imperial-purple carpeting. Suites include kitchenettes, two-person

Jacuzzis, and gas fireplaces. If you're a light sleeper be sure to request a room at the back. One of the best features of the Hall of Fame is its location, within a 5- to 10-minute walk of the Osmonds, Ozark Jubilee, Presleys, Grand Palace, Americana, Andy Williams, Roy Clark, John Davidson, Jim Stafford, and Mickey Gilley theaters.

Hi-Ho Motor Inn. The Hi-Ho would be just another ho-hum motel, were it not for the friendly service and Jacuzzi suites. The medium-size rooms are decorated in light pastels. The pool is the only amenity, but most guests stay here because it's inexpensive and is within walking distance of several theaters, including the John Davidson, Mickey Gilley, Jim Stafford, Roy Clark, Osmonds, Ozark Jubilee, and Pump Boys and Dinettes venues.

Holiday Inn Crowne Plaza. This new property, built in 1994, is Branson's largest and is just steps from the Andy Williams, Bobby Vinton, and Grand Palace theaters. Better yet, it's on a side street, just off the Strip, so it's less noisy than hotels on the main drag. The Crowne Plaza appellation is reserved for top properties in the Holiday Inn chain. Rooms are huge and done in elegant, dark mountain colors. **McGuffey's Highway 76 Cafe** (*see* Chapter 8, Dining) is on the premises. Other amenities include indoor and outdoor pools, a hot tub and a sauna, an exercise room, a convention center, an executive concierge floor, a gift shop, an art gallery, and a beauty salon. Children 19 and under stay free in their parents' room.

Lodge of the Ozarks. One of the most elegant options on the Strip, this hotel combines the ambience and comfort of a resort with the location and reasonable prices of a chain property. The small but sophisticated lobby, with marble, tile, and polished-wood furnishings, strikes an immediate note of class as you enter. There are several categories of accommodations, from oversize standard rooms in soothing earth tones to suites with wet bar and Jacuzzi. Facilities include three restaurants; the **Club Celebrity Lounge,** which offers live music and dancing after the shows, as well as other nightly entertainment; a convention center; three gift shops; a boutique; a beauty salon; a spa; and an indoor pool with hot tub. The location is excellent—with the Roy Clark Theater next door, and the Mickey Gilley, Jim Stafford, John Davidson, and Osmonds theaters within a few minutes' walk.

Mountain Music Inn. Two blocks off of the Strip but within walking distance of theaters such as the Cristy Lane, Boxcar Willie, and Five Star, Mountain Music Inn is a good bet for those who want proximity to the action without hassle. The decor is uniform from room to room, with mint and beige predominating. Ask to stay in the

newer wing; the older section could use renovation. Some new Jacuzzi suites are available. Facilities include indoor and outdoor pools, an indoor hot tub, a coffee shop, and an exercise room.

Music Capital Inn. This inn across from the Shoji Tabuchi Theater is an easy drive to the Shenandoah South, Country Tonite, and Mel Tillis theaters. Built in 1993, it sits right off time-saving access roads that feed into the Strip. Amenities include laundry facilities, a sauna, an indoor pool and hot tub, a game room, and a gift shop. Rooms favor mountain colors such as dusky rose and wine.

Music Country Motor Inn South. This basic motel's advantages are good rates and a central location across from the Baldknobbers and within walking distance of the Andy Williams, Bobby Vinton, Americana, Presleys, and Grand Palace theaters. The rear-building rooms are much quieter than those near the street; royal blue is the dominant color throughout. Facilities include indoor and outdoor pools and an indoor hot tub.

Palace Inn. The Palace Inn, next door to the Grand Palace and Grand Village shopping center, is another Branson bargain, considering the high quality of its rooms and facilities. The hospitable lobby evokes a genteel southern sitting room. Although accommodations are on the small side, they are pleasingly decorated in jade and dusky rose and have a tiny balcony overlooking either the Strip or woodlands. Amenities include a coffee shop, a beauty salon, indoor and outdoor pools and hot tubs, a sauna, laundry facilities, and Buckingham's, a fine restaurant (*see* Chapter 8, Dining).

Queen Anne Motel. Sister properties Queen Anne I and II combine the amenities of a motel with the ambience of a B&B. Exterior Victorian touches include turrets, frosted-glass doors, and gables galore. The larger-than-average rooms are daintily decorated in coral and salmon colors, with dark, polished headboards and armoires. The Queen Anne II is the preferred property because it overlooks woods and bluffs and is two blocks off of the Strip, but still convenient to several theaters, including the Five Star, Cristy Lane, and Boxcar Willie. Service is exceptionally friendly, even by Branson standards.

Settle Inn. The huge green-and-white buildings recall grand hotels of a bygone era. Average-size rooms have two-poster hardwood beds, burgundy carpets, and curtains with floral trim. The hotel is noted for its theme suites, which are at once kitschy and fun. (The mounted "knight" in shining armor that welcomes you outside is a giveaway that interesting times await.) Among the theme quarters are the Jungle Room (decorated with plants, stuffed parrots, and primary colors), the Aloha Room (with wind chimes, fishnets, tropical prints, trompe l'oeil beach murals, and papier-mâché parrots), the OK Corral Room (with a rough-hewn-timber bar and paintings of ranchers and cowboys), the Big Top Room (with elephant murals and bean bag chairs), the Medieval Room (with a papier-mâché "stone" arch and another suit of armor), and the Coca Cola Room (a '50s-theme room with movie posters and a small jukebox). All of the special rooms have Jacuzzis. Other offbeat attractions include a murder-mystery dinner theater, and there are more traditional features such as indoor pools and hot tubs, a conference room, a game room, laundry facilities, and a sandwich bar.

Seven Gables Inn. You'll receive a gracious welcome at this cozy property just off the Strip, one block from the Pump Boys and Dinettes show and within easy walking distance of the Osmonds, Roy Clark, Jim Stafford, John Davidson, and Mickey Gilley theaters. Standard rooms have maroon carpets and cherry two-poster beds; several Jacuzzi rooms are available. Amenities include indoor and outdoor pools, an outdoor hot tub, and laundry facilities. A new wing, slated for completion in 1995, will add 50 slightly larger rooms, all decorated in similar fashion.

Ye English Inn. Listed on the National Register of Historic Sites in Hollister (across Lake Taneycomo from Branson; *see* Chapter 5, Excursions in Ozark Mountain Country), the 1912 Ye English Inn has the mock-Tudor look common to all of the buildings on Downing Street. The theme is not carried out in the funky guest rooms, however, where you'll be transported back to the '50s: the burnt-orange and rust-brown couches and oddly mixed, bulky furniture seem to be left over from someone's garage sale. Somehow, though, the vintage style is part of the charm at this different (by Branson standards) establishment.

HOUSEBOATS

Houseboat Holidays (tel. 417/335–3042) and **Table Rock Lake Houseboat Vacation Rentals** (tel. 417/779–5214 or 800/833–5214). Renting a houseboat is a unique, delightful Branson experience that children seem especially to adore. The boat can remain moored, or you can happily explore the many coves and nooks of the lake. Don't expect to find a quaint nautical theme on these sleek cruisers, which typify houseboating on Table Rock Lake. You'll appreciate the air-conditioning, fully equipped kitchen, and utilitarian decor. Many boats have such features as sun decks and even water slides. The largest houseboats (64 feet long) can sleep up to 10 people comfortably. Before you indulge, remember that you're responsible for incidental expenses, including gas and food. Depending on the size of the boat, there may be tiny cabins (and berths around the dining room table) or a large stateroom. Quarters are always close on a boat, so if you're traveling with a group, make sure everyone is reasonably compatible.

RESORTS AND CONDOMINIUMS

Big Cedar Lodge. Nestled in a cove of Table Rock Lake, this impressive property ranks among the top resorts in the Midwest, if not in the country. At Bass Pro, the largest outdoors store in the country (*see* Springfield in Chapter 5, Excursions in Ozark Mountain Country), the owner, spared no expense in creating the ultimate retreat for both heavy corporate hitters and true romantics. The lush grounds and pristine lakefront are the Ozarks at their loveliest. The designer strived to duplicate authentic frontier-style architecture, with rough stone and rich woods. Choose among a variety of accommodations, from standard hotel rooms with handsome, Old World, hunting-lodge decor to luxurious private log cabins with full kitchen, a whirlpool bath, wrought-iron or hand-carved beds, vaulted ceilings, enormous stone fireplaces, stained-glass windows, hammered-iron fixtures, mounted trophies, antler chandeliers, and huge bearskin rugs. The woodwork throughout the property is wonderfully textured, contrasting logs with planks and assorted polished hardwoods. Turndown service includes fresh-baked ginger snaps by your bed. Among the facilities are the fine **Devils Pool** restaurant, a gift shop, a marina, tennis courts, jogging/hiking trails, stables, a fitness room, an outdoor pool and hot tub, a playground, miniature golf, and a private, 5,000-acre wilderness reserve called Dogwood Canyon, an unspoiled expanse of deep green pools, forested ridges, and limestone bluffs that is a trout angler's paradise.

Clarion at Fall Creek Resort. The selling point at this condo complex on a quiet curve of Lake Taneycomo is that it's somewhat removed from the action of Branson but is much closer than most of the condos at the other lakes. There are plenty of back roads nearby that you can use to bypass the Strip and get to a show within 10 or 15 minutes. Choose between deluxe condominiums and luxury log homes. All units have a full kitchen and washer/dryer, except the studio (kitchenette only) and an oversize motel room (bath only), both of which are less expensive than standard units. Some of the larger units have a sleeping loft, a bathtub with jets, and a fireplace. All of the amenities of a full-scale resort are available, including a tennis court, four pools (one indoor), a fitness center, a miniature golf course, a volleyball court, and a marina with private fishing dock.

Kimberling Inn Resort. This sprawling resort on Table Rock Lake includes everything from standard motel rooms to deluxe two-bedroom condominiums, some lavishly furnished, depending on the owners' taste. More units are scheduled for completion between 1995 and 1997. The inn is noted for its fine restaurants, including the romantic **Pier,** whose classic Continental menu, specializing in steaks and seafood, is prepared with panache; and **Ahoy's Lounge,** where a pianist and guitarist play relaxing music nightly for locals in the know. Other facilities include tennis courts, five pools (one indoor), a health club (with sauna and steam room), a playground, a marina, and an 18-hole miniature-golf course.

Pointe Royale. Celebrities are among the many people who have purchased condos in this upscale development on Lake Taneycomo below Table Rock Dam. Residents enjoy the highly rated 18-hole golf course and the awe-inspiring views from their decks, of the emerald greens, towering bluffs, or the imposing dam itself. In addition to the gorgeous surroundings, there is a tennis center (courts lighted for night play), an Olympic-size pool, a restaurant, a mini-mart, and a clubhouse with men's and women's saunas. One-, two- and three-bedroom units are individually decorated, most of them with impeccable taste. Full kitchen and washer/dryer are standard amenities.

Rock Lane Resort. This Best Western property is beautifully situated on a point of land jutting into Table Rock Lake. You'll get a stunning view from almost every room, especially from the individually decorated one- and two-bedroom condominiums located on the water. The glass-enclosed **Windows on the Lake** restaurant is that rare place where the food nearly equals the fabulous views. Full-scale facilities include a marina, two pools, and two tennis courts.

Sammy Lane Resort. The resort has been a beloved Branson institution since 1924, hosting several generations of families that have vacationed on this secluded neck of Lake Taneycomo. The complex, hidden amid banks of towering shade trees, offers cozy, fully equipped cottages of various sizes that can sleep 2 to 10 people comfortably. Several units have barbecue grills and/or fireplaces. The resort is famed for its leviathan pool, the largest in Missouri. Other facilities include a playground, game room, hot tub, fishing pier, and boat dock.

Tribesman Resort. This is one of the premier family resorts on Table Rock Lake, thanks to its inventive children's programs. There's a fishing hole just for kids (the staff excels at teaching young ones how to angle) and a family of ducks who love to be fed and petted. "Injun" signs are posted all over the resort, offering rewards for capturing Geronimo. The owner, Arno II (his nickname), is a font of fascinating Ozarks tales (tall and otherwise) that keep the entire family entranced. Fully equipped accommodations range from one-bedroom condo cabins to four-bedroom Swiss houses. The decor is nothing special, but the quarters are clean, functional, and lived-in. Promotional deals are offered throughout the year, and every guest is welcomed by the *Smokesignals* newsletter, which includes plenty of coupons for local attractions and restaurants.

Turkey Creek Ranch. This 400-acre working ranch possesses a herd of cattle and saddle horses, giving it a dude-ranch flavor; kids love traipsing through the stables and petting their favorites. The 17 fully equipped housekeeping cottages are appealing, unassuming, and decorated predominantly in pastels. The white-washed, red-roof buildings blend with the surroundings, as is typical of Bull Shoals resorts. There is a wide range of recreational facilities on tap, from shuffleboard to a video arcade to tennis and, of course, fishing.

BED & BREAKFASTS

Accommodations	Rates	Credit Cards	Number of Rooms	Months Closed	Accessibility	Senior Discount	Children Free	Pets Allowed	No Smoking Rooms	Restaurants	Room Service	Lounge/Disco/Nightclub	Exercise Room	Pool	Tennis Courts	Golf Courses	Marina	Shops
Aunt Sadie's Garden Glade 163 Fountain St. 417/335-4063	$70–$89	AE,D,MC,V	3	none	no	no	no	no	yes	no	no	no	no	no	no	no	no	no
Barger House Bed and Breakfast 621 Lakeshore Dr. 800/335-2134	$95	none	3	none	no	no	no	no	yes	no	no	no	yes	yes	no	no	yes	no
Bird's Eye View Bed and Breakfast 718 Acacia Club Rd., Point Lookout 417/336-6551	$75–$95	AE,D,MC,V	3	none	no	no	no	no	yes	yes	no	no	no	no	no	no	no	no
Branson Hotel Bed and Breakfast Inn 214 W. Main St. 417/335-6104	$85–$95	none	9	mid-Dec.–Mar.	no	no	no	no	yes	yes	no	no	no	no	no	no	no	no
Branson House Bed and Breakfast Inn 120 N. 4th St. 417/334-0959	$65–$85	none	7	mid-Dec.–Mar.	yes	yes	no	no	yes	yes	no	no	no	no	no	no	no	no
Brass Swan 202 River Bend 417/334-0959	$70–90	D,MC,V	4	none	no	yes	no	no	yes	no	no	no	no	no	no	no	no	no
Cameron's Crag 738 Acacia Club Rd. 417/335-8134	$75–$95	AE,D,MC,V	3	none	yes	yes	no	no	yes	no	no	no	no	no	no	no	no	no
Cinnamon Hill 24 Wildwood La. Kimberling City 417/739-5727	$55–$65	MC,V	4	none	no	no	under 5	no	yes	no	no	no	no	no	no	no	no	no
Emory Creek B&B and Gift Shop, 143 Arizona Dr. 417/334-3805 800/482-1090	$64–$95	D,MC,V	7	none	no	no	no	no	yes	no	no	no	no	no	no	no	no	yes
Fall Creek 4988 Fall Creek Rd. 417/334-3939	$55–$110	AE,MC,V	19	none	yes	yes	no	no	yes	no	yes	yes	yes	yes	no	no	no	no
Gaines Landing Bed and Breakfast 521 W. Atlantic 417/334-2280	$75–$95	D,MC,V	3	none	no	no	no	no	yes	no	no	no	no	yes	no	no	no	no

Name	Price	Credit Cards	No.															
Grandpa's Farm Bed and Breakfast Box 476, HCR 1, Lampe 417/779-5106	$65–$85	D,MC,V	4	none	no	yes	yes	no	no	no	yes	no	yes	no	no	yes	no
Inn at Fall Creek Bed and Breakfast 391 Concord Ave. 417/336-3422	$70–$95	MC,V	4	none	no	yes	yes	no	no	no	yes	no	yes	no	yes	yes	no
Josie's Peaceful Getaway HCR 1, Box 1104, Indian Point Rd. 417/328-2678	$36–$95	MC,V	4	none	no	no	yes	no	yes	yes	yes	no	yes	no	no	no	no
Kite House 397 Esplanade 417/334-7341	$60–$95	MC,V	8	none	no	no	yes	yes	no	no	yes	no	yes	no	no	no	no
Light in the Window Rte. 160, Walnut Shade 417/561-2415	$50–$75	none	4	none	no	yes	yes	no	no	no	yes	no	yes	under 10	yes	no	no
Lodge at We Lamb Farm 760 Gobbler's Knob 417/334-1485	$85	D,MC,V	4	none	no	no	yes	no	no	no	yes	no	yes	under 12	no	yes	no
Ozark Mountain Country B&B Service Box 295; 417/334-4720, 800/695-1546	$40–$95	AE,D,MC,V	100	none	yes	yes	yes	yes	yes	yes	yes	no	yes	no	yes	yes	yes
Red Bud Cove HC 1, Box 446 417/334-7144	$70–$90	AE,D,MC,V	7	none	no	no	yes	no	no	no	yes	no	yes	under 3	no	yes	no
Schroll's Lakefront Bed and Breakfast 418 N. Sycamore 417/335-6759	$45–$95	D,MC,V	5	none	yes	yes	yes	no	no	no	yes	no	yes	no	yes	no	no
Show Me Hospitality 391 Concord Ave. 800/280-3422 417/337-5210	$70–$95	MC,V	5	none	no	yes	yes	no	no	no	yes	no	yes	no	no	no	no
Thurman House Bed and Breakfast 888 State F. Hwy. 417/334-6000	$85 and up	AE,MC,V	1	none	no	yes	yes	no	no	no	yes	no	no	under 2	yes	yes	no
CAMPGROUNDS																	
Acorn Acres RV Park and Campground, W. Rte. 76 417/338-2500	$15–$23	D,MC,V	83	none	yes	no	no	no	no	no	yes	no	yes	under 6	no	no	yes
America's Best Campground, Inc. 499 Buena Vista Rd. 417/336-4399	$21.50–$23	D,MC,V	154	none	yes	yes	yes	no	no	no	yes	no	yes	no	yes	yes	yes

Accommodations	Rates	Credit Cards	Number of Rooms	Months Closed	Accessibility	Senior Discount	Children Free	Pets Allowed	No Smoking Rooms	Restaurants	Room Service	Lounge/Disco/Nightclub	Exercise Room	Pool	Tennis Courts	Golf Courses	Marina	Shops
Aunts Creek Resort Rte. 5, Box 570 417/739-5267	$15	MC,V	23	none	yes	no	no	yes	no	no	no	no	no	yes	no	no	no	yes
Blue Mountain Campground 4590 W. Rte. 76, Box 8410 417/338-2114 800/779-2114	$25 cabins $11-17 sites	D,MC,V	3 cab. 65 sites	none	yes	yes	under 10	yes	no	no	no	no	no	yes	no	no	no	no
Branson City Campground 300 S. St. Limas Dr., Box 1309 417/334-2915	$13	none	350	none	yes	no	yes	yes	no	no	no	no	no	no	no	no	no	no
Branson Shenanigans 3675 Keeter St. 417/334-1920	$18.31-$22.89	MC,V	30	Dec.-Mar.	yes	no	no	yes	no	no	no	no	no	yes	no	no	no	no
Carson's Country Court 2166 Rte. 248 417/334-3084	$15	none	35	none	yes	no	no	yes	no	no	no	no	no	no	no	no	no	no
Castle View Estates HCR 4, Box 3679 Reeds Spring 417/338-2156	Members only	AE,D,MC,V	134	none	yes	no	no	yes	no	no	no	yes	yes	yes	yes	no	yes	no
Cedar Falls Campground & RV Park Rte. 65 S, Hollister 417/334-2770	$14-$16	MC,V	42	none	no	no	yes	yes	no	no	no	no	no	yes	no	no	no	yes
Chastains S. Branson RV Park 397 Animal Safari Rd. 417/334-4414	$17.50-$26.50	D,MC,V	218	none	yes	yes	no	yes	no	no	no	no	no	yes	no	no	no	no
Compton Ridge Campground HCR 9, Box 1180 417/338-2911	$17-$25	MC,V	234	mid-Dec.-mid-Mar.	yes	no	under 5	yes	no	no	no	no	no	yes	no	no	no	yes
Gerth Camper Park 139 Irish La. 417/334-5849	$15-$20	none	150	none	yes	yes	yes	yes	no	no	no	no	no	yes	no	no	no	no
Headwaters Campground 1025 Headwaters Rd. 417/334-7450	$15-$23	none	108	none	no	yes	under 4	yes	no	no	no	no	no	yes	no	no	no	no

Indian Point's Deer Run Camp *HCR 1, Box 1168, Indian Point Rd.* *800/908–3337*	$8–$18	D,MC,V	140	none	yes	yes	no	yes	no	no	no	no	no	yes	no	no	no	yes
Lakeview Campground *Indian Point Rd.* *417/338–5211*	$15–$20	D,MC,V	47	Nov.–May	yes	yes	under 5	yes	yes	no	no	no	no	no	no	no	no	yes
Musicland KOA Campground *116 N. Gretna Rd.* *417/334–0848*	$21.95–$27.95	MC	130	Nov. 1–Apr. 1	no	no	no	yes	no	no	no	no	no	yes	no	no	no	yes
Ozark Country Campground *679 Quebec Dr.* *417/334–4681*	$11–$19	MC,V	76	none	yes	yes	no	yes	yes	no	no	yes	no	yes	no	no	no	no
Silver Dollar City Campground *Rte. 265* *417/338–8189*	$14–$23	AE,D,MC,V	186	none	yes	no	no	yes	no	no	no	yes	no	yes	no	no	no	yes
Stagecoach Stop RV Park/Campground *5751 Rte. 165* *417/334–4681*	$15–$18	D,MC,V	41	none	yes	no	under 6	yes	no	yes	no	no	no	yes	no	no	no	no
Stormy Point Resort & Campground *HCR 9, Box 1401* *417/338–2255*	rooms: $50–$152 sites: $15–$20	MC,V	18 rms. 65 sites	mid-Dec.–mid-Mar.	yes	no	campers under 11	no	yes	no	no	no	no	yes	no	no	yes	yes
Table Rock State Park *Rte. 165* *417/334–4704*	$6–$11	none	165	none	no	yes	yes	yes	no	no	no	no	no	no	no	no	yes	no
Tall Pines Campground *HCR 9, Box 1175, Rte. 265* *417/338–2445*	$12–$21	D,MC,V	8	Nov.–mid-Mar.	yes	yes	under 12	yes	no	no	no	no	no	yes	no	no	no	yes
Treasure Lake Camping Club *1 Treasure Lake Dr.* *417/334–1040*	Members only	AE,D,MC,V	600	none	yes	no	yes	yes	no	no	no	no	no	yes	yes	no	no	no
Wilderness Club RV Resort *Rte. 165* *417/336–6401*	$20–$25	none	150	none	yes	no	yes	yes	yes	no	no	no	yes	yes	no	no	no	no
➧ MOTEL/HOTEL																		
Alpenrose Motor Inn *2875 Green Mountain Dr.* *800/324–9494*	$49–$62	AE,D,DC,MC,V	50	Jan.–Feb.	no	yes	under 12	no	yes	no	no	no	no	yes	no	no	no	no
Amber Light Motor Inn *Box 177* *417/334–7200*	$40–$55	D,MC,V	60	Dec. 22–Jan. 15	no	yes	under 13	no	yes	no	no	no	no	yes	no	no	no	no

Accommodations	Rates	Credit Cards	Number of Rooms	Months Closed	Accessibility	Senior Discount	Children Free	Pets Allowed	No Smoking Rooms	Restaurants	Room Service	Lounge/Disco/Nightclub	Exercise Room	Pool	Tennis Courts	Golf Courses	Marina	Shops
America's in 4 Less 1031 W. Rte. 76 417/334-7380	$32.95–$39.95	D, MC, V	23	none	no	yes	under 13	no	no	no	no	no	no	yes	no	no	no	no
Atrium Inn 3005 Green Mountain Dr. 417/336-6000 800/656-5555	$29.95–$85	MC, V	102	mid-Dec.–mid-Jan.	yes	yes	under 13	no	yes	no	no	yes	no	yes	no	no	no	yes
Baldknobber's Motor Inn 2843 W. Rte. 76 417/334-7948	$48–$70	AE,D,MC,V	75	mid-Dec.–Feb.	yes	yes	yes	no	no	no	no	no	no	no	no	no	no	no
Barrington Hotel 265 Shepherd of the Hills Expressway; 417/334-8866 800/760-8866	$39.95–$98	AE, D, MC, V	149	none	yes	yes	under 13	yes	yes	no	no	no	no	yes	no	no	no	no
Ben's Wishing Well Inn 2935 W. Rte. 76 417/334-6950	$33–$55	AE,D,MC,V	150	none	no	no	yes	no	yes	no	no	no	no	yes	no	no	no	yes
Bentree Lodge HCR 1, Box 967, Indian Point Rd. 800/272-6766	$35–$300	D,MC,V	74	none	no	yes	under 14	no	yes	no	no	no	no	yes	yes	no	no	no
Best Inns of America 3150 Green Mountain Dr. 800/404-5013	$30–$75	AE,D,MC,V	66	none	yes	yes	yes	no	no	no	no	no	no	yes	no	no	no	no
Best Western Branson Inn 248 Rte. 65 417/334-5121	$40–$135	AE,D,DC,MC,V	272	none	yes	yes	under 18	no	yes	no	no	no	no	yes	no	no	no	no
Best Western Knights Inn 3215 W. Rte. 76 417/334-1894	$50–$95	AE,D,DC,MC,V	166	Jan.–mid-Feb.	yes	yes	under 12	no	yes	yes	yes	yes	no	yes	yes	no	no	no
Best Western Mountain Oak Lodge W. Hwy. 76 417/338-2141	$49–$69	AE,D,MC,V	150	Jan.–Mar.	no	yes	yes	no	yes	yes	yes	yes	no	yes	yes	no	no	yes
Best Western Music Capital Inn, 3257 Shepherd of the Hills Expressway 417/334-8378	$50–$95	AE,D,DC,MC,V	93	Jan.–mid-Mar.	yes	yes	under 12	no	yes	no	no	yes	no	yes	no	no	no	yes

Property	Price	Credit Cards	Rooms	Closed	Children Discount	A	B	C	D	E	F	G	H	I	J	K
Best Western Rock Lane Resort, HCR 1, Box 920, Indian Point Rd. 417/338-2211	$60–$90	AE,D,MC,V	100	Nov.–mid-Apr.	yes	yes	yes	no	yes	yes	no	yes	no	yes	yes	no
Best Western Rustic Oak Motor Inn, 403 W. Main St. 800/528-1234	$36–$67	AE,D,MC,V	109	none	yes	no	no	no	no	yes	no	no	yes	no	yes	no
Big Valley Motel, 2005 W. Rte. 76 800/332-7274	$29–$65	AE,D,MC,V	99	mid-Dec.–Feb.	yes	yes	no	no	no	yes	no	yes	no	no	no	yes
Blue Bayou Motor Inn, 3400 W. Rte. 76 800/633-3789	$49–$68	AE,D,MC,V	124	mid-Dec.–mid-March	yes	no	no	no	no	yes	no	yes	no	yes	yes	yes
Boxcar Willie Motel, 3454 W. Rte. 76 417/334-8873	$65	AE,D,MC,V	88	mid-Dec.–Feb.	yes	yes	no	no	no	yes	no	yes	no	no	no	yes
Bradford Inn, Rte. 265 417/338-5555	$49–$89	D,MC,V	15	none	yes	yes	no	no	no	yes	no	yes	no	yes	yes	yes
Branson Grand Ramada, 245 N. Wildwood 800/850-6646	$80–$130	AE,D,MC,V	200	none	yes	yes	no	no	no	yes	yes	yes	yes	yes	yes	yes
Branson Lodge, 2456 Rte. 165 417/334-3105	$45–$69	D,MC,V	32	none	yes	no	no	no	no	yes	no	yes	no	yes	yes	yes
Branson Motor Court, 615 S. Commercial St. 417/334-3420	$28–$40	D,MC,V	30	none	no	yes	no	no	no	yes	no	yes	no	no	no	no
Branson Park Inn, 2801 Green Mountain Dr. 417/336-2100	$49–$68	AE,D,DC,MC,V	120	none	under 16	no	no	no	no	no	yes	no	no	no	no	yes
Branson Plaza Motel, 1106 W. Rte. 76 417/334-7511	$32.95–$38.95	AE,D,MC,V	33	Dec. 20–Jan.	under 12	no	no	no	no	yes	no	yes	yes	no	no	no
Branson Suites, 3706 W. Rte. 76 417/335-3233	$45–$130	AE,D,DC,MC,V	40	none	no	no	no	no	no	yes	no	yes	yes	no	yes	yes
Branson Towers Inn, 236 Shepherd of the Hills Expressway 417/336-4500	$42–$76	AE,D,DC,MC,V	210	none	under 12	yes	no	no	no	yes	no	yes	yes	no	yes	yes

Accommodations	Rates	Credit Cards	Number of Rooms	Months Closed	Accessibility	Senior Discount	Children Free	Pets Allowed	No Smoking Rooms	Restaurants	Room Service	Lounge/Disco/Nightclub	Exercise Room	Pool	Tennis Courts	Golf Courses	Marina	Shops
Caprice Motor Inn 3410 W. Rte. 76 417/334-8555	Call for rates	AE,D,MC,V	80	Dec 1.-Apr.	no	no	under 12	no	yes	yes	no	yes	no	yes	no	no	no	no
Cascades Inn 3226 Shepherd of the Hills Expressway 417/335-8424	$39.95-$79.95	AE,D,DC,MC,V	160	none	yes	yes	under 18	no	yes	no	no	yes	yes	yes	no	no	no	yes
Cedar Cliff Motel 150 Church Rd. 417/335-2543	$39-$55	D,MC,V	60	none	yes	no	under 12	yes	no	no	no	no	no	yes	no	no	no	no
Cinnamon Inn 3601 Shepherd of the Hills Expressway 417/334-8694	$39.95-$61.95	AE,D,MC,V	95	none	yes	yes	under 12	no	yes	no	no	no	no	yes	no	no	no	no
Classic Motor Inn 2384 Shepherd of the Hills Expressway 417/334-6991	$38-$58	AE,DC,MC,V	62	Jan.-Feb.	yes	yes	under 19	no	yes	no	no	no	no	yes	no	no	no	yes
Colonial Mountain Inn Box 2068, W. Rte. 76 417/272-8414	$32-$50	D,DC,MC,V	52	none	yes	no	under 12	yes	no	no	no	no	no	yes	no	no	no	no
Comfort Inn 203 S. Wildwood Dr. 417/335-4727	$55.95-$74.95	AE,D,DC,MC,V	108	Jan.-Feb.	yes	yes	under 12	no	no	no	no	no	yes	yes	no	no	no	no
Compton Ridge Lodge HCR 9, Box 1180 417/338-2949	$55-$75	MC,V	25	Dec. 23-Feb.	yes	no	under 6	no	no	no	no	no	no	no	no	no	no	no
Country Music Inn 3060 Green Mountain Dr. 417/336-3300	$45-$79	AE,D,DC,MC,V	82	Jan.-Feb.	yes	yes	under 13	no	no	no	no	no	no	yes	no	no	no	no
Country Western Motor Inn Box 1452, W. Rte. 76 417/334-6978	$29.95-$54.95	D,MC,V	38	mid-Dec.-Feb.	no	yes	under 9	no	no	no	no	no	no	yes	no	no	no	no
Days Inn of Branson 3524 Keeter St. 417/334-5544	$39-$85	AE,D,DC,MC,V	425	Jan.-mid-Feb.	yes	yes	under 12	yes	yes	yes	no	no	no	yes	no	no	no	yes

Name / Address / Phone	Price Range	Credit Cards	Units	Closed														
Deer Run Motel, Indian Point HCR 1, Box 1168 417/338-2223	$39.95–$65	AE,D,MC,V	89	none	yes	yes	under 13	no	yes	no	no	no	no	yes	no	no	no	no
Dutch Kountry Inn 2425 W. Rte. 76 417/335-2100	$35–$85	D,MC,V	291	none	yes	yes	under 17	no	yes	yes	no	no	no	yes	no	no	no	no
Eagle's View Cottages (formerly Red Eagle Resort) HCR 1, Box 996 417/338-2227	$41–$139	AE,D, MC,V	15–20	none	no	no	under 1	no	no	no	no	no	no	yes	no	no	yes	no
The Eagles 3221 Shepherd of the Hills Expressway 417/728-2664	$40–$60	D,MC,V	66	mid-Dec.–mid-Mar.	yes	yes	under 12	no	yes	no	no	no	no	yes	no	no	no	no
Econo Lodge 230 S. Wildwood Dr. 417/336-4849	$45–$70	AE,D,DC, MC,V	62	none	yes	yes	under 19	no	yes	no	no	no	no	yes	no	no	no	no
Econo Lodge of Hollister Rte. 65 417/334-2770	$36.95–$45.95	AE,D,MC,V	43	none	yes	yes	under 12	yes	yes	no	no	no	no	yes	no	no	no	no
Edgewood Motel W. Rte. 76 417/334-1000	$40–$80	AE,D,MC,V	297	none	yes	yes	no	no	yes	yes	no	no	no	yes	no	no	no	yes
Expressway Inn 691 Shepherd of the Hills Expressway 417/334-1700	$40–$63	D,MC,V	106	mid-Dec.–Mar.	yes	yes	under 13	yes	yes	no	no	no	no	yes	no	no	no	no
E-Z Center Motel Box 6370 417/334-8200	$23.95–$44.95	AE,D,DC, MC,V	19	none	no	no	under 8	no	yes	no	no	no	no	no	no	no	no	no
Fairfield Inn 220 Rte. 165 417/336-5665	$29–$81.95	AE,D,DC, MC,V	100	none	yes	yes	under 18	yes	yes	no	no	no	no	yes	no	no	no	no
Falls Parkway Inn 3245 Falls Pkwy. 417/336-3255	$39–$68	AE,D,DC, MC,V	117	Jan.–Feb.	yes	yes	under 12	no	yes	no	no	no	no	yes	no	no	no	no
Family Inn 208 Old County Rd. 417/334-2113	$22–$90	D,MC,V	25	Jan.–Mar.	yes	yes	under 2	no	no	no	yes	no	no	no	no	no	no	no
Fiddler's Inn 3522 W. Rte. 76 417/334-2212	$39–$60	AE,D,MC,V	80	mid-Dec.–Mar. 20	yes	yes	yes	yes	yes	yes	yes	no	no	yes	no	no	no	no

Accommodations	Rates	Credit Cards	Number of Rooms	Months Closed	Accessibility	Senior Discount	Children Free	Pets Allowed	No Smoking Rooms	Restaurants	Room Service	Lounge/Disco/Nightclub	Exercise Room	Pool	Tennis Courts	Golf Courses	Marina	Shops
Five Star Lodge 422 N. Business Rte. 65 800/653-1800	$24.50–$59	D,MC,V	17	mid-Dec.–Mar.	no	no	no	no	yes	no	no	no	no	no	no	no	no	no
Foxborough Inn 589 Shepherd of the Hills Expressway 417/335-4369	$24–$65	AE,D,DC,MC,V	175	Jan.–mid-Mar.	yes	no	under 12	no	yes	no	no	no	no	yes	no	no	no	yes
Frontier Inn Motor Lodge 3340 W. Rte. 76 417/334-5704	$35–$52	AE,D,DC,MC,V	54	mid-Dec.–mid-Mar.	no	no	no	no	yes	no	no	no	no	yes	no	no	no	no
Friendship Inn (formerly Williamsburg Inn) 3015 Green Mountain Dr. 417/335-4248	$39.95–$59.95	AE,D,DC,MC,V	100	none	yes	yes	yes	no	no	no	no	no	no	yes	no	no	no	no
Gazebo Inn 2424 W. Rte. 76 417/335-3826	$49.95–$129.95	AE,D,MC,V	73	mid-Dec.	yes	yes	yes	no	no	no	no	no	no	yes	no	no	no	yes
Good Shepherd Inn 1023 Main St., W. Rte.. 76 417/334-1695 800/324-3457	$29.95–$49.95	AE,D,DC,MC,V	63	none	yes	yes	under 15	yes	no	no	no	no	no	yes	no	no	no	no
Grand Oaks Hotel 2315 Green Mountain Dr. 417/336-6423	$49–$75	AE,D,DC,MC,V	111	none	yes	yes	under 18	no	no	no	no	yes	no	yes	no	no	no	no
Great Western Inn 3110 W. Rte. 76 417/334-8998	$24.50–$68.50	AE, D, MC, V	41	Jan.–mid-Feb.	no	no		no	no	no	no	no	no	yes	no	no	no	no
Greenbrier Inn 3518 W. Rte. 76 417/334-0444	$30.95–$52.95	AE,D,MC,V	106	mid-Dec.–mid-Mar.	no	yes	under 17	no	no	no	no	no	no	yes	no	no	no	no
Guest House Hotel 495 Shepherd of the Hills Expressway 417/336-3132	$45–$55	AE,D,MC,V	98	none	yes	yes	under 19	no	yes	no	no	no	no	yes	no	no	no	no
Hall of Fame Motor Inn 3005 W. Rte. 76 417/334-5161	$45–$64.50	AE,D,MC,V	160	mid-Dec.–mid-Mar.	yes	yes	under 19	no	yes	no	no	no	no	yes	no	no	no	no

Name / Address / Phone	Price	Credit Cards	Rooms	Closed	1	2	3	4	5	6	7	8	9	10	11	Age	12	13
Hampton Inn 2350 Green Mountain Dr. 417/334-6500	$39–$78	AE,D,DC,MC,V	113	none	no	no	no	yes	no	no	no	no	yes	no	yes	no	no	no
Hampton Inn West 3695 W. Rte. 76 417/337-5762	$55–$99	AE,D,DC,MC,V	110	none	no	no	no	no	yes	no	no	no	no	yes	no	under 18	yes	yes
Heritage Inns 220 S. Wildwood Dr. 417/335-4500	$38.50–$68.50	D,MC,V	105	mid-Dec.–mid-Mar.	no	no	no	no	yes	no	no	no	no	yes	no	under 12	yes	yes
Hi-Ho Motel 3325 W. Rte. 76 417/334-2204	$39.50–$58	D,MC,V	56	mid-Dec.–Mar. 1	no	no	no	no	yes	no	no	no	no	yes	no	under 10	no	yes
Hillbilly Inn 1166 W. Rte. 76 417/334-3946	$38–$48	AE,D,MC,V	51	mid-Dec.–Mar.	no	no	no	no	yes	no	no	no	yes	yes	no	under 12	yes	yes
Holiday Inn 1420 W. Rte. 76 417/334-5101	$65–$100	AE,D,DC,MC,V	220	none	no	no	no	no	yes	yes	yes	yes	yes	yes	no	under 19	yes	yes
Holiday Inn Crown Plaza 120 S. Wildwood Dr. 417/335-5767	$65–$99	AE,D,DC,MC,V	500	none	yes	no	no	no	yes	yes	yes	yes	yes	yes	no	under 19	yes	yes
Holiday Inn Express 1000 W. Main St. 417/334-1985	$49.50–$93.50	AE,D,DC,MC,V	90	none	no	no	no	no	yes	no	no	no	no	yes	no	under 19	yes	yes
Holiday Inn North I-44 2720 N. Glenstone Ave. Springfield 417/865-8600	$78.50–$200	AE,D,DC,MC,V	188	none	no	no	no	no	yes	yes	yes	yes	yes	yes	yes	under 19	yes	yes
Hollister Inn 1250 Rte. V Hollister 417/334-5950	$18.95–$36.95	D,MC,V	30	none	no	no	no	no	yes	no	no	no	no	yes	no	under 16	yes	yes
Honeysuckle Inn & Info. Center, 3598 Shepherd of the Hills Expressway 417/335-2030	$39.95–$49.95	AE,D,MC,V	215	none	no	no	no	no	yes	no	no	no	no	yes	no	under 13	yes	yes
Hotel Grand Victorian 2325 W. Rte. 76 417/336-2935	$62.95–$99.95	AE,D,MC,V	152	Jan.–Feb.	yes	no	no	no	yes	no	no	no	no	yes	yes	under 18	yes	yes
Howard Johnson 3027-A W. Hwy. 76 417/336-5151	$55–95	AE,D,DC,MC,V	344	mid-Dec.–mid-Feb.	yes	no	no	no	yes	no	no	no	yes	yes	yes	under 13	yes	yes

Accommodations	Rates	Credit Cards	Number of Rooms	Months Closed	Accessibility	Senior Discount	Children Free	Pets Allowed	No Smoking Rooms	Restaurants	Room Service	Lounge/Disco/Nightclub	Exercise Room	Pool	Tennis Courts	Golf Courses	Marina	Shops
K Royal Motel 3775 W. Rte. 76 417/335-2232	$30–$70	AE,D,MC,V	55	mid-Dec.–Feb.	yes	yes	under 12	no	no	no	no	no	no	yes	no	no	no	no
Kimberling Suites Rte. 13 and Oak Dr. Kimberling City 417/739-5547	$52.65–$79.50	AE,D,MC,V	28	none	yes	yes	no	yes	no	no	no	no	no	yes	no	no	no	no
Kings Quarters 580 Shepherd of the Hills Expressway 417/334-5464	$49.95–$59.95	AE,D,DC,MC,V	104	mid-Dec. Mar.	yes	yes	under 12	yes	no	no	no	no	no	yes	no	no	no	no
Lakeview Inn W. Rte. 76 417/272-8195	$19.95–$39.95	AE,D,MC,V	66	none	no	yes	under 12	no	no	no	no	no	no	yes	no	no	no	no
Leisure Country Inn 3350 W. Rte. 76 417/335-2425	$42.50–$65	AE,D,DC,MC,V	101	Jan.–mid-Feb.	yes	yes	under 13	yes	no	no	no	yes	no	yes	no	no	no	no
Lighthouse Inn 2375 Green Mountain Dr. 417/336-6161	$39.50–$67.50	AE,D,DC,MC,V	91	mid-Dec.–mid-Jan.	yes	yes	under 18	yes	no	no	no	no	no	yes	no	no	no	no
Lodge of the Ozarks 3431 W. Rte. 76 417/334-7535	$60–$130	D,MC,V	190	none	yes	no	yes	no	yes	yes	yes	no	no	yes	no	no	no	yes
Lowe's Fall Creek Inn Rte. 165 and Fall Creek Rd. 417/334-0428	$28–$69.95	D,MC,V	100	none	yes	yes	under 16	no	yes	no	no	no	no	yes	no	no	no	no
Lynina Inn 2772 Shepherd of the Hills Expressway 800/435-4883	$29.95–$49.95	AE,D,DC,MC,V	51	Jan.–Feb.	yes	yes	yes	no	no	no	no	no	no	yes	no	no	no	yes
Magnolia Inn 3311 Shepherd of the Hills Expressway 417/334-2300	$45–$62	AE,D,MC,V	152	none	yes	no	under 12	yes	no	no	no	no	no	yes	no	no	no	yes
Marriot Residence Inn 280 Wildwood Dr. S 417/336-4077	$59–$179	AE,D,DC,MC,V	85	none	yes	yes	under 18	yes	no	no	no	yes	yes	yes	no	no	no	no

Name / Address	Price	Credit Cards	No.	Closed	1	2	3	4	5	6	7	8	9	10	11	12	13
Marvel Motel 3330 W. Rte. 76 417/334-4341	$40–$45.95	D,MC,V	71	mid-Dec.–Mar.	yes	yes	yes	no	yes	no	no	no	no	yes	no	no	no
Melody Lane Inn 2821 Rte. 76 W 417/334-8598	$39.50–$62	AE,D,MC,V	140	Jan.–Feb.	yes	yes	under 12	no	yes	yes	no	no	no	yes	no	no	yes
Motel 9 210 N. Gretna Rd. 417/334-4836	$32.95–$44.95	AE,D,DC,MC,V	50	Jan.–Feb.	no	no	yes	no	yes	no	no	no	no	yes	no	no	no
Mountain Country Motor Inn Rte. 5, Box 720 Reeds Spring 417/739-4155	$30–$50	D,MC,V	30	none	no	yes	under 10	no	yes	no	no	no	no	yes	no	no	no
Mountain Music Inn 300 Schaefer Dr. 417/335-6625	$32–$80	AE,D,MC,V	140	none	yes	yes	under 16	no	yes	no	no	no	yes	yes	no	no	yes
Music Capital Inn, Best Western, 3257 Shepherd of the Hills Expressway 417/334-8378	$50–$125	AE,D,MC,V	93	Jan.–Mar.10	yes	yes	no	no	yes	no	no	no	yes	yes	no	no	yes
Music Country Motor Inn South 2834 W. Rte. 76 417/334-1194	$45–$99	AE,D,MC,V	113	Jan.–Feb.	yes	yes	yes	no	yes	no	no	no	no	yes	no	no	no
Notch Inn (inn and condos) W. Rte. 76 800/336-6824	$34–$125	AE,D,MC,V	226	Jan.–Mar. for the inn discount	yes	yes	yes	yes	no	no	no	no	yes	no	no	no	no
Old Southern Inn 2 mi south of Rte. 76 on Rte. 265 417/338-2900	$31–$51	AE,D,MC,V	24	mid-Dec.–mid-Mar.	yes	no	under 5	no	yes	no	no	no	no	yes	no	no	no
Old Weavers Inn, 2651 Shepherd of the Hills Expwy. 417/336-6088 800/884-8224	$39–$65	MC,V	52	none	yes	yes	yes	no	yes	no	no	no	no	yes	no	no	no
Orange Blossom Inn 3355 Shepherd of the Hills Expressway 417/336-6600	$65–$75	AE,D,DC,MC,V	77	Jan.–Mar.	yes	yes	yes	no	yes	no	no	no	no	yes	no	no	no
Ozark Mountain Inn 1415 W Rte. 76 417/334-8300	$40–$95	AE,D,MC,V	27	Jan.–early Mar.	no	yes	yes	no	yes	no	no	no	no	yes	no	no	no
Ozark Regal Hotel 3010 Green Mountain Dr. 417/336-2200	$49–$69	D,MC,V	100	none	yes	yes	yes	no	yes	yes	no	yes	yes	yes	no	no	no

Accommodations	Rates	Credit Cards	Number of Rooms	Months Closed	Accessibility	Senior Discount	Children Free	Pets Allowed	No Smoking Rooms	Restaurants	Room Service	Lounge/Disco/Nightclub	Exercise Room	Pool	Tennis Courts	Golf Courses	Marina	Shops
Ozark Valley Inn, 2693 Shepherd of the Hills Expwy. 417/336-4666 800/947-4666	$45–$60	D,DC,MC,V	66	none	yes	yes	yes	yes	yes	no	no	no	no	yes	no	no	no	no
Ozark Western Motel 2719 W. Rte. 76 417/334-7000 800/343-9302	$50–$60	AE,D,DC,MC,V	133	Jan.–mid-Mar.	yes	yes	under 19	no	no	no	no	no	no	yes	no	no	no	no
Ozarka Lodge Rte. 6, Box 8 Eureka Springs, AR 501/253-8992	$40–$68	AE,D,MC,V	45	none	yes	yes	under 18	no	yes	yes	no	no	no	yes	no	no	no	yes
Palace Inn 2820 W. Rte. 76 417/334-7666	$50–$105	AE,D,MC,V	166	none	yes	no	no	no	yes	yes	yes	no	no	yes	no	no	no	yes
Parkview Lodge 5477 Rte. 165 417/334-4041	$18–$35	AE,D,DC,MC,V	10	none	no	yes	under 7	no	no	no	no	no	no	yes	no	no	no	no
Peach Tree Inn 2450 Green Mountain Dr. 417/335-5900	$45–$64	AE,D,DC,MC,V	64	Jan.–Feb.	yes	yes	under 12	no	no	no	no	no	no	yes	no	no	no	yes
Plantation Inn 3460 W. Rte. 76 417/334-3600	$50–$59	D,MC,V	78	Jan.–Feb.	no	no	yes	no	yes	no	yes	no	no	yes	no	no	no	no
Polar Bear Inn 3545 Arlene Dr. 417/336-5663	$29–$49	AE,D,MC,V	40	none	yes	yes	under 12	no	no	no	no	no	no	yes	no	no	no	no
Quality Inn 3269 Shepherd of the Hills Expressway 417/335-6776	$39–$65	AE,D,MC,V	215	none	yes	yes	yes	no	yes	yes	no	no	no	yes	no	no	no	no
Quality Inn 3050 N. Kentwood Springfield 417/833-3108	$45–$64	AE,D,MC,V	198	none	yes	yes	under 17	no	yes	yes	yes	yes	yes	yes	no	no	no	no
Quality Inn-76 245 Jess Jo Pkwy. 417/336-6288	$45–$55	AE,D,MC,V	132	none	yes	yes	yes	no	no	no	no	no	no	yes	no	no	no	no

Name / Address / Phone	Price	Credit Cards	Rooms	Closed													
Queen Anne Motel 3510 W. Rte. 76 417/335-8100	$40–$65	AE,D,MC,V	40	none	yes	yes	under 12	no	yes	no	no	no	no	yes	no	no	no
Ridgeview Motel HCR 9, Box 1278 417/338-2438	$30–$48	D,MC,V	19	Jan.–Mar.	no	no	under 5	no	yes	no	no	no	no	yes	no	no	no
Rodeway Inn 2422 Shepherd of the Hills Expressway 417/336-5577	$39–$68	AE,D,DC,MC,V	66	Jan.–Feb.	yes	yes	yes	no	yes	no	no	no	no	yes	no	no	yes
Rosebud Inn 2400 Roark Valley Rd. 417/336-4000, 800/767-3522	$39–$59	AE,D,MC,V	64	none	yes	yes	yes	no	yes	no	no	no	no	yes	no	no	yes
Rustic Gate Motor Inn Rte. 13, Box 1088 417/272-3326	$33–$46	AE,D,MC,V	65	Dec.–Feb.	yes	yes	under 12	no	yes	yes	no	no	no	yes	no	no	yes
Scottish Inns 730 Rte. 165 417/334-5555	$29–$61	D,MC,V	85	none	yes	yes	under 10	no	yes	no	no	no	no	yes	no	no	no
Settle Inn 3050 Green Mountain Dr. 417/335-4700	$33–$129	AE,D,MC,V	300	none	yes	yes	yes	yes	yes	yes	yes	yes	yes	yes	no	no	yes
Seven Gables Inn 305 Rte. 165 S 417/334-7077, 800/280-7077	$29.95–$69.95	AE,D,MC,V	130	none	yes	no	no	no	no	no	no	no	no	yes	no	no	no
76 Mall Inn, Inc. 1945 W. Rte. 76 417/335-3535	$41–$59	AE,D,MC,V	319	none	yes	yes	under 12	no	yes	yes	no	no	no	yes	no	no	yes
Shadowbrook Motel W. Rte. 76 800/641-4600	$50–$60	AE,D,MC,V	60	Jan.–Feb.	yes	yes	yes	no	yes	yes	no	no	no	yes	no	no	no
Silver Slipper Motel 3705 W. Rte. 76 417/334-3326	$25–$40	AE,D,MC,V	40	none	no	no	under 10	no	yes	no	no	no	no	yes	no	no	yes
Silver Fountain Inn 1425 W. Rte. 76 417/334-5125	$35–$140	AE,D,MC,V	80	Mid-Dec.–mid-Mar.	no	no	no	no	no	no	no	no	no	yes	no	no	no
Sleep Inn 210 S. Wildwood Dr. 417/336-3770	$55–$79	AE,D,DC,MC	68	Jan.–mid-Feb.	yes	yes	yes	no	yes	no	no	no	no	yes	no	no	no

Accommodations	Rates	Credit Cards	Number of Rooms	Months Closed	Accessibility	Senior Discount	Children Free	Pets Allowed	No Smoking Rooms	Restaurants	Room Service	Lounge/Disco/Nightclub	Exercise Room	Pool	Tennis Courts	Golf Courses	Marina	Shops
Southern Air Motel 549 N. Business Rte. 65 417/334-2417	$26.50–$42.95	AE,D,MC,V	24	none	no	yes	no	yes	no	no	no	no	no	no	no	no	no	no
Southern Country Inn 2316 Shepherd of the Hills Expressway 417/337-5207	$45–$78	AE,D,DC,MC	90	none	yes	yes	yes	yes	yes	no	no	no	no	yes	no	no	no	no
Southern Oaks Inn 3295 Shepherd of the Hills Expressway 800/324-8752	$40–$62	D,MC,V	150	none	yes	yes	under 12	no	yes	no	no	no	no	yes	no	no	no	no
Spinning Wheel Inn 235 Schaefer Dr. 800/215-7746	$33–$58	AE,D,MC,V	50	Jan.–Mar.	yes	yes	under 16	no	yes	no	no	no	no	yes	no	no	no	no
Stonewall Motor Inns 511 S. Commercial St. 417/334-3416	$32–$48	AE,D,MC,V	17	Jan.–Mar.	no	yes	yes	no	no	no	no	no	no	yes	no	no	no	no
Stonewall West Motor Inn 1030 W. Main W. Rte. 76 417/334-5173	$32–$52	AE,D,DC,MC	25	Jan.–Feb.	yes	yes	under 11	no	yes	no	no	no	no	no	no	no	no	no
Stonybrook Inn HCR 9, Box 1176 417/338-2344	$34.95–$39.95	D,MC,V	19	Jan.–Feb.	yes	yes	yes	no	yes	no	no	no	no	yes	no	no	no	no
Summer House Inn 1360 W. Rte. 76 417/334-0040	$34.95–$54.95	AE,D,MC,V	99	none	no	yes	yes	no	yes	no	no	no	no	yes	no	no	no	no
Super 8 Motel-Branson 2490 Green Mountain Dr. 417/334-8880	$48.88–$79.88	AE,D,DC,MC	73	none	yes	yes	under 12	no	yes	no	no	no	no	yes	no	no	no	no
Surrey Inn 430 Rte. 165 S 417/335-5090 800/452-2716	$40–$55	AE,D,MC,V	151	Dec.20–Mar. 1	yes	yes	under 19	no	yes	no	no	yes	no	no	no	no	no	yes
Table Rock Inn 5631 Rte. 165 800/234-5890	$30–$50	AE,D,MC,V	17	none	yes	yes	no	yes	Apr.–Oct.	no	no	no	no	yes	no	no	no	no

Name / Address	Rates	Credit Cards	Rooms	Closed			Children									
Tara Inn 245 Shepherd of the Hills Expressway 800/525-8272	$40–$95	AE,MC,V	63	none	yes	yes	yes	no	yes	no	no	no	yes	no	no	yes
Travelers Inn 1970 W. Rte. 76 417/336-1100	$50–$80	AE,D,DC,MC	159	none	yes	yes	under 11	yes	yes	no	no	no	yes	no	no	no
Travelers Motel, Downtown 402 N. Business Rte. 65 417/334-3868	$39.75–$69.75	AE,D,MC,V	33	Jan.–Feb.	no	yes	no	yes	yes	no	no	no	yes	no	no	no
Travelodge Forget-Me-Not Inn 3102 Falls Pkwy. 800/899-1097	$45–$83	AE,D,DC,MC,V	81	Jan.–Feb.	yes	yes	under 17	no	yes	no	no	no	yes	no	no	yes
Twelve Oaks Inn 205 Schaefer Dr. 417/334-7340	$29.95–$75.95	AE,D,MC,V	66	Jan.–Feb.	yes	yes	under 16	yes	no	no	no	no	yes	no	no	no
Twin Pines Motel 141 Montgomery Dr. 417/335-3740	$25–$35	D,MC,V	18	none	no	no	yes	no	yes	no	no	no	yes	no	no	no
Uncle John's Inn HCR 1 Box 833 417/338-2820	$35–$59.50	D,MC,V	23	mid-Dec.–Mar.	yes	yes	under 4	yes	no	no	yes	no	yes	no	no	no
Victorian Palace 600 Schaefer Dr. 417/334-8727	$48–$185	AE,D,MC,V	68	Jan.–Feb.	yes	yes	under 12	no	yes	no	no	no	yes	no	no	no
Village At Indian Point HCR 1, Box 1158 417/338-8800	$79–$99	D,MC,V	24	none	no	no	no	no	yes	no	no	no	yes	no	no	no
White Oak Inn W. Rte. 76 and 13 Junction 800/822-6159	$34.95–$44.95	D,DC,MC	30	Jan.–Mar.	yes	yes	under 12	yes	yes	no	no	no	yes	no	no	no
The Woods Resort Hotel 2201 Gretna Rd. 800/935-2345	$64–$140	AE,D,MC,V	223	none	yes	yes	under 12	yes	no	yes	yes	no	yes	yes	no	no
Ye English Inn/Banjo's Pub 24 Downing St. Hollister 800/554-7188	$30–$45	AE,D,MC,V	22	none	no	no	no	no	no	no	no	no	yes	no	no	no
▶ **RESORTS & CONDOS** **Allendale Resort, Inc.** 420 N. Commercial St. 417/334-3411	$21–$52	D,MC,V	42	none	no	yes	no	no	no	no	no	no	yes	no	yes	no

Accommodations	Rates	Credit Cards	Number of Rooms	Months Closed	Accessibility	Senior Discount	Children Free	Pets Allowed	No Smoking Rooms	Restaurants	Room Service	Lounge/Disco/Nightclub	Exercise Room	Pool	Tennis Courts	Golf Courses	Marina	Shops
Alpine Lodge Resort HCR 1, Box 795 417/338-2514	$45–$135	D,MC,V	17	Jan.–Feb.	no	no	yes	no	no	no	no	no	no	yes	no	no	yes	no
Antlers Resort and Campground HCR 1, Box 858 417/338-2331	rooms: $32–$126 sites: $14–$18	AE,D,MC,V	19 rms. 19 sites	none	yes	no	yes	no	no	no	no	no	no	yes	no	no	yes	no
Artilla Cove Resort HCR 1, Box 839 417/338-2346	$32–$63	AE,D,MC,V	10	Jan.–Feb.	no	no	no	no	no	no	no	no	no	yes	no	no	yes	no
Aunts Creek Resort Rte. 5, Box 497 Reeds Spring 417/739-4411	$47–$136	none	16	Nov.–Feb.	yes	no	yes	no	no	no	no	no	no	yes	no	no	yes	no
Bavarian Village Resort HCR 1, Box 797 800/322-8274	$39–$85	MC,V	17	Nov.–Feb.	no	no	no	no	no	no	no	no	no	yes	no	no	yes	no
Benson Spring Resort Rte. 1, Box 813 Green Forest, AR 501/438-6729	$100	MC,V	2	none	yes	yes	no	yes	no	no	no	no	no	no	no	no	no	no
Bentree Lodge, HCR 1, Box 967, Indian Point Rd. 417/338-2218	$34.95–$300	D,MC,V	74	none	yes	yes	under 14	yes	yes	no	no	no	no	yes	yes	no	no	no
Big Cedar Lodge 612 Devils Pool Rd. Ridgedale 417/335-2777	$79–$850	AE,D,MC,V	195	none	yes	yes	under 12	no	yes	yes	yes	yes	yes	yes	yes	yes	yes	yes
Big Bear Resort and Campground 353 Clevenger Cove Rd. 800/334-4131	$15–$150	AE,D,MC,V	241	Nov.–Mar.	yes	no	yes	yes	no	no	no	no	no	yes	no	no	no	yes
Blue Haven Resort 1851 Lakeshore Dr. 417/334-3917	$39–$55	D,MC,V	31	none	yes	no	no	no	no	no	no	no	no	yes	no	no	no	yes
Boomerang Resort Rte. 4, Box 3450 Reeds Spring, 417/338-2358	$35–$84	D,MC,V	30	none	yes	no	yes	yes	no	no	no	no	no	yes	no	no	no	no

Resort	Rates	Credit Cards	Units	Closed	1	2	3	4	5	6	7	8	9	10	11	12	13	14
Branson Bluffs, Inc., *Rte. 3, Box 3440, Galena, 417/538-2291, 800/640-1550*	$34.95–$65	AE,D,DC,MC	52	none	yes	yes	under 12	no	yes	yes	no	yes	no	yes	yes	yes	yes	yes
Branson Lakes Resort *200 Lake St. Rockaway Beach 800/886-9184*	$26–$89	D,MC,V	23	none	yes	yes	yes	no	yes	no	no	no	no	yes	no	no	no	no
Briarwood Resort *1685 Lake Shore Dr. 417/334-3929*	$37–$135	none	16	Dec.–Feb.	yes	yes	yes	yes	no	no	no	no	no	yes	no	no	yes	yes
Brills Rainbow Resort *414 N. Sycamore 417/334-3955*	$22–$52	D,MC,V	29	none	no	no	under 2	no	no	no	no	no	no	yes	no	no	yes	no
Cardinal Hills Cottages *Rte. 9, Box 1176-1 417/338-8732*	$60–$80	D,MC,V	16	none	yes	yes	under 6	no	yes	no	no	no	no	yes	no	no	no	no
Cedar Point Resort *261 Cedar Pt. Rd. Forsyth 417/546-3326*	$25–$45	none	7	mid-Dec.–mid-Jan.	no	no	no	yes	no	no	no	no	no	yes	no	no	yes	no
Cedar Resort *HCR 9, Box 1418 417/338-2653*	$29–$256	D,MC,V	20	none	yes	yes	no	no	no	no	no	no	no	yes	no	no	yes	no
Clarion at Fall Creek Resort *1 Fall Creek Dr. 417/334-6404 800/562-6636*	$59–$189	AE,D,DC,MC,V	320	none	yes	yes	under 13	no	yes	yes	no	no	yes	yes	yes	no	yes	yes
Cloud Nine Resort *1575 Lakeshore Dr. 417/334-6273*	$34–$55	D,MC,V	9	none	no	yes	under 3	yes	no	no	no	no	no	yes	no	no	yes	no
Coleman's Resort *HCR 1, Box 1009 417/338-2849*	$36–$120	D,DC,MC	19	none	no	yes	under 5	no	yes	no	no	no	no	yes	no	no	yes	no
Cooper Creek Resort & Campground *471 Cooper Creek Rd. 417/334-4871*	$15.75–$113	MC,V	111	none	yes	no	no	yes	no	no	no	no	no	yes	no	no	no	yes
Corvair Resort *HCR 1, Box 1006 417/338-2231*	$36–$93	D,MC,V	18	Dec.–Feb.	yes	no	under 5	no	no	no	no	no	no	yes	no	no	no	no
Cottage Resort and Market *HCR 1, Box 1030 417/338-2621*	$30–$85	D,MC,V	19	Nov.–Feb.	yes	yes	under 8	no	yes	no	no	no	no	yes	no	no	yes	no

Accommodations	Rates	Credit Cards	Number of Rooms	Months Closed	Accessibility	Senior Discount	Children Free	Pets Allowed	No Smoking Rooms	Restaurants	Room Service	Lounge/Disco/Nightclub	Exercise Room	Pool	Tennis Courts	Golf Courses	Marina	Shops
Cozy Cove Condominium Community 78 Cozy Cove Rd. Reeds Spring 417/335-2644	Yearly rentals only	none	58	none	yes	no	no	yes	no	no	no	no	yes	yes	no	no	yes	no
Crest Lodge Resort HC 5, Box 348 Reeds Spring 417/739-4456	$54–$94	none	14	end. Oct.–mid-Mar.	yes	no	no	yes	no	no	no	no	no	yes	no	no	yes	no
Crow's Nest Resort HCR 1, Box 792 417/338-2524	$29–$54	MC,V	15	Nov.–Mar.	yes	no	no	no	no	no	no	no	no	yes	no	no	yes	no
Del Mar Resort 1993 Lakeshore Dr. 417/334-6241	$33–$60	none	14	none	yes	no	no	no	no	no	no	no	no	yes	no	no	yes	no
Double Oak Resort Rte. 3, Box 4650 Galena 800/525-3625	$44–$58	AE,D,DC, MC	10	Nov.–Feb.	no	no	under 1	yes	no	no	no	no	no	yes	no	no	yes	yes
Driftwood Resort HCR 9, Box 1421 417/338-2243	$38–$72	D,MC,V	15	none	no	no	no	no	no	no	no	no	no	yes	no	no	yes	no
Edgewater Villa Resort Rte. 5, Box 314 Reeds Spring 417/739-4585	$49–$57	none	18	Nov.–Feb.	no	no	no	no	no	no	no	no	no	yes	no	no	yes	no
Fox Fire Resort HCR 1, Box 794 417/338-2119	$42–$120	none	12	Jan.–mid-Mar.	yes	yes	yes	no	no	yes	no	no	no	yes	no	no	no	no
Gage's Long Creek Lodge Main Rte. 2, Box 958 Ridgedale 417/334-1413	$42.50–$95.50	AE,D,MC,V	36	none	yes	no	under 5	no	yes	no	no	no	no	yes	no	no	yes	no
Gobblers Mountain Resort HCR 4, Box 1372 Reeds Spring 417/338-2304	$37–$68	D,MC,V	9	none	yes	no	no	yes	no	no	no	no	no	yes	no	no	yes	no
Golden Arrow Resort HCR 1, Box 977 417/338-2245	$40–$100	MC,V	20	Jan.–Feb.	yes	no	under 5	no	no	no	no	no	no	yes	no	no	no	no

Name	Rate	Credit Cards	Units	Closed													
Green Mountain Lodge 204 Merriam Blvd. Rockaway Beach 417/561-4324	$25–$100	AE,D,MC,V	20	none	no	yes	under 15	yes	no	no	no	no	no	no	yes	no	yes	no
Green Valley Resort Rte. 4, Box 3470 Reeds Spring 417/338-2241	$62–$85	MC,V	17	Dec.–Mar.	yes	no	under 2	no	yes	no	no	no	no	yes	no	yes	yes
Happy Hollow Resort 248 Hammock Way Blue Eye 417/779-4360	$38–$75	MC,V	11	none	yes	no	under 2	no	no	no	no	no	no	yes	no	yes	no
Happy Valley Lodge HCR 1, Box 849 417/338-2342	$34–145	D,MC,V	22	Jan.–Mar.	no	no	under 1	yes	no	no	no	no	no	yes	no	yes	no
Hiawatha Resort HCR 9, Box 1411 417/338-2605	$35–$48	D,MC,V	20	Nov.–mid-Mar.	yes	no	under 2	yes	no	no	no	no	yes	yes	no	yes	no
Holiday Hills Nightly Condos 640 East Rockford Dr. 417/334-4443	$59.50–$129.50	AE,D,MC,V	100	none	yes	yes	yes	no	no	yes	no	no	no	yes	no	no	yes
Indian Point Lodge HCR 1, Box 982 417/338-2250	$50–$199	AE,D,MC,V	50	mid-Dec.–Jan.1	yes	no	no	no	no	no	no	no	no	yes	yes	yes	yes
Indian Trails Resort HCR 1, Box 999 417/338-2327	$43–$141	MC,V	18	mid-Dec.–Jan.	yes	no	no	no	no	no	no	no	no	yes	no	no	no
Kimberling Arms Resort/Best Western Rte. 13, Kimberling City 417/739-2461	$66–$99	AE,D,DC,MC,V	38	Dec.–Feb.	yes	yes	no	yes	no	no	no	no	no	yes	no	yes	no
Kimberling Heights Motel/ Resort HCR 4, Box 980, Kimberling City 417/779-4158	$39–$59	AE,D,DC,MC,V	14	Nov.–Feb.	no	yes	no	yes	no	no	no	no	no	yes	no	no	no
Kimberling Inn Resort and Conference Center, Box 159, Kimberling City, 417/739-4311, 800/833-5551	$39.50–$159.50	AE,D,MC,V	350	none	yes	no	under 13	no	yes	yes	no	yes	yes	yes	yes	yes	no
Lakefront Resort & Campground, HCR 2, Box 127, Rte. UU10, Blue Eye 417/779-4154	rooms:– $50–$150 sites: $10–$15	MC,V	11 rms 34 sites	none	no	no	under 2	yes	no	no	no	no	no	yes	no	yes	yes
Lakeshore Resort 1773 Lakeshore Dr. 417/334-6262	$46–$125	AE,D,MC,V	15	none	yes	yes	under 2	yes	yes	yes	no	no	no	yes	no	yes	yes

Accommodations	Rates	Credit Cards	Number of Rooms	Months Closed	Accessibility	Senior Discount	Children Free	Pets Allowed	No Smoking Rooms	Restaurants	Room Service	Lounge/Disco/Nightclub	Exercise Room	Pool	Tennis Courts	Golf Courses	Marina	Shops
Lantern Bay Resort & Condos 100 Lantern Bay Rd. 417/338-3000	$69–$109	AE,D,MC,V	100	none	yes	yes	yes	no	no	no	no	no	yes	yes	yes	no	yes	no
Last Resort 207 St. Limas 417/335-6697	$30–$60	D,MC,V	12	none	no	yes	yes	yes	yes	no	no	no	no	yes	no	no	no	no
Lazy Lee's Resort HCR 4, Box 1840 Reeds Spring 417/338-2253	$49–$123	MC,V	20	Nov.–mid-Mar.	yes	no	under 1	no	no	no	no	no	no	yes	no	yes	yes	yes
Lazy Valley Resort 285 River La. 417/334-2397	$47–$100	none	16	none	yes	no	no	no	no	no	no	no	no	yes	no	yes	yes	yes
Lilleys' Landing 367 River La. 417/334-6380	$45–$130	D,MC,V	23	none	yes	no	under 5	yes	no	no	no	no	no	yes	no	yes	yes	yes
Lost Tree Condominium Rte. 65 N 417/335-3936	Yearly rentals only	none	60	none	yes	yes	yes	no	no	no	no	no	no	yes	no	no	no	no
Lucky '13' Resort Rte. 5, Box 615 417/739-4414	$49–$99	MC,V	15	Nov.–Mar.	yes	no	no	yes	yes	no	no	no	no	yes	no	yes	no	no
Meadow Lane Resort 402 N. St. Limas 417/334-3442	$32–$42	D,MC,V	15	none	yes	no	under 6	yes	yes	no	no	no	no	no	no	no	no	no
Night Hawk Resort HJR-1, Box 838-5 417/338-8963	$32–$90	D,MC,V	15	Dec.–Apr.	no	no	under 4	no	yes	no	no	no	no	yes	no	yes	no	no
Notch Estates Condos/Motel W. Rte. 76 417/338-2941	(C) $75–$105; (M) $43.50–$56.50	AE,D,MC,V	226	condos: none; motel: mid-Dec.–mid-Apr.	no	yes	under 11 (motel)	no	no	no	no	no	no	yes	no	no	no	no
Oak Hill Resort Rte. 5, Box 520 417/739-4566	$46–$132	none	13	Nov.–Feb.	no	no		no	no	no	no	no	no	yes	no	no	yes	no

	Price	Credit cards	Units	Closed			Children											
Ozark Trout Resort 347 River La. 417/335-4619	$38–$86	D,MC,V	8	none	yes	no	under 5	yes	yes	no	no	no	no	yes	no	no	yes	yes
Paradise Shores Condo Rentals 2213 Mountain Grove Rd. 417/334-6800	$65–$90	MC,V	10	none	no	no	under 16	no	yes	no	no	no	no	yes	no	no	yes	no
Pine Valley Resort 195 Canonball Loop 417/334-2738	$38–$57	none	31	none	yes	no	no	no	yes	no	no	no	no	yes	no	no	no	no
Pointe Royale Prop., Inc. 4 Point Royale Dr. 417/334-5614	$57–$199	AE,D,MC,V	300	none	no	yes	under 1	no	yes	yes	yes	yes	no	yes	yes	yes	no	yes
River Lake Resort 146 Riverlake Circle Hollister 417/334-2800	$45–$91	D,DC,MC,V	27	none	yes	yes	under 2	no	yes	no	no	no	no	yes	no	no	yes	yes
River Point Estates & Condos 184 River Point Rd. Hollister 417/334-6721	$50–$155	MC,V	22	none	yes	yes	under 12	no	yes	no	no	no	no	yes	yes	no	yes	yes
Rock Lane Resort HCR 1, Box 920 417/338-2211	$55–$200	AE,D,DC,MC,V	148	condo: Jan.–Feb.; motel: Nov.–Apr.	yes	yes	under 13	no	yes	yes	yes	yes	no	yes	yes	no	yes	no
Rock View Resort 1049 Parkview Dr. 417/334-4678	$48–$70	AE,D,MC,V	12	none	yes	no	under 2	no	no	no	no	no	no	yes	no	no	yes	no
Rockwood Resort Box 1162 417/338-2470	$35–$130	D,MC,V	25	Nov.–Apr.	yes	yes	under 1	no	no	no	no	no	no	yes	no	no	yes	no
Rustic Acres Resort, Inc. 2120 Rustic Acres Rd. Kirbyville 417/334-5964	$24–$48	D,MC,V	9	Nov.–Apr.	no	no	under 12	yes	no	no	no	no	no	yes	no	no	yes	no
Sammy Lane Resort 320 E. Main St. 417/334-3253	$55–$160	none	33	Dec.–Mar.	yes	no	yes	no	no	no	no	no	no	yes	no	no	yes	no
Shady Lane Resort 404 N. Sycamore 417/334-3823	$36–$60	D,MC,V	27	none	no	no	no	no	no	no	no	no	no	yes	yes	no	no	no
Shore Acres Resort Rte. 4, Box 2010 417/338-2351	$48–$73	MC,V	17	none	no	no	under 1	no	no	no	no	no	no	yes	no	no	no	no

Accommodations	Rates	Credit Cards	Number of Rooms	Months Closed	Accessibility	Senior Discount	Children Free	Pets Allowed	No Smoking Rooms	Restaurants	Room Service	Lounge/Disco/Nightclub	Exercise Room	Pool	Tennis Courts	Golf Courses	Marina	Shops
Sleepy Hollow Resort HCR 3, Box 348 Kimberling City 417/739-4525	$45–$156	D,MC,V	17	Nov.–Apr.	yes	no	under 1	yes	no	no	no	no	no	yes	no	no	yes	no
Spiltrail Resort HCR 4, Box 3580 Reeds Spring 417/338-2350	$65–$75	none	5	Jan.	no	no	no	no	no	no	no	no	no	no	no	no	yes	no
Still Waters Beach & Resort HCR 1, Box 928 417/338-2323	$49–$169	AE,D,MC,V	90	mid-Dec.–Jan.2	yes	no	under 6	no	yes	no	no	no	no	yes	yes	yes	yes	no
Sunshine Resort 405 N. Commercial St. 417/334-2100	$20–$60	none	15	none	no	no	under 2	no	no	no	no	no	no	yes	no	no	no	no
Sun Valley Resort 249 Sun Valley Circle Hollister 417/334-3346	$47–$72	D,MC,V	14	yes	yes	no	under 3	no	no	no	no	no	no	yes	no	yes	yes	yes
Tacomo Resort 1458 Acacia Club Rd. Hollister 417/334-2332	$36–$63	D,MC,V	21	none	no	yes	under 4	yes	no	no	no	no	no	yes	no	yes	yes	yes
Taneycomo Resort Box 158 417/334-7375	$36–$42	MC,V	23	Dec.	yes	no	under 5	no	no	no	no	no	no	yes	no	yes	yes	no
Tanglewood Lodge Box 1217 417/334-1642	$34–$44	MC,V	17	none	no	no	under 5	yes	no	no	no	no	no	yes	yes	yes	yes	no
Thousand Hills Condo Rental 2700 Green Mountain Dr. 417/336-5873	$99–$139	AE,MC,V	150	none	no	yes	yes	no	yes	no	no	no	yes	yes	yes	no	no	no
Trail's End Resort & RV Park HCR 1, Box 982 417/338-2633	$39–$125	AE,D,MC,V	31	mid-Dec.–Jan. 6	yes	no	under 1	no	no	no	no	no	no	yes	no	yes	no	no
Treehouse Condo Rentals HCR 1, Box 1163-12, Indian Point Rd. 417/338-5199	$65–$145	MC,V	32	Jan.	no	no	yes	no	no	no	no	no	no	yes	no	no	no	no

Name / Address	Price	Credit Cards	No.	Closed	1	2	3	4	5	6	7	8	9	10	11	12	13	14	15
Tribesman Resort *Rte. 1, Box 1032* *417/338-2616*	$46–$148	AE,D,DC,MC,V	54	none	no	yes	no	no	yes	no	no	no	no	no	no	under 5	no	yes	no
Turkey Creek Ranch *HCR 3, Box 3180* *Theodosia* *417/273-4362*	$42–$117	none	24	Dec.–Feb.	no	yes	no	yes	yes	no	no	no	yes	no	no	no	no	yes	no
Twin Island Resort *4134 Rte. 86* *Richdale* *417/779-4361*	$37.50–$75	D,MC,V	17	none	yes	yes	no	no	yes	no	no	no	no	no	no	under 4	no	no	no
Vacation Place Resort *416 N. Sycamore* *417/334-6250*	$22–$50	D,MC,V	12	none	no	no	no	no	yes	no	no	no	no	yes	no	under 4	no	no	no
Village at Indian Point *HCR 1, Box 1158* *417/338-8800*	$79–$110	D,MC,V	20	none	no	yes	no	no	no	no	no	no	no	no	no	no	yes	yes	no
Water's Edge Cottages *Box 125* *Rockway Beach* *417/561-4146*	$40–$80	MC,V	45	Nov.–Mar.	no	no	no	no	yes	no	no	no	no	no	no	no	no	no	no
Whispering Woods Resort *HCR 3, Box 674, Kimberling City, 417/739-4951* *800/226-4951*	$39–$70	MC,V	13	none	no	yes	no	no	yes	no	no	no	no	no	no	no	no	no	no
White Wing Resort *HCR 1, Box 840* *417/338-2318*	$28–$104	none	18	Nov.–mid-Mar.	no	yes	no	no	yes	no	no	no	no	no	no	under 1	no	yes	no
Windwood Resort Lodge *4173 Rte. 86* *Blue Eye* *417/779-4366*	$25–$68	AE,D,MC,V	9	none	no	yes	no	no	yes	no	no	no	no	no	yes	under 17	no	no	no

Index

Fodor's cannot be responsible for changes of ownership, unforeseen occurrences, closing and the like. Read each coupon before using. Discounts only apply to the items and terms specified in the offer at participating locations. If in doubt, please check with the establishment.

Fodor's cannot be responsible for changes of ownership, unforeseen occurrences, closing and the like. Read each coupon before using. Discounts only apply to the items and terms specified in the offer at participating locations. If in doubt, please check with the establishment.

Fodor's cannot be responsible for changes of ownership, unforeseen occurrences, closing and the like. Read each coupon before using. Discounts only apply to the items and terms specified in the offer at participating locations. If in doubt, please check with the establishment.

Fodor's cannot be responsible for changes of ownership, unforeseen occurrences, closing and the like. Read each coupon before using. Discounts only apply to the items and terms specified in the offer at participating locations. If in doubt, please check with the establishment.